D1135307

INDUSTRIAL RELATIONS IN THE COAL INDUSTRY

By the same author

WAGES
INTRODUCING ECONOMICS (*co-author*)

Industrial Relations in the Coal Industry

B. J. McCormick

First published 1979 by
THE MACMILLAN PRESS LTD
London and Basingstoke
Associated companies in Delhi
Dublin Hong Kong Johannesburg Lagos
Melbourne New York Singapore Tokyo

Printed in Great Britain by
William Clowes & Sons Limited
London, Beccles and Colchester

British Library Cataloguing in Publication Data

McCormick, Brian Joseph
Industrial relations in the coal industry
1. Coal miners – Great Britain
2. Industrial relations – Great Britain
I. Title
331′.042′2330941 HD6976.M62G7

ISBN 0–333–24108–8

This book is sold subject to the standard conditions of the Net Book Agreement

To
Monica, Isobel and Fergus

Contents

Preface

In 1962 my distinguished teacher, H. A. Turner, published *Trade Union Growth, Structure and Policy* (Allen and Unwin, London). It was a double book. On the one hand, it was a history of trade unions and industrial relations in the cotton industry, using the technique of comparative analysis to examine the varying experiences of the spinners, weavers, tapesizers and so on. On the other hand, it attempted to use the cotton industry as a yardstick by which to understand the evolution of British industrial relations: it was British industrial relations viewed from the cotton industry, from Lancashire. *Trade Union Growth, Structure and Policy* was a successful book and many of its concepts and theories walked the rounds, crept into official thinking and became clichés.

Coal and cotton were the two major industries of the Industrial Revolution but whereas cotton has languished, since 1952 coal has experienced a decade of contraction followed by a recent revival. Furthermore, coal has been nationalised, has transformed its wage structures and has toppled a government. Therefore the idea of analysing industrial relations in the coal industry has its attractions. But there are other influences than those of Turner's ideas on my education.

My knowledge of the coal industry is secondary and derivative. Only the burnt-out embers of the Cheshire coalfield existed around Stockport and my early awareness of the industry was through cycle racing and its interrelations with colliery racing clubs coupled with the tendency of some racing circuits to run alongside pits. My first serious encounter, however, came through the day-release courses organised by the National Coal Board and the National Union of Mineworkers (Yorkshire and Derbyshire Areas). On the academic side this brought me into contact with John Hughes, Royden Harrison and the late J. E. Williams, whose *Derbyshire Miners* (Allen and Unwin, 1962) was to exert such a considerable influence upon the writing of trade-union history in the mining industry. It also brought me into contact with a large number of distinguished students such as Tom Ryan (Aldwarke, Denaby and Cadeby), Barry Yates (Rossington), Dennis Skinner (Glapwell and Westminster), Eric Varley (Central workshops and Westminster). And it brought me into contact with large numbers of miners who never left the industry, and who fitted their studies in between shifts at work.

In addition to these influences there have been the more robust effects of being trained as an economist by Professor J. C. Gilbert. My colleague Mr G. P. Marshall has exercised a considerable influence upon my thinking about industrial relations. I am also grateful to Mr J. E. MacFarlane, whosc unrivalled knowledge of the South Yorkshire coalfield has been indispensable to me. His work on Denaby Main will, when published, become the classic work on the interrelations of pit and village and the making of an industrial community. I am also indebted to Professor J. C. Wood, who thinks that the difference between us is seven blacks at snooker. I have also benefited from the help of numerous officials in the National Coal Board and the National Union of Mineworkers but, like all those so far mentioned, they are not responsible for any of my idiosyncrasies and blunders. Finally, I have to thank my wife Monica, who has had to put up with an ever increasing slag heap of notes, memoranda and books.

The Douglas Knoop Research Fund of the University of Sheffield provided my bus fares to the pits on the grounds that going to Wombwell must constitute research.

January 1978 B. J. M.

Acknowledgements

The author and publishers would like to thank the following who have kindly given permission for the use of copyright material.

The *Economic History Review* and A. J. Taylor for a table from the article 'Labour Productivity and Technological Change in the British Coal Industry' in *Economic History Review*, 2nd Series, XIV (1960–1), and D. J. C. Forsyth for the tables from *Studies in the Coal Industry*, edited by D. M. Kelly and D. J. C. Forsyth. The Controller of Her Majesty's Stationery Office for the tables and graphs based on data from the Department of Employment *Gazette*, 'Digest of Energy Statistics' and an extract from the written *Evidence of Sir Harold Emmerson* to the Royal Commission on Trade Unions and Employer's Associations, Appendix 6, and Manchester University Press for a table from *Pay and Productivity Bargaining* by R. G. Searle-Barnes.

The National Coal Board for figures from their Annual Reports and from the documents 'Investing in Coal' (April, 1956) and 'Revised Plan for Coal' (October, 1959), and The Post Office, Central Headquarters, for a graph 'Post Office Sickness Absence Since 1934' from a Post Office report.

1 The Coal Industry, 1550–1947

Coalmining occupies a unique place in the history of the British economy. For it was the exploitation and utilisation of coal which reduced the dependency upon use of wood and created the possibilities of an industrial sector to complement an agricultural sector, but supplies of wood were limited and were gradually being exhausted by the sixteenth century. In contrast stocks of coal seemed boundless. The problem was how to use the coal. In the Elizabethan period there was a minor industrial revolution which enabled glass and non-ferrous metals to be smelted with coal. Mining took place everywhere but because of their access to ports the coalfields of Northumberland, Durham and the Firth of Forth underwent greater development than the inland fields and they enjoyed a thriving coastal trade with London. In the sixteenth century Northumberland and Durham accounted for 33 per cent of total production and Scotland contributed a further 20 per cent.[1] Coal was not the first industry to create an industrial wage-earning class; that honour belongs to the medieval building industry with its highly mobile labour force and its mass-produced alabaster saints.[2] But coal produced a wage-earning class long before those of nineteenth-century textiles and engineering and it was a class located in isolated communities and working in unusual conditions.

The major expansion in the use of coal came with the smelting and refining of iron and steel in the eighteenth and nineteenth centuries. From 1700 to 1913 the industry grew, particularly after the canals and the railways allowed the development of the inland fields. And this stimulus permitted an even greater surge in industrial activity. Coal was used to produce manufactures which were exchanged for the agricultural products of other countries in many latitudes and the dependence on British agriculture was reduced and a more even flow of agricultural crops was achieved.

In 1913 the coal industry achieved its peak, behind it lay an Indian summer, before it lay crises. Between 1920 and 1939 the industry languished and the British economy stagnated. The Second World War provided an interruption, and from 1940 to 1957 coal was in short supply and the growth of the economy was constrained by the inability to expand the supply of coal. The emergence of oil as a competitor produced another crisis and, from 1957 to 1972, the industry was in the doldrums once more. The sharp rise in oil prices in 1972 provided a temporary reprieve, which may be extended if the energy crisis is prolonged.

Coal created the industrial economy and its characteristic features have been the pit, the factory and the town. And because of the dependence of industrial activity upon coal, the mining industry stamped its influence upon the British system of industrial relations. The exchange of dependence upon wood for dependence upon coal permitted the emergence of an industry marked by violent fluctuations in output, long drawn-out strikes over wages and employment, terrible accidents and loss of life, political intervention and, ultimately, the transfer of ownership from private to public hands. In no other industry is it possible to find industrial and political issues so deeply intertwined. And the long-standing support of the Liberal Party by the miners was a decisive factor in determining the emergence and growth of the Labour Party.

THE BEGINNINGS, 1550–1840

PROBLEMS OF LABOUR SUPPLY

The expansion of coalmining, taking place as it did in rural areas, created a labour shortage. There is little evidence to suggest that workers were brought in from the Continent and most of the influx must therefore have come from domestic sources until the relatively high birthrates of mining villages in the nineteenth century created an internal labour supply. Nef cites Staffordshire men being employed in the Forest of Dean in the sixteenth century and Radford noted an influx of miners from the declining lead mines of Derbyshire into the adjacent coalfields in the nineteenth century.[3]

In Scotland the scarcity of labour led to the development of serfdom. The Scottish Poor Laws of 1579 and 1597 allowed vagrants to bind themselves for life to any employer willing to receive them on these terms and some use may have been made of the Acts by coal-owners. But it was the Act of 1606 which led to the widespread development of servitude by not allowing workers to move between jobs without the production of a certificate of clearance from their former employer. The Act did not refer to servitude but the concept of a black list and its application by employers did create serfdom. And subsequent legislation, framed by coal-owners anxious to hold and obtain labour and statesmen conscious of the revenue to be derived from a valuable export commodity, tightened the bonds. Most coal-owners did assume that their miners were their bondsmen.

Collier serfs were well-cared-for as compared with miners in England or workers in other industries. Adam Smith observed that: 'They have indeed privileges which slaves have not. Their property after maintenance is their own, they cannot be sold but along with their work, they enjoy marriage and religion'.[4] But though wages and conditions of employment were better than those of free workers, they still attempted to escape and were often brought back to their employers. And it was because of the stigma attached to working in the mines that the system had finally to be abandoned. For the expansion of the coal industry created a demand for labour that was greater than the supply made possible by the enserfment of vagrants. Some employers tried to enforce the system and extend it, but it was difficult. The only solution to the labour shortage lay in getting rid of the serfdom which was an obstacle to the recruitment of freemen. And it was the employers who took the initiative. In 1774 they got an Emancipation Bill introduced into the Commons but it was limited in scope and it was not until 1779 that an Amending Act removed the last traces of serfdom from Scotland. Its immediate effect was to cause a movement of labour from the pits and additional supplies of labour were only forthcoming in large quantities when the Irish migrated to the coalfields.

Serfdom of the medieval or Scottish kind was not practised in England but long hirings were common.[5] In Northumberland and Durham there was the yearly bond which at its inception ensured security of labour supply to the employer and guaranteed high wages and regularity of employment. Subsequently, and throughout the eighteenth and early nineteenth centuries, there were attempts by employers to modify the terms of the bond and strikes by workers to alter and, later, abolish it. Thus in 1765 there was a big strike resulting from the efforts of the employers to switch the time of hiring from October to April in order to take advantage of the greater bargaining power afforded by slack demand for coal in the spring. And on the miner's side there were demands for the removal of the bond when technological change increaed the job security of the hewer. The original form of work organisation took the form of pairs of hewers working the coal face, with the haulage being undertaken by boys. Later, improvements in blasting increased the speed of operations and the two hewers divided the working day into two shifts of six hours each, whilst the haulage workers continued to work one long shift. At the same time improvements in haulage and the increasing size of pits led to a growth in the number of haulage workers and intensive division of labour among them. These forces combined to increase the numbers of steps in the job hierarchy and to give the hewers greater job security since it was impossible to become a hewer without first climbing all the other rungs of the ladder. In the 1840's there was considerable litigation concerning the terms of the bond and the miners employed W. P. Roberts, the Chartist who became known as the Miners' Solicitor, to undertake the defence of miners in breach of contract. As a result of the costs of litigation the employers abandoned the Annual Bond – though there were attempts to revive it in 1853 and 1864. Strikes over the bond occurred frequently in the eighteenth and nineteenth centuries and the more prominent strikes took place in 1765, 1810, 1831, 1844, 1853 and 1864.

There are only scattered references to the use of the bond in other parts of England. Challinor suggests that it would have been extremely difficult to enforce in densely populated areas such as Lancashire.[6] Some workers may have operated under a kind of bond system which permitted employment in agriculture in the summer and in the mines in the winter, though even that could be difficult since coal was often mined in the summer in order to avoid the difficulties of transporting it in the winter. In most areas labour was probably recruited through the agency of sub-contractors – *the big butty system.* A butty would provide his own capital and be responsible for the running of an entire mine or seam which he would lease from the owners. The income of the butty would be based on the difference between the revenue from the sale of the coal, on the one hand, and the lease price and the wage bill, on the other hand: a difference which would be heavily dependent upon how hard the butty drove his workers. Normally, the workforce was paid a fixed price for the shift or fortnight which contrasted strongly with the payment by results system under which the miners of the North East were employed. Taylor, following Ashton and Sykes, suggests that the butty system existed where the size of pit was small and there was an absence of professional managers employed by the coal owners.[7] Hence the butty system did not exist in Northumberland and Durham. But when the size of pits grew the butty system did not disappear entirely. Instead it was transformed into *the little butty system* in which a sub-contractor might be responsible for a district or face. The little butty system showed remarkable persistence. For example, it spread into the Doncaster coalfield in the first two decades of the twentieth century when that coalfield was being developed. And in North Staffordshire it was not eliminated until the 1950s when the Coal Board introduced a fixed payment on top of shift earnings for face chargemen – a practice that was also introduced into other coalfields. The willingness of nineteenth-century miners' unions to accept piecework stemmed from a desire to avoid exploitation by the butty master.

The problem of labour scarcity also led to the employment of women and children. Indeed it is noticeable that coal and textiles, the new industries of the sixteenth and eighteenth centuries, both figure prominently in nineteenth-century legislation concerning the employment of women and children. For unlike the old gild trades, such as building and printing, and the new gild trades, such as engineering – which was merely turning and fitting in metal instead of wood – coal and textiles had no tradition of recruitment and restriction upon which to draw. The impact of economic activity upon the printing industry took the form of an expansion of the scale of output and though it became progressively more difficult for the journeyman to set up as a master, there was no technological revolution to threaten his skill until late in the nineteenth century. What the journeyman did, therefore, was to restrict the labour supply by restricting the number of apprentices. The apprenticeship ratio was also adopted in the engineering trades. In contrast, the newer industries of coal and cotton fell back not upon the gild system but upon the domestic system. The Butty became the putter-out who employed men, women and children and because there was no tradition of fixed hours of work in the domestic system long hours came to be worked in mines and factories. So the nineteenth century witnessed the attempts of workers in coal and textiles to create some form of restriction on labour supply analogous to that imposed by the gild system.

The problems of ensuring a labour supply partially explain the development of the truck system and its association, in some instances, with the butty system. The payment of truck involves arrangements whereby some form of consumption is tied to employment. Typically, part of the wage took the form of foodstuffs, and sometimes clothing, which had to be bought from a shop owned by the employer. In other cases, truck meant that the worker was paid in tickets which could be used to buy goods at a shop owned by the employer or a shopkeeper who gave the employer a fee based on worker's purchases. A failure to accept the truck system would result in a worker's dismissal.

The truck system developed before the Industrial Revolution but achieved notoriety in the eighteenth and nineteenth centuries. In 1831 an Act was passed prohibiting truck but the practice persisted and in 1877 further legislation had to be passed. The motives behind truck were complex and not all of them were as distasteful as some of the literature implies. In North Wales miners petitioned their employers to provide truck shops in order to destroy the monopoly of local shopkeepers.[8] Also a lack of shops in rural areas may have been a general reason for the emergence of truck. In other instances truck was used as a means of preventing drunkenness and reckless habits. It was a tax on riotous living. In South Wales wage payments were monthly and a worker who waited until the end of the month for his wages was under no compulsion to buy from the truck shop. Between pay days many Welsh pits held a 'draw day' when workers could drawn on some of their wages and, again, there was no compulsion to buy from the truck shop. But where a worker wanted a 'sub', to anticipate his wages, then he might be required to spend some of his wages at the truck shop. The use of truck to discipline workers seems to be the most general explanation for its use in the coal industry. But it does beg the question: why not sack or reprimand the workers by other methods such as fines? The lame answer seems to be that truck was the least costly method.

But if the discipline argument is weak then none of the other suggestions are wholly convincing. Thus, Ashton and Sykes, following Unwin, pointed to the problems of credit and the shortage of coins. But why should it be more easy to obtain credit on groceries than on coal? And if coins were scarce, why not cut wages instead of providing goods which, presumably, had either to be financed by credit or paid for with coins? Another argument was that truck, by allowing workers to go into debt, rendered them immobile. But this argument depended upon the ability of workers to recover debt. And in the case of married men, who would be heavy spenders at the tommy shops, the existence of wives and children might be an *a priori* reason for immobility. Finally, there remain fraud and extortion arising out of ignorance. Cases of fraud did occur though they do not appear to have been widespread. Prices in truck shops could be higher than in other shops but profits tended to be swallowed up in inefficient administration. Extortion did occur though it is not obvious why it had to take the form of buying goods at relatively high prices.

The truck system was compatible with a variety of management systems but in the Midlands it became identified with the butty system. It was common for butties to pay out wages in pubs and many butty masters were publicans. But again the question has to be asked: why did the cut-back take the form of beer? Truck was common in Yorkshire in the 1820s, but seems to have disappeared in the North East around 1832. It was, however, still prevalent in South Wales in the 1860s. In its early phase it was probably beneficial but it later became the subject of criticism from those who objected to long way periods and the practice of asking the majority to accept a system designed to discipline the minority.

TRADE UNIONS

The lack of written records, the physical isolation of miners in many areas and the nature of hiring systems makes it difficult to trace the origins and modes of behaviour of the early unions. In the eighteenth century the Combination Acts must have acted as a deterrent. There was also the problem of labour turnover. In some areas, such as Lancashire and Yorkshire, workers moved easily between pits, farms and factories according to the availability of work. Many pits were small, owners were often paternalistic and wages were usually higher than those earned by agricultural workers. What written evidence exists tends to suggest that unions were often short-lived: emerging in boom periods, fighting against wage cuts in the downswings and disappearing in the slumps. But such evidence may be misleading. During the slumps some form of organisation may have been kept alive through the cohesiveness of the workgroup and the village. Thus the Brotherly Union Society was formed in Pemberton, Lancashire, in 1974, its rules were amended in 1804 and again 1830.[9] Many unions functioned as friendly societies in order to conceal their activities and the evidence of extensive organisation can be detected in the simultaneity of strikes in different localities as, for example, in Flintshire and Denbighshire between 1823 and 1825.[10]

The early phase of unionism seems to reveal two distinct subperiods. In the first, activity is directed not against employers but against merchants and shopkeepers who were accused of raising food prices in years of bad harvest. The idea of asking for wage increases to compensate for price increases does not appear to have been considered by the rioteers. It is in the second phase that rioting against merchants becomes transformed into rioting against employers. And the riot, the destruction of machinery and the burning of pit-head gear, as at Bedlington in County Durham in 1831, was ideally suited to an age when employers could respond to strikes by importing blacklegs.[11] Violence was also extended to non-union labour and in South Wales, in the first quarter of the nineteenth century, the Scotch Cattle – unknown bands of miners – attacked those who accepted low wages.[12]

There is some evidence that the unions of the 1830s had links and the upsurge of militancy in 1831 in which miners' unions, as far apart as Northumberland and North Wales, demanded and obtained wage increases and reductions in hours suggests some central direction. Some miners' unions were associated with Doherty's National Association for the Protection of Labour. On the other hand, other groups remained aloof from the general movements of the thirties. Owen's Grand National struck no roots in Yorkshire. And a similar view must be taken of miners and Chartism in the 1840s. Williams found only slight evidence of a connection in Derbyshire and Leicestershire the miners positively disassociated themselves from Chartism and political causes. On the other hand, Challinor detected a Chartist influence and prominent Chartists, such as W. P. Roberts, were involved with some miners' unions. In periods when unionism was at a low ebb, miners, like other working men, turned to political movements.[13]

THE VICTORIAN ECONOMY, 1840–50

THE MINERS' ASSOCIATION

The first national union was The Miners' Association of Great Britain and Ireland, formed at Wakefield in 1842. The impetus to organisation came from Yorkshire but control passed to Northumberland and Durham when the latter affiliated. About two-thirds of the membership came from the North East and the bulk of the remainder came from Lancashire and Yorkshire. Behind the creation of the Union lay the stimulus of low wages and the exposure of conditions of employment in the mines through the publication of the report of the Childrens' Employment Commission, 1842.[14] The objectives of the Union were to unite all mineworkers, equalise working conditions, increase wages and reduce hours of work. It lasted four years and its short-lived history was to illustrate all the difficulties that were to beset miners' unions throughout the nineteenth and twentieth centuries.

A problem that confronted any miners' union in the nineteenth century was how to prevent its policies being undermined either by the import of blacklegs or by the import of coal from other regions. The import of blacklegs was extensively practised and men were transported over considerable distances. Lancashire and Staffordshire miners were used to break strikes in North Wales and Derbyshire miners were employed in the North East. Furthermore, the canals and railways tended to break monopolies by permitting the cheap import of coal. What the Miners' Association therefore attempted to do was to prevent employers from using these measures by pursuing policies designed to produce a general scarcity of coal. Unfortunately, the Association was unable to control the policies of its constituent associations. During 1842 and 1843 there was widespread strike activity in different coal fields and, in some areas, gains were easily obtained as industrial activity was increasing. But in the North East conditions were unfavourable. There had been a period of heavy investment which turned out to have been based upon false expectations. Excess capacity emerged and the Newcastle Vend, the local monopoly which had managed to control prices in the London market, began to crumble as new entrants started to cut prices.[15] The pressure on the Vend, in turn, removed the protection which monopoly in the product market extended to the unions in the labour market. So the demand for wage increases met with resistance and a four-month strike ensued. During the strike the Association failed to prevent the movement of labour into the North East and its financial support was meagre. The strike ended with the defeat of the Northumberland and Durham miners and their surrender presaged the collapse of the Association.

Despite the fall of the Association there was a useful legacy. The Union had been actively involved in both the legal and political aspects of miners' employment and it had dealt with issues concerning the interpretation of the miners' bond. Its secretary, David Swallow, had visited various coalfields and had given evidence on the employment of women and children to the 1842 Commission. The Association had mobilised support in 1844 to defeat the Master and Servant Bill and it had canvassed for legislation to regulate safety in mines. Strike activity in the Midlands had served, in some instances, to remove the truck system and to arouse considerable public criticism of the practice. There were also gains from reductions in hours in some areas. Furthermore, the collapse of the national union did not lead automatically to the extinction of the county unions, many of which continued in existence in an attenuated form. And their survival pointed to the problems for the future. Either a national union could attempt to pursue a single industrial policy which would require a reduction in the power of its constituents or it could allow affiliates complete autonomy on industrial matters whilst seeking to pursue common political objectives, such as safety legislation. The choice between these alternatives was to dominate policies in the miners' unions until the last decades of the nineteenth century and then re-emerged in the twenties and thirties. Often the choice was not even available because of the intertwining of industrial and political issues. Thus, the achievement of a satisfactory working day and minimum wage required political action which disturbed the regional autonomy of the coalfield unions.

1860–80

THE NATIONAL

The next significant phase in unionism begins in the 1850s and continues until the collapse of coal prices in 1874. Throughout the period county unions were created or reconstituted, of which the following are a sample:

1858 South Yorkshire Miners' Association
West Yorkshire Miners' Association

1863 Derbyshire and Nottinghamshire Miners' Association
South Staffordshire Miners' Association

1864 Northumberland Mutual Confident Association
Leicestershire Miners' Association

1869 Durham Miners' Association
North Staffordshire Miners' Association

1870 Fife and Kinross Miners' Association

1872 Somersetshire Miners' Association

In Lancashire, according to Challinor, intense individualism obstructed the development of a county union and the sixties witnessed the re-emergence of district unions:

1862 Wigan Miners' Provident Benefit Society

1863 Farnworth and Kearsley Provident Benefit Society
Worsley Miners' Association
Ashton-under-Lyne Miners' Association
Oldham Miners' Association
St Helen's Miners' Association

1863 Haydock Miners' Association

Challinor's emphasis upon Lancashire individualism should not, however, obscure the fact that unions in other coalfields were federations of pit unions and that these pit unions or collections of unions into district unions could often insist upon their autonomy. Thus Sheffield and Rotherham miners had their own association outside the South Yorkshire Association. Sometimes these divisions arose out of employers' policies which had their basis in different costs and markets. The distinction between West and South Yorkshire, which was to persist at the formal level until the amalgamation of the two unions in 1881, reflected the fact that West Yorkshire pits were thin seam pits, operating in areas of diversified industry, selling their output to the mill towns of the West Riding, and were less prosperous than the pits in the south of the county. And even within West Yorkshire a division was drawn between the western and eastern halves. These differences within Yorkshire persisted after amalgamation and exerted an influence on industrial relations in the inter-war years and since nationalisation. Another area where individualism was strong was the West Midlands where district unions persisted even after nationalisation. But having emphasised individualism and sectionalism it is worth noting the pressures to nationalism created by competition within and between coalfields. In the 1860s and 1870s the South Yorkshire Miners devoted considerable assistance to developing unionism in Derbyshire.

The upsurge of unionism in this period seems to begin in the slump that occurred after the boom of the fifties. Before the boom we know little about unions after the collapse of the Association. In the North East some form of organisation existed as a result of the partial monopoly of the London market that persisted after the downfall of the Vend. But despite the apparent lack of unions miners did well in the boom of 1851–4. New pits were sunk, the price of coal rose by about 50 per cent and wages rose by about 30 per cent. Absenteeism increased partly as a result of the rise in wages and partly out of a fear that the expansion of output would cause employers to produce for stock which would, in turn, lead to increased competition, falling prices and wages. The limitation of output, however, led to the recruitment of inexperienced miners and accidents increased from 1851–4.[16] By 1865 there was a glut of coal and the Mining Association, an informal organisation of coal owners, proposed a reduction of wages. But it was not until after the crisis of 1857 that wage cuts were attempted and these attempts produced a rash of strikes throughout the country while attempts were made to form unions.

At the national level Alexander MacDonald created the Miners' National Association in 1863. Initially, the Association interested itself in industrial matters and raised funds to support coalfield strikes. But the difficulties of raising funds and controlling strike activity caused a shift towards political and legislative activity – a programme for which MacDonald was suited both by ability and by temperament. During the sixties there were important changes in the law relating to employment. The South Yorkshire Miners demanded the right to have a representative of the men at the pit bank to check the weighing of coal and, with the help of MacDonald, the Association secured an amendment to the Mines Regulation Act of 1860 which allowed miners at each pit to appoint a check-weighman. Although the Act was often evaded, the workers who became check-weighmen were often victimised, and the Act had to be subsequently strengthened, the creation of such a legally protected post gave the unions a base from which to secure effective unionisation at pit level. Also the abandonment of the butty system in many pits provided a supply of local leadership.

But the tendency of the National Association to withdraw from collective bargaining and to adopt a conciliatory attitude led to sliding scales in 1877 and 1878 respectively. West Yorkshire Miners asked for a scale in 1874 but it was not until 1880 that the coal-owners would agree on the details. South Yorkshire also introduced a scale in 1880.

THE EDWARDIAN SUMMER, 1889–1913

THE MINERS' FEDERATION OF GREAT BRITAIN AND IRELAND

The fourth phase of unionism began with the revival of trade in the eighties and the formation of new unions. It was a period when unions established a firm foothold not only in the coal industry but also in other industries. Labour, even unskilled labour, was tending to become scarce relative to capital and in some industries, such as gas, there was emerging a stability of employment conducive to unionism. Even in the highly unstable trades, such as the docks, the compact location and immobility of labour made unionism feasible. But though unionism had been made legal by the 1871 Trade Union Act and made possible by changing economic circumstances, it was still subject to attack and in the two decades before the First World War there was a major onslaught on unions by employers. The sources of conflict lay in the changing economic conditions of those years. International competition was intensifying and employers were caught between rising wages and downward pressures on prices. The effect was to cause employers to attempt to cut wages and to eliminate restrictions on the use of machines by semi-skilled labour. Thus there was an attack on the newly-formed unions of unskilled workers and on the long-established craft unions. In the general picture of attack and counterattack mining unions occupied an important place. Mining was expanding and the mining unions contained a quarter of all trade unionists. But the expansion contained problems. Output was expanding but productivity was tending to decline as the easy and better seams were worked-out and as more and more labour had to be employed on haulage and surface operations (see Table 1.1). There was a movement away from the high-cost areas to the more productive coalfields of the Midlands but it was a slow process. There was also a tendency for the price of coal to rise so that increasing costs were covered; which in turn served as a stimulus to search for substitutes and for other countries to develop their coalfields – but these effects only began to be felt after the First World War.

In 1889, on the wave of a rise in coal prices, the Miners' Federation of Great Britain and Ireland was formed. It arose out of informal meetings of miners in the inland coalfields under the leadership of Thomas Ashton of Lancashire and Ben Pickard of Yorkshire. Ashton had managed to bring together the various Lancashire district unions, following an attempt by employers to avoid the provisions of the Employers' Liability Act of 1880 by insisting that all workers join the Lancashire and Cheshire Permanent Relief Society which they controlled. The stratagem failed. In 1881 the South and West Yorkshire Miners' Associations had amalgamated and, given the sheer numbers of miners in Yorkshire, the YMA came to dominate the Federation. In the

TABLE 1.1 Output, Productivity, Prices and Wages in the Coal Industry, 1887–1913

	(1) Output (m. tons)	(2) Miners employed underground (th.)	(3) Total manpower (th.)	(4) Annual output/man below gr'd (tons)	(5) An. output/man below & above gr'd (tons)	(6) 5) Adjusted*	(7) F.O.B. price of coal (d.)	(8) Pit-head price of coal (d.)	(9) Howers' wages	(10) Miners' earnings	(11) Value of Coal raised (£)
1887	162.1	414.8	509.5	391	318		67.4	55.2	65.9	71.4	39.1
1888	169.9	422.9	529.6	401	321		68.1	58.1	70.2	77.9	43.0
1889	176.9	447.6	562.2	395	315		83.2	72.4	82.1	91.3	56.2
1890	181.6	490.5	612.4	370	297		102.5	94.3	93.1	99.1	75.0
1891	185.5	520.7	649.2	356	286		99.1	91.5	93.7	98.2	74.1
1892	181.8	536.5	668.0	339	272		90.1	82.9	88.5	89.3	66.1
1893	164.3	536.0	666.2	307	247		80.5	78.1	87.1	84.9	55.8
1894	188.3	555.6	688.0	339	274		85.3	75.2	82.4	84.0	62.7
1895	189.7	549.4	681.7	345	278		76.4	68.6	78.5	81.1	57.2
1896	195.4	540.5	672.4	361	291		72.2	66.7	77.9	82.0	57.2
1897	202.1	541.9	675.2	373	299	307	72.9	67.6	78.7	83.8	59.7
1898	202.1	550.6	686.7	367	294	295	80.5	72.4	85.2	89.5	64.2
1899	220.1	566.4	708.7	389	311	300	86.0	86.7	90.5	97.4	83.5
1900	225.2	607.7	759.9	371	296	285	136.2	123.8	108.3	112.6	121.7
1901	219.0	632.3	787.7	346	278	286	113.5	106.7	101.8	104.0	102.5
1902	227.1	646.9	805.1	351	282	285	100.4	94.3	94.8	97.5	93.5
1903	230.3	660.4	822.0	349	280	290	95.6	87.6	92.0	95.2	88.2
1904	232.4	664.8	826.8	350	281	292	90.8	82.9	89.2	92.4	83.9
1905	236.1	673.8	837.1	350	282	295	86.0	79.0	87.8	90.6	82.0
1906	251.1	691.6	860.4	363	292	293	89.4	82.9	90.4	95.4	91.5
1907	267.8	739.8	918.4	362	292	279	104.6	102.9	104.3	110.1	120.5
1908	261.5	778.7	966.3	336	271	274	104.6	101.9	101.1	102.8	116.6
1909	263.8	800.7	992.3	329	266	273	92.2	92.4	96.6	97.4	106.3
1910	264.4	830.5	1027.5	318	257	258	96.3	93.3	97.1	96.4	108.4
1911	271.9	845.6	1045.3	322	260	261	93.6	93.3	96.2	99.5	110.8
1912	260.4	862.2	1068.8	302	244	237	103.9	103.8	101.6	98.5	117.9
1913	287.4	892.6	1106.8	322	260	246	114.2	116.2	108.5	108.2	145.5

Source: A. J. Taylor, 'Labour productivity and technological change in the British Coal Industry', *Economic History Review*, XIV (1960–1), 68–9.

TABLE 1.2 Mining Unions formed after 1880

1880	Derbyshire Miners' Association
1881	Yorkshire Miners' Association – merger of South and West Yorkshire
	Nottinghamshire Miners' Association
1885	Warwickshire Miners' Association
1886	Ayrshire Miners' Federal Union
	Forest of Dean Miners' Association
	Shropshire Miners' Association
1887	Clackmannanshire Miners' Association
	Cannock Chase Miners' Association
	Leicestershire Miners' Association
1888	Somerset Miners' Association
1889	South Derbyshire Miners' Association
	Mid and East Lothian Miners' Association
1892	North Wales Miners' Association
1896	Lanarkshire Miners' Association
1897	Lancashire and Cheshire Miners' Association
1898	South Wales Miners' Federation

1880s the Yorkshire Miners' Association was fourth largest union in Britain.

The principal objects of the federation were the abolition of the sliding scale method of wage determination and the eight-hour day. The pursuit of these policies was to bring the Federation into conflict with Northumberland and Durham, both unions being wedded to sliding scales, opposed to the eight-hour day and affiliated to the Miners' National Union, which they dominated. Also outside the Federation were South Wales, South Staffordshire and Fife. The Federation was fortunate in being formed in a boom period, as between 1889 and 1891 coal prices rose by about 60 per cent; wages rose by 10 per cent in 1889 and, subsequently, two further increases of 10 per cent were granted. But the rapid increase in prices led to a further demand for 10 per cent and strike notices were posted in March 1890. The effect was to compel the coal-owners in the Federated Area to form an association and, though the strike lasted for only a week, the wage increases were granted. But the main achievement of the strike was to establish that in the future wage movements were to be determined for the whole of the Federated Area by joint negotiations.

THE 1893 LOCKOUT

The Federation gained from the period of rising prices from 1889 to 1891. But in 1892 prices began to fall and the first attempts to cut wages were made in the exporting fields. At the beginning of the year the Durham coal-owners asked for a reduction of 10 per cent. Patterson, the general secretary of the Durham Miners, proposed acceptance but the men voted to strike and refused arbitration. The owners locked out the men and the dispute lasted twelve weeks. During the stoppage the Federation contributed to the support of Durham in the hope that it would secure the Association's affiliation. This hope was realised and Northumberland also joined, following the efforts of the Federation's missionaries in that coalfield.

When prices fell, in 1892, the Federation responded by calling for a restriction of output by working fewer days and having a spring holiday. But as the recession deepened the employers demanded a return to the wage level of 1888. The Federation rejected the proposal whilst Durham, just emerging from a long strike, opted for arbitration and Northumberland voted against a strike. In July 300,000 miners stopped work and did not return until November. The strike resulted in the loss of 21 million working days, was the biggest strike yet experienced and was more dramatic than the struggle for the dockers' tanner in 1889. Miners' families suffered extreme hardship, public subscriptions were opened and financial support came from all quarters. As the strike progressed there was rioting in some areas as miners tried to stop the use of blacklegs. In Featherstone a 'massacre' occurred when troops fired on a crowd, killed two men and injured others.

The strike was brought to an end by the intervention of the government Waiving all principles of laissez faire, Gladstone wrote to Ashton:

> The Government have not, up to the present, considered that they could advantageously intervene in a dispute, the settlement of which would far more usefully be brought about by the action of those concerned, than by the good offices of others. But having regard to the national importance of a speedy termination of the dispute, and the fact that the conference which took place on the 3rd and 4th November did not result in a settlement, Her Majesty's Government have felt it their duty to

> make an effort to bring about a resumption of negotiations between the employers and the employees under conditions which they hope may lead to a satisfactory result.[17]

A conference, under the chairmanship of Lord Rosebery, was established and produced a settlement. It provided for the introduction of a conciliation board, with an independent chairman, to cover the Federated Area. The board was to have the power to determine wages from February 1894. In the meantime the miners were to receive pre-stoppage wages.

Ever since the publication of J. E. Williams, *The Derbyshire Miners*, there has been a dispute concerning the outcome of the 1893 lockout. Williams challenged the traditional view that the miners won a notable victory. He admitted that the miners returned on pre-stoppage terms but pointed out that the effect of the dispute was to create a shortage of coal which allowed high wages. He conceded that within the Federated Area the operation of the Conciliation Board did not allow wages to fall below a minimum wage of 30 per cent above the 1888 level while in other coalfields there were reductions, but he argued that the trend of wages and prices was upward, that the Board acted as a restraining influence on wages and that a more militant policy might have pushed up wages by more than the Board allowed. Williams, following Rowe,[18] also argued that the principle that wages must follow prices had been reasserted whereas the Federation had entered the dispute determined to have some say in the determination of prices and the right to a minimum living wage. Because of the failure to maintain these principles the 1893 lockout merely delayed the inevitable struggle over a minimum wage which eventually exploded in the Cambrian lockout of 1910 and which was partially resolved by the Minimum Wage Act, 1912.

We need to distinguish between the short-run and long-run effects of the 1893 settlement. In the short run the Federation believed it had won a great victory. The miners had entered the stoppage because they believed that they had to defend the living wage – 30 per cent above the 1888 basis. 'Notwithstanding all the teachings of political economists, all the doctrines taught by way of supply and demand', said Sam Woods, the Federation's vice-president, 'we say there is a greater doctrine of humanity. We believe that the working man is worthy of his hire, and hold at the present moment that wages are as low as they ever ought to be.' And as the dispute proceeded 30 per cent became a symbol which transcended the economist's calculus. The view that the settlement was a victory for the Federation stands unqualified, despite the early return of the North East on reduced wages, because the first issue was the defence of the Federation and because the Federation had previously supported the North East. The Federation entered a summer campaign having expended funds on a non-member and it won. And the verdict stands despite the reference to the effect of the dispute in creating a temporary shortage because both sides were aware that a strike or a holiday would create scarcity; but the expectations concerning the outcome went beyond that piece of arithmetic.

It is the medium and long-term results that are the subject of uncertainty. Neville and Benson state that part of the argument centres around an assessment of the conciliation procedures established by the Rosebery settlement of 1893 and that these procedures have now been clarified by Porter.[19] Unfortunately, Porter's analysis contains some obscurities. He suggests that in the coal industry the pattern of development of third-party intervention was for arbitration to be succeeded by sliding scales which in turn were superseded by conciliation boards. Thus in the 1870s arbitration was first adopted because initially compromise was difficult and therefore the burden of reconciliation was thrust upon the arbitrators. But he then goes on to conclude that the unions were prepared to accept compromise.[20] A more compelling reason for the pattern of developments, however, lies in the rules that were developed to resolve disputes. Since third-party intervention was acceptable to both sides the crucial issue was: What were the principles to be followed in finding a settlement within the implicit area of agreement? The answer to this question may not have been obvious either to employers or unions. And when it was realised that the arbitrators tended to use 'the state of the trade' as codified in the selling price of coal then both parties were able to dispense with the outsiders and appoint a less costly, impersonal arbitrator – the selling price of coal. The adoption of the selling price schedules was a development of arbitration. What finally broke this form of arbitration was that in a period of falling prices and slow productivity growth the selling prices provided no guaranteed minimum wage. This was in contrast to the iron and steel trades where rising productivity raised basic rates and offset the fall in the percentage additions dictated by falling prices. Hence the move towards conciliation was an attempt to move away from 'the state of trade' as a basis for wage determination. But the state of trade could not be ignored except by the introduction of a minimum wage and a possible contraction of employment.

We are now in a position to analyse the effects of the Conciliation Board of 1893. The first point to note is that the Board was concerned with only one component of earnings – the percentage addition. As well as the percentage, earnings comprised the basis or price list items which were negotiated at pit level and the allowances for abnormal conditions. In accepting the Conciliation Board the Federation was creating one element common to all coalfields whilst allowing branches to screw up wages locally and thereby creating pressure for revision at pits. Thus, the assertion that the Federation could have got higher wages by more militant action ignores the fact that in the years immediately after the lockout the Federation could not afford a strike, that the miners wanted to enjoy the victory and that local pressure could be very effective. In Nottinghamshire, as Griffin observed, it was possible for the County Union to use the wage gains in the Leen Valley to pull up wages in the Erewash Valley.[21] Indeed one result of the 1893 victory was to strengthen unionism at pit level and to lead to the extensive negotiation of price lists. It is true that there were occasional conflicts between the rank and file and the leadership, notably in Durham. But these never presented any serious challenge to the leadership, which suggests that most miners opted for security. As for the criticism that the strike failed to protect earnings because earnings fell when short-time working was introduced; that point of view ignores the nature of the working-class mind which accepts shared adversity. And the assertion that the 1893 settlement failed to establish a minimum wage, and that that failure led to the dispute of 1910 and the need for a minimum wage in 1912, ignores the fact that the problems of 1910 arose because the employers chose not to attack the percentage which was determined on an industry-wide basis but to cut allowances which were determined at pit level. Furthermore, the attack on allowances took place in South Wales and in 1893 South Wales was not a member of the Federation. Had South Wales been affiliated then the 1893 outcome might have been different. South Wales might have seceded at an earlier date, as did Northumberland and Durham, or the combined weight of the export fields might have dragged down the Federation. But that is conjecture. The Federation held together, it won and the employers were left in disarray. The fact that the State had to intervene, and did so on the side of the miners, was a portent for the future. When the Federation did establish a minimum wage for South Wales – it was not necessary in the Federated Area – it chose to use the machinery of the State. And the intervention by the State set a precedent for future industrial conflicts. In 1895 it stepped into the boot and shoe industry's biggest ever dispute and in 1896 it became involved in a railway dispute. In 1896 the Government passed the Conciliation Act which allowed the State to provide conciliators for industrial disputes. And though Baldwin attempted in the twenties to take the State out of industrial relations it became exceedingly doubtful after 1893 whether the distribution of income could be left to negotiation between private parties. 1893 was the year in which the State became a party to industrial matters and voluntary collective bargaining started to decline.

THE DENABY MAIN DISPUTE

The Denaby Main dispute of 1903, sometimes referred to as 'The Bag Muck Strike' was parochial in incidence but national in effect.[22] Its repercussions were felt as late as 1972 when it was cited in the case of *Heatons v The Transport and General Workers' Union* which was heard by the Industrial Court established under the 1971 Industrial Relations Act.

Denaby Main Colliery was located in the Don Valley between Mexborough and Doncaster, at the junction of the exposed and concealed coalfields. Its sinking in 1868 was an extremely speculative and hazardous affair because the shafts had to be put down to greater depths than had hitherto been reached and through heavily faulted and water-bearing rocks. The owners, Denaby and Cadeby Colliery Company, built a complete village, which, for the period, was extremely well designed, though it did have all the economic and social atmosphere of a company town. The pit always seems to have had an unhappy history. In 1885 there was a big strike and there were wholesale evictions when the owners attempted to introduce riddles and differential payments for large and small coal. There was the 1903 strike which we are about to analyse. And after nationalisation the pit acquired a bad reputation for strikes; in the fifties and sixties it became one of the most strike-bound pits in the country. There was a strike in 1962 to remove the manager and when that failed the branch left the Yorkshire NUM and industrially and socially ostracised the manager and his family. Even the owners in the private enterprise period seem to have been unusually obstinate by Yorkshire standards and, on occasions, left the coal-owners' association.

The dispute which began on 29 June 1902 concerned the payment for the removal of dirt. The company refused extra payment and dissatisfaction increased when there was a reduction of 10 per cent on the standard rate by the wages board. A branch meeting was held but was only attended by 400 out of the 5,000 workforce. At the meeting the branch officials proposed a strike and this was carried by those present. Pickets were set up, there was a certain amount of violence and evictions took place. The branch appealed to The Yorkshire Miners' Association for strike pay. This was refused when it was discovered that the men were in breach of contracts of employment, which required 14 days notice, and that a two-thirds majority for strike action had not been obtained at the ballot. County Officials advised the men to return to work and conduct a fresh ballot. At this juncture an unfortunate incident occurred. The Home Secretary had passed new regulations governing timbering which the Union had refused to accept. The colliery owners asked the men to sign new contracts of employment which embodied these regulations. The men refused and the County Officials then regarded the dispute as a lockout and began to pay strike pay. An injunction was applied for against the Yorkshire Miners' Association by a worker at the pit named Howden who alleged that funds were being misapplied. The injunction was granted and the strike pay which had been granted from 24 August 1902 ceased in February 1903. The strike then began to collapse and ended in March 1903. The Denaby and Cadeby Colliery Company sued the Yorkshire Miners for damages.

Both cases – *Howden v Yorkshire Miners Association* (1905) and *Denaby and Cadeby Collieries v Yorkshire Miners Association* (1906) must be seen in the light of the growing reaction to trade unions at the turn of the century and the attempts of the courts to curtail their activities. The *Howden case* involved the rights of the individual member against his union and as such was a forerunner of the Osborne Judgement as well as of many more recent cases such as *Bonsor v Musician's* Union (1955) and *Rookes v Barnard* (1964). The *Denaby and Cadeby Colliery case* concerned the ability or inability of a union to control its members and the right to sue a trade union for damages caused by its members. Just before the Denaby case lay the famous Taff Vale decision in which a railway company was able to sue the Amalgamated Society of Railway Servants for damages arising out of a strike. Ahead lay the Industrial Disputes Act 1906 which removed the problems raised by the Taff Vale decision by stipulating that a trade union could not be sued for damages arising out of or in contemplation of a trade dispute. More recently there has been the 1971 Industrial Relations Act and the decision in *Heatons v Transport and General Workers Union* in which a company attempted to claim damages from a union even though the union disagreed with the actions of its members. It was the Heatons case which led to the downfall of the Industrial Relations Act and during the course of the case reference was made to the Denaby decisions.

So much for the general context of the Denaby dispute. The details of the Howden issue can now be considered. Before the 1871 Trade Union Act trade unions were illegal and therefore members could not bring actions to enforce rights against their officials. After the Act unions were legalised, but Section 4 of the Act stated that: 'Nothing in this Act shall enable any Court to entertain any legal proceedings instituted with the object of directly enforcing or recovering damages for the breach of any of the following agreements'. The agreements set out in sub-sections referred to the use of funds. Howden wanted an injunction to prevent the officials from giving strike pay because it was in contravention of the Union's rule requiring a two-thirds majority decision. The issue turned, therefore, on the interpretation of the word 'directly'. Howden's injunction arose not because he wanted the rules to be directly enforced but because the rules were not being applied. It was the negative rather than the positive action that he wished to have enforced, and it was this interpretation which the judges upheld.

The second case, involving the colliery company, took place at a time when the Taff Vale decision was still reverberating around the trade union world. The decisions in the Denaby and Cadeby case were that the County Officials were not responsible for the damages caused by the strike, that the County Union does not prevent strikes but prescribes rules governing their conduct and that the County Officials did not enter a conspiracy but spoke against the strike and tried to get the men to return to work. The fact that strike pay was given did not constitute actionable grounds since the officials were acting contrary to the rules of the Union – this was the decision in *Howden v Yorkshire Miners*. The result also implied that branches were, to some extent, independent of the associations to which they were affiliated.

The verdicts in the Denaby dispute had a profound influence on union thinking. The dispute followed quickly on the Taff Vale case. Legal decisions operate on the periphery of industrial relations; they describe a magic circle within which the parties are expected to operate and usually the circles are drawn in such a way as to imply that their transgression will be rare. Taff Vale was a symbol and did not create many incidents. The Denaby case was one of the few exceptions. An obstinate employer, who was also suspected of financing a workman to bring an action against his union, was prepared to take up the precedent, and the union was frightened by the precedent. Had the union decided to continue financing the strike, the dispute would have continued. But it did not. When the Denaby case was referred to in the Heatons case there was a parallel. In the 1960s employers had asked for the means to punish unions, and for the balance of power to be restored. The 1971 Industrial Relations Act was passed to restore the balance but it was never intended that the Act was to be invoked, since it was hoped that unions would be able to control their shop stewards, and the Act was merely to be symbolic.[23] The Denaby and the Heaton's cases illustrate the bad effects of the law. In 1906 when Taff Vale was revoked most employers showed no anxiety even though Conservatives in the House of Lords were anxious to reject the Bill. When the 1971 Act was passed most employers did not want to use it and few regretted its passing.

THE EIGHT-HOUR DAY

A central plank in the platform of the Federation was the eight-hour day. The idea of reducing hours of work to create more employment was long established in trade union thinking and the miners had practised in the nineteenth century the policy of 'playing the pits' in order to clear stocks of coal. There were also the arguments that reductions in hours were necessary in order to ensure that people were not overworked and therefore prone to accidents. There was also the belief that some of the increase in output should take the form of increased leisure. But what distinguished the discussion at the turn of the century was the emphasis upon the desirability of state regulation of men's hours of work. It was the pros and cons of a statutory eight-hour day that divided the trade union world. The division split the Old Unions (New Model Unions) from the New Unions, though to emphasise the break in those terms is to ignore 'the accidental prominence' of particular forms of unions in particular periods.[24] The real distinction, as the Webbs observed, was between the closed and open unions.[25] The closed unions felt that they could achieve reductions in hours through collective bargaining and feared state intervention lest it widen out into a more general interference in the activities of unions. The open unions wanted a statutory eight-hour day because, as Marshall noted, it was the only method by which they thought a reduction in the supply of unskilled labour could be achieved.[26]

Within the coal industry the distinction between closed and open unions could be detected in the clash between Northumberland and Durham, on the one hand, and the Federation, on the other hand. In the North East the methods of working had evolved to produce two hewing shifts of seven hours and one long shift of ten hours for haulage. If an eight-hour day were introduced the employers would have to adopt one of three policies. Either, they could introduce a single shift of eight hours for haulage in which case output would fall and many hewers would have to be dismissed, or they could introduce double shifts for both hewers and haulage workers which would increase the work of hewers and necessitate the employment of more haulage workers. Finally, they could introduce two shifts for hewers and three shifts for haulage workers. But whichever policy was adopted the hewers stood to lose, and there was the added problem that costs of production could rise sharply. To the possible change in working conditions had also to be added the existence of conflict in mining unionism. The North East dominated the Miners' National Union, the descendant of the Miners' National Association, and the exponent of passive industrial policies and common political and legal policies. But the Federation threatened to turn the flank of the Union by fusing industrial and political measures. Thus in 1893 Northumberland and Durham left the Federation and did not return until 1907 and 1908.

Elsewhere the length of the working day was complicated by the definition adopted. By an eight-hour day the Federation meant 'eight hours from bank to bank'; that is, from the time the first man was wound down to the time when the first man returned to the surface. So one winding time had to be added to the time during which coal was raised. Unfortunately, not everyone adhered to this definition. In some areas winding times were excluded; in others both winding times were included, and hence various surveys produced conflicting evidence. But if care is taken to steer through the various definitional entanglements it would appear that the longest hours were worked in Lancashire and South Wales and the shortest were worked in Somerset, the Midlands and Scotland.

The Act which was introduced in 1908 omitted winding times and therefore specified a working day of about nine hours. But even so it had an effect. In the North East it led to strikes as workers protested against new methods of working. In the Midlands the employers tried to eliminate mealtimes from the calculation of eight hours and in Yorkshire some employers tried to introduce a Saturday afternoon shift, or a full Saturday shift, to keep costs down. In South Wales productivity fell, costs rose and the Act made a not insignificant contribution to the problems of the coalfield. And everywhere there seemed to be an increase in the number of men at the face with a consequent fall in productivity and, to a lesser extent, earnings. There were also wider repercussions. The Act applied to coalface workers but its introduction led to demands by haulage workers and surface workers, many of whom were unorganised, for a shorter working day.

THE MINIMUM WAGE 1912

The Coal Mines (Minimum Wage) Act, 1912, was a product of the upsurge in labour discontent during the period 1900 to 1912. It was a time when real wages declined and there was a wholesale attack on trade unions which was exemplified in the Taff Vale decision and the Osborne case. It was a period in which the educational revolution, which began in 1871, was making workers aware of their condition, and it was also an era in which the existing order was once more being challenged and doctrines of workers' control, nationalisation and socialism were being espoused.

The demand for a minimum wage arose directly out of the problem of payments for working in abnormal places. Miners' wages were determined by price lists, allowances and the percentage addition. The price list governed the payments to be made for working in average conditions but when conditions were abnormal the practice was to pay an allowance which would bring wages up to some agreed level. These allowances were ex gratia payments dependent upon the attitudes of managers. In 1907 the South Wales Miners had tried to secure their legal enforcement but failed in the case of *Walters v Ocean Coal Ltd.* During the first decade of the twentieth century allowances began to be reduced or withdrawn at pits where the impact of the eight-hour day, the Workmen's Compensation Act, the Coal Tax and the Board of Trade's new regulations governing timbering and safety increased costs. This pressure to nibble at allowances was not universal. We have noticed that it occurred at Denaby, but the Denaby and Cadeby Colliery Company was a rogue elephant by Yorkshire standards. It was in South Wales, a high cost–low productivity area, that pressure became greatest.

In September 1910 miners at the Ely Colliery of the Cambrian Combine struck over the payment of insufficient allowances. The dispute then spread from the Rhondda to the Aberdare and Ogmore valleys and eventually 30,000 miners were out. There were riots and disturbances at Tonypandy and other places where blacklegs were brought in, and there were clashes with the police. Churchill, the Home Secretary, sent in the troops. The South Wales Miners Federation appealed to the MFGB for support and the Federation raised a levy to finance the strike. But South Wales wanted action and not finance. An attempt by the Federation to produce a compromise settlement was rejected by a South Wales delegate Conference which demanded a general stoppage throughout the Federated Area for the purpose of securing a guaranteed minimum wage. The proposal split the Federation into two camps – the Old Liberals and the Syndicalists. The Old Liberalists wanted the dispute treated as a local issue which the Federation was being asked to assist in solving, while the Syndicalists wanted to widen the front and sought a national confrontation. At a national conference in June 1911 Ashton's view that there should be a return to work received general support, leaving the South Wales Federation to continue the strike until August.

Meanwhile the problem of a minimum wage was receiving wider discussion. The decline of real wages was universal and there was the fact that, though mechanisation was being introduced to offset the inexorable tendency to diminishing returns, the collier was not sharing in the benefits of increased productivity. He was being downgraded to becoming a mere shoveller of coal.

The Coal-owners were as divided over the issue of a minimum wage as were the Federation. In the high-cost areas, such as Scotland and South Wales, there was considerable opposition. An increase in wages, it was argued, would raise costs and result in some pits having to close, and might also bring about an increase in absenteeism. In the inland coalfields there was little resistance to the idea of a minimum wage because wages were thought to be already higher than any expected minimum wage. It was these differences which led the employers to resist the proposal.

In February 1912 the Federation balloted its members on the desirability of strike action and received the necessary two-thirds majority.[27] The government attempted to intervene through the use of the Industrial Council under the chairmanship of G. R. Askwith.[28] By February there were 115,000 men idle and the number climbed to 1,803,000 in March. The government then offered to introduce a Bill which would provide for the establishment of Joint Boards in each district to fix district minima. The Federation agreed to call off the strike once the Bill had been passed by Parliament and provided that it gave a guaranteed national minimum of five shillings a shift for adult workers and two shillings for boys as well as a schedule of district minimum rates. Asquith, the Prime Minister, refused to incorporate these proposals into the Bill which was hurriedly passed through Parliament and became law on 29 March.

The Federation then balloted its members on the desirability of continuing the strike. There was a great deal of support for continuance but it failed to secure the necessary two-thirds majority; the voting was 201,013 for a resumption of work and 244,011 against a resumption. Lancashire, Yorkshire, Derbyshire, Northumberland and Durham were strongly against a return to work. The only two big coalfields to vote in favour of acceptance of the Act were Scotland and South Wales. The return to work caused a great deal of bitterness and recriminations against the leadership at national and district levels, because no guidance was given to the rank and file on how to vote on the contents of an Act which still left everything to be determined at district level. There were hints of a breakaway in the Doncaster Area and demands for periodic elections in order to produce a more responsive and militant leadership. In the inland coalfields most men got nothing out of the legislation, whilst the coalowners were able to sub-divide the coalfields so as to ensure the viability of uneconomic pits. The high wages of South Yorkshire were not allowed to pull up wages in West Yorkshire and the prosperous Leen Valley was kept isolated from the Erewash Valley in Nottinghamshire.

The strike resulted in the loss of 30,800 working days. Its short-run importance lay in the fact that it provided a basis for unionism in South Wales. The strike was the price exacted for giving South Wales statutory minimum wage legislation and keeping South Wales within the Federation. Its long-run importance was two-fold. First, it sowed the seed of the idea that districts could be treated as autonomous units for the purposes of wage determination. This was to sprout in 1926 for Spencerism (see page 59) was the application of the 1893 settlement as reinforced by the 1912 conclusion. But by 1926 the Federation's idea had moved on to the idea of a national minimum wage and Spencerism became a term of abuse. The second lesson of 1912 was that it demonstrated the possibilities of using minimum wage legislation to protect collectively bargained rates. In 1908 statutory wage boards had been set up to fix wages in the unorganised trades, mainly domestic trades of chainmaking, paper-box making and tailoring. However, these were not typical trades but ones which were being replaced by factory production. The big expansion of statutory wage fixing came in 1918, 1943 and 1945 – the forerunner was the Coal Mines (Minimum Wages) Act, since the successful application of statutory wages boards requires the prior existence of some degree of organisation of both employers and workers and it was this idea that Ernest Bevin developed in 1943 and 1945, when he introduced minimum wage legislation for catering and retail distribution in order to protect the wages obtained by unions for some workers in those trades and for workers in other trades. The wages to be extended and applied to the unorganised were to be those determined by the organised. Despite the recent trend towards the abolition of wages councils, unions have shown no reluctance to invoke the aid of the state and future policy will see the unions relying on section 8 of the Employment Protection Act, 1975, which allows a union to insist on an unorganised employer paying the same wages as have been determined by collective bargaining. The advantage that this alternative method has over the old system may lie in the pressure it exerts on non-unionists to join unions in order to have their cases presented to the arbitration service. The clause in the Act embodies the same principle that was contained in the Fair Wages Clause of 1911 and the Industrial Disputes Order No. 1376, 1951. The effects of these two instruments have been mixed. On the one hand, there is evidence that unions in the public sector failed to invoke the Fair Wages Clause in order to get government employees paid in line with those in the private sector, with the result that many were very badly paid.[29] On the other hand, Order 1376 was successfully used by NALGO in the fifties to compel some local authorities to pay union rates.

THE ABANDONMENT OF LIBERALISM

The final event of the decade before the First World War was the abandonment of liberalism by the miners and their affiliation to the Labour Party. The change was part of that great transformation which overcame unions. Coal and cotton had symbolised the Industrial Revolution and its progress through the nineteenth century, and the large numbers of workers in both industries had deeply influenced political and social thought and action. Cotton had stood for the Conservative working man and Coal for the Liberal working man and as long as the two great concentrations of unionists had been able to get what they wanted by acting as pressure groups on the established political parties there appeared to be a profound continuity in political life and little scope for the creation of a working-class political party.

There were, of course, other reasons for the slow emergence of a workers' party. There was the slow growth of the working class. Domestic service – that hangover from feudalism – was still a large source of employment in the 1870s. Change was also dependent upon the development of stable mass workers' unions and they only emerged around the turn of the century. Also, among the miners the opportunities for establishing a separate party were limited until the Third Reform Act gave the vote to the counties. Even then, when the opportunities came there were retarding influences. Men like Ben Pickard of Yorkshire for example, saw no point in financing a political party which would benefit the weak and poorly organised. There was also the influence of non-conformism which encouraged individualism, discouraged drinking and emphasised the importance of education. As such, conformism tended to strengthen the links between the pit villages and the Liberal Party. There was also the undeniable fact that the Liberal leaders of the miners' unions could be tough and militant and were not averse to conducting long and gruelling strikes against the employers. It was their record that the young socialists had to challenge.

Conversion when it came was uneven in its incidence; there were leaders and laggards. Northumberland and Durham were traditional areas of cautious unionism but there had been an earlier history of radicalism and there was the fact that at the turn of the century the two coalfields were being confronted by many problems. There was discontent with the customary policies, there were difficulties with hours of work, and there was increasing competition from other countries. In Scotland the incursion of socialism was swifter. Scotland was a low-wage area and many early socialists were Scots. In Lancashire there was the desire to overcome the problems created by the fact that many miners were Tories and some were Liberals; there was a need to find a political party which would cement differences.

South Wales was slow to change but when it came the conversion was dramatic. The coalfield expanded in the first decade of the twentieth century. South Wales was an export coalfield and when exports rose South Wales sucked in workers from neighbouring regions, especially England. As Table 3.1 reveals there was an alternation in the expansion of the export and inland coalfields. When exports were slack then the inland coalfields expanded; when exports boomed labour migrated to

TABLE 1.3 Migration Balances in the Coalfield of England and Wales 1851–1911

	Net gain or loss by migration (in thousands)	
	English coalfields	*Welsh coalfields*
1851–61	+63	+42
1861–71	+82	+ 9
1871–91	+63	+10
1881–91	−30	+86
1891–1901	+18	+40
1901–1911	+35	+126

Source: B. Thomas, *Migration and Urban Development*, Methuen, London, 1972.

South Wales. The years before the First World War witnessed a boom. The labour force in the Welsh valleys became more cosmopolitan and this tended to erode the influence of leaders such as W. J. Abraham (Mabon), who used to exploit Celtic passion to create an insular union. In the eighties the sliding scale came under attack and with it went those who had sponsored it. Northumberland, Durham, Scotland and Lancashire were the leaders and South Wales was a good second. The laggards were mainly to be found in the inland coalfields such as Yorkshire, Derbyshire and Nottinghamshire. But even in these coalfields the unions were disturbed by the Taff Vale decision, while in the background there was falling productivity, rising costs and mounting industrial unrest. In the light of such experiences it was difficult for the unions to be associated with a political party which was also supported by the coal-owners. In 1909 the Federation affiliated to the Labour Party. The miners were slow to change but their conversion hardened with time, and in the debacle of 1931 it was the miners who returned the bulk of the Labour MPs to Westminster.

THE INTER-WAR YEARS, 1919–39

The problems of the coal industry during the inter-war years represented a continuation of the difficulties experienced before the war and intensified by lack of adjustment during the war. Before the war the industry was experiencing a rise in costs due to diminishing returns in the old coalfields. These rising costs were encountering resistance in markets and encouraging an internal movement towards the new coalfields of the east while abroad there was growing development of coalfields. There was also the introduction of mechanisation at the coalface and on haulage in which Scotland pioneered, plus increasing efficiency in the use of fuel and the use of substitutes such as oil and electricity. What the war did was to restrict the adjustment of the industry to the new competition and to magnify the problems of adaptation by increasing the scale of output and employment in existing coalfields. After the immediate post-war boom the size of the adjustment problem was revealed; the industry had excess capacity. Market forces responded to the problem but the problem was too big to be handled by the slow forces of competition.

The difficulties of change were, of course, not peculiar to coal. They were present in the other staple trades, such as textiles, iron and steel and engineering and shipbuilding – all of which were badly affected by the war. Table 1.4 throws a great deal of light upon the issues and sources of conflict. A distinction is revealed between the export trades and the sheltered trades, such as shipbuilding, printing and railways. During the war some of these industries gained from the expansion of demand for their services, while others strengthened their position after the war. Thus, railways were amalgamated and a monopoly position was established, in which railwaymen, who were poorly paid and worked long hours before the war, benefited. The sheltered trades were characterised by relatively high wages and low levels of employment. In contrast, the collapse of markets led to a fall in wages in the export trades and, because their workers tended to be immobile, to relatively high levels of unemployment. The export trades employed the bulk of the labour force and the fall in incomes acted as a multiplier to reduce demand in the sheltered trades so that the general level of unemployment was higher than before the war. The overall position was that wages were too high for the export trades to remove unemployment and too low to give a decent standard of living to those employed whilst unemployment pay provided a disincentive to move to those other trades which, though relatively better off, were also somewhat depressed.

The distinction between export and sheltered trades was one that occurred within industries as well as between industries. In

TABLE 1.4 Unemployment and Wage Rates

	Relative levels of weekly rates of wages (September, 1927), as percentage of August 1914	*Percentage of insured persons unemployed (Great Britain and Northern Ireland), 26 September 1927*
All trades	170—5	9.3
Building	197	9.1
Coal (earnings)	152	19.1
Engineering: skilled	149	10.0[a]
labourer	182	
Shipbuilding: shipwright	135	21.8
labourer	168	
Electrical installation	191	5.7
Iron and steel	120—70	11.8—32.4
Cotton	161	9.3
Wool textile	180—90	8.2
Hosiery (Midlands)	158⅓	5.7
Boot and shoe	200	8.2
Railway services	200—45	4.6
Docks etc.	190—240	22.1
Printing: compositor	207	4.3
Furniture: cabinet-maker	184	4.5
Baking	214	6.0
Pottery	150—61¼	12.3
Heavy chemicals	205—15	6.2[b]

[a] *'General Engineering: Iron and Steel-founding.'*
[b] Average of 'Chemicals Manufacture and 'Explosives'.
Source: H. Clay, *The Problem of Industrial Relations* (Macmillan, London, 1929).

the coal industry it was the export fields of South Wales and Northumberland and Durham whilst some of the inland fields such as Yorkshire, Derbyshire, Leicestershire and Nottinghamshire were relatively prosperous. Also to the depressed export regions could be added the high-cost inland fields as well as the export areas seeking alternative markets. These differences between coalfields explain much of the internal discord and conflict and failure to reach agreement that marked the period up to the 1926 lockout. Within the ranks of the coal-owners it was those who came from South Wales, such as D. A. Thomas and Evan Williams, who tended to be the most obdurate, the most willing to seek a confrontation, whereas the coal-owners of South

Yorkshire, Derbyshire and Nottinghamshire seemed the most willing to seek peaceful solutions to the difficulties. At the Markham pits in Yorkshire there was no lockout in 1926; instead there were sympathy strikes. The differences between the coal-owners paralleled the differences between the miners and their leaders. The most militant areas tended to be the export and high-cost coalfields, and what prevented a split for so long was the solidarity that had been created within the Federation, a solidarity more ardently expressed in Yorkshire than anywhere else. If Yorkshire had decided not to support the depressed coalfields then, almost certainly, the conciliatory unionism that emerged in Nottinghamshire after 1926 would have developed earlier. It was the consciousness of the Yorkshire miners, expressed more in the form of industrial militancy than the political militancy of South Wales, that kept the Federation on a cohesive and determined policy for so long.

Given the circumstances depicted by Table 1.4 governments could have pursued a variety of policies. One solution would have been to impose tariffs, increase internal demand by monetary measures and attempt a change in the industrial structure by a judicious mixture of taxes and subsidies.[30] But though tariffs were imposed on some goods there was a reluctance to pursue a thorough going protectionist policy and unbalanced budgets were a thing of the future. A second possibility would have been to devalue in the hope of stimulating exports and reducing the rate at which adjustment would have had to be achieved in the staple trades. Devaluation would have been possible in the relatively prosperous world conditions of the twenties. But when the decision was made to fix the exchange rate it was decided to restore the pre-war parity. The policy that was adopted was compounded of hesitancy and uncertainty and the hope that the Americans would allow a domestic expansion sufficient to expand world trade and boost British exports. Whether devaluation would have worked is a moot point. There would have been some prices at which Britain could have sold coal, iron and steel and textiles and retained people in existing jobs but the resulting standard of living might have been exceedingly low. A more far-sighted policy would have been to hasten the movement to the newer industries instead of relying on the market.

The effects of the war were to increase the swing to the left in the Federation and, as a result of State control and national wage agreements, to increase the power of the Executive. In 1919 the Union proposed a substantial increase in wages, a six-hour day and nationalisation of the mines, and a ballot on strike action was carried by a large majority. Lloyd George's response was to set up the Coal Industry Commission (sometimes referred to as the Sankey Commission) to enquire into the condition of the industry and the strike was called off when Lloyd George stated that he would accept the Commission's findings. The Commission was composed of representatives of the miners, the coal-owners and three independent Government nominees, under the chairmanship of Mr Justice Sankey. The Commission issued three interim reports of which the third, signed by the Chairman and the three government nominees recommended a seven-hour day with effect from 16 July 1919, a six-hour day (depending upon the circumstances of the industry) with effect from 13 July 1921, an increase of wages of two shillings a day and a radical reorganisation of the industry either through nationalisation or joint control. Bonar Law, speaking for the Government, said that the Government accepted the spirit of the report, which the Federation took to be a promise of nationalisation. The Federation then withdrew its strike threat. The Commission went on to produce four final reports, of which the one signed by the Chairman and the miners' sympathisers advocated nationalisation but the other reports were opposed to state control.

Although many coal-owners had come to accept the inevitability of nationalisation, the Government showed no sense of urgency and preferred to play a waiting game. Coal prices were increased to pay for the higher wages and reduced hours and the effect was to lose the miners much sympathy. Finally, a strike in Yorkshire which had the support of the Area officials but not of the MFGB Executive allowed Lloyd George to declare his opposition to nationalisation because, he argued, it was still under some form of State control and yet strikes still occurred. Nationalisation was not, therefore, a solution to the industry's problems, and he recommended State purchase of mineral rights, subsidies to inprove amenities in mining areas and amalgamation of companies to improve efficiency.

THE DATUM LINE STRIKE 1920

With the hopes of nationalisation dwindling the Federation

decided to press for an increase in wages. Prices were still rising and miners' real wages were falling, but when wage increases were granted the Government tended at the same time to increase coal prices in order, as the Federation believed, to turn public opinion against the miners. The Federation therefore decided in 1920 not merely to seek an increase in wages but also to press for a reduction in prices and it received the support of the Triple Alliance.[31]

The Government hedged on the question of a wage increase and suggested that increased wages should be conditional upon increased output – this was the origin of the datum line from which increases should be calculated. The Federation rejected arbitration and thereby lost the support of the Alliance. Strike action was threatened for September 1920 and began on 16 September. On 21 October the National Union of Railwaymen threatened to come out in sympathy and this caused the Government to re-open negotiations. The miners then called off their strike, though not without considerable bitterness and hostility being expressed against the leadership.

THE 1921 LOCKOUT

The next stage in the industry's fortunes occurred when state control was suddenly abandoned. In 1920 the post-war boom ended and the slump began at the time the coal-owners and the miners were preoccupied with the nature of the future wage structure. The miners wanted to consolidate various wartime increases and the post-war additions and allow future changes to take the form of flat rate increases or decreases which would narrow differentials. They also wanted to retain a system of pooling revenues so as to perpetuate cross-subsidisation, but the coal-owners were opposed to these proposals. On 31 March 1921 the industry was suddenly and hastily decontrolled because the export markets had collapsed and the pits were making losses. Both the miners and the owners protested against the drastic change. Faced with the removal of subsidies the owners demanded that wages should be determined by the financial position of each district which implied an average reduction in wages of 22 per cent with the range extending from 48 per cent in

Cumberland to 1 per cent in Derbyshire, Nottinghamshire and Leicestershire.

The MFMGB Executive suggested that each district should seek the most advantageous settlement, but this was rejected by South Wales and later by a National Conference vote. A lockout began on 1 April 1921. There was the suggestion of a sympathetic strike by transport workers to be started on Friday 15 April, but it did not take place and thereafter 15 April was known as 'Black Friday'. The lock-out lasted from April to July. At the end of April the Government, which was opposed to a National Pool but was not averse to a National Wages Board to supervise district wage agreements, offered a subsidy of £ 10 million if a settlement was achieved. The offer was turned down and the Prime Minister threatened to withdraw the subsidy.

Faced with the possible loss of the subsidy the coal-owners made a revised offer in June which proposed to use the subsidy to ensure that any immediate cuts in wages would not exceed two shillings a day. They did, however, want a return to district wage agreements with the possibility of a National Wages Board to lay down the general principles of wage determination. The offer was put to the membership of the Federation without any guidance from the Executive and was rejected. Large majorities for continuing the strike were recorded in Scotland, South Wales, Lancashire and the Forest of Dean; these were the high-cost areas. Finally, in June the Executive recommended the districts to accept substantially the same terms as the membership had rejected earlier. The district vote was in favour of a return to work, with only Lancashire, of the large districts, being in favour of a continuance of the stoppage.

THE SAMUEL COMMISSION

The French occupation of the Ruhr and the dislocation of that coalfield brought a temporary improvement in trading conditions, and during the little boom of 1923–4 the Federation pressed for a wage increase and threatened strike action. The owners' offer was rejected and a Court of Inquiry was set up which supported the Federation's claim. A new settlement was reached which made wages the first charge upon the industry; standard profits were to be 15 per cent of standard wages and any surplus was to be divided in the ratio 88 to 12. The agreement was to run for twelve months.

But the improvement in trade was short-lived and the situation was further aggravated by the return to gold at the pre-war parity in 1925. In June 1925 the coal-owners proposed the termination of the 1924 Agreement and a return to district negotiations and a rejection of the notion that wages were a first charge upon the industry. The effect of the owners' proposals would have been to reduce the percentage on base rates by 9 per cent in the Eastern Area (Nottinghamshire, Derbyshire and Yorkshire) and by as much as 48 per cent in Northumberland, Durham and Scotland. The Federation flatly refused to consider the offer and also refused to be involved with a Court of Inquiry set up by the Government. The Inquiry Report found a great deal of substance in the miners' claims and factors outside the control of both the miners and the masters. A proposed lockout was averted by the promise of a full-scale inquiry and, until the inquiry was complete, there was to be financial assistance. In the interim the miners were to return to work on the 1924 terms.

The Samuel Commission of 1925 rejected nationalisation and opposed any further subsidies, whether permanent or temporary, but it agreed with many of the arguments in the miners' case. It stated that wages should be determined by national agreements in order to avoid cut-throat competition between the districts at the expense of wages. It was also opposed to any lengthening of the working day. The commission also believed that the industry could and should be made more efficient by amalgamations, closure of uneconomic pits and the establishment of a central selling agency. It suggested that the State should acquire possession of mineral rights and indicated that the transfer price at which companies sold coal to their other plants should be fixed by an independent body in order to prevent firms subsidising ancillaries and keeping coal wages down. Finally, the Commission stated that any wage reductions were to be conditional upon reorganisation.

The Commission's Report was accepted by the Government. It confirmed Baldwin's view that there had been too much political meddling in the industry's affairs and that the industry must be left to work out its own solutions.[32] The Report was rejected by the miners and the coal-owners.

THE GENERAL STRIKE AND THE MINERS' LOCKOUT

The General Strike has been well-documented and only the barest details will suffice. The coal-owners posted notices of reductions in wages and increases in hours of work and the miners were locked out on 1 May 1926. Three days later the TUC called a general strike in support of the miners. The strike lasted nine days and was accompanied by considerable violence. On 12 May the TUC called off the General Strike. It had failed to get the miners to accept a draft set of recommendations which closely followed the recommendations of the 1925 Samuel Commission and it was frightened of the charge that the strike was political and not industrial in intent.

Having rejected the leadership of the TUC and the proposed terms of settlement the miners were left to continue the struggle alone. The lockout eventually ended in November 1926 when a National Conference advised the districts to seek local negotiations. There had been a steady trickle back to work in some areas and breakaway unions formed in Nottinghamshire. The last districts to return to work were South Wales, Durham and Yorkshire: the former two having the most to lose from any settlement, the latter staying out through obdurate loyalty.

The effects of the General Strike and the Miners' Lockout on the miners were traumatic. Wages were cut and hours of work were increased. The Federation was subjected to the disintegrative forces of district wage bargaining. In Nottinghamshire a breakaway union under the leadership of George Spencer conducted negotiations with employers. Spencerism emerged in the Leen Valley and spread into the Mansfield coalfield at Harworth, which was owned by the Barber Walker Company.[34] From Harworth it crossed into the Doncaster pits of Bentley and Bullcroft which were also owned by the Barber Walker Company. It also travelled into Durham but seems to have been rejected by the coal-owners as well as the miners. Company unionism also developed in Wales. In Scotland the union broke up as the left developed their own union in Fife.

Despite the reductions in wages and increases in hours the conditions of the industry did not improve, and supply still exceeded demand. In 1930 restriction of output was given Parliamentary approval when the Coal Mines Act was passed. The Act established the system of output quota and attempted to encourage amalgamation and the elimination of inefficient pits but it foundered on the problems of disentangling technical from commercial efficiency. Many of the pits which came into being in the post-war boom were saddled with high fixed charges and impeded by quotas which did not allow them to attain economies of scale. In contrast, older pits had paid off their overheads and could operate as long as they covered running costs. It was these problems that complicated amalgamations. The Samuel Commission assumed that size meant efficiency but this dictum was relative and by no means universal. It was true of South Yorkshire and Nottinghamshire but it was not so obvious in Scotland and South Wales where the average size of pit tended to be small.[35]

But what of the rest of British industry? The Trades Disputes Act and the Trade Union Act of 1927 outlawed the general strike and some sympathetic strikes prevented the development of trade unionism in the civil service. Also the Act substituted 'contracting-in' for 'contracting—out' of the political levy. There was a fall in strike activity after 1926. Between 1919 and 1925 28 million working days were lost in disputes of which three-quarters were due to national strikes. Between 1927 and 1939 just over 3 million working days were lost in stoppages of which two-thirds involved national disputes, mainly in textiles. Thus the main effect of 1926 seems to have been a fall in disputes connected with the establishment or reaffirmation of national agreements. But the 1927 Act seems to have played little part in causing a reduction in strikes. It was seldom invoked and its main effect, as with so many pieces of labour legislation, was mainly symbolic.[36]

Unions may not have engaged in national strikes but this fact does not appear to have been due to the debacle consequent upon the support they gave to the miners. Many continued to believe that, if called upon to do it again, they would have done so. It was the lack of a call rather than the absence of a response that accounts for the absence of a large-scale sympathetic strike after 1926. Most union leaders were moderates in 1926 and it was moderates who continued to run unions after 1926. As for the general absence of national strikes after this date, might not that be accounted for by their irrelevance? Unions have tended to operate by putting the screws on locally and the drift to national bargaining was a development produced by employers' opposition to plant – level bargaining. In the full employment years after 1945 unions went back to plant – level bargaining which suggests that it was the peculiar circumstances of depression that preserved national bargaining and national conflict.

THE SECOND WORLD WAR 1939–45

The Second World War brought tremendous changes in the organisation of industrial relations in the industry, though the changes were not immediate. At the beginning of the war the Government was able to set up an indirect form of control through the use of the machinery which had been set up under the 1930 Coal Mincs Act. During 1939 the task was to increase the supply of coal of France, but with the collapse of France in 1940 there was a switch of coal to domestic markets and excess supply developed. Many miners were allowed to join the Forces but they were to be missed later on.

With the increasing conversion to a war economy after 1940 there was an expansion of the demand for coal by the munitions industries, and shortages developed in 1941. At the same time coal output started to fall and the Government placed restrictions on the movement of workers out of the industry and set up pit production committees. But output still continued to fall. Absenteeism was cited as a cause of falling output but this was doubtful because attendances were also rising. The main cause was falling productivity in the older coalfields which was not offset by rising productivity in the newer regions. Also behind the statistics lay the legacy of the inter-war years; the labour force was getting older, population was declining in the mining areas and most miners were reluctant to let their children go down the pits.

BETTESHANGER 1941

In 1941 a strike occurred at Betteshanger Colliery in Kent which was to have far-reaching implications since it was referred to in the deliberations of the 1968 Royal Commission on Trade Unions and Employers' Associations. No account of the dispute could match that provided by Sir Harold Emmerson to the Commission:

MASS PROSECUTION IN WAR TIME

1. Doubts about the practicability of prosecuting large numbers of men for going on strike illegally were put to the test at the Betteshanger Colliery in Kent, in December 1941. There had been trouble at this colliery about allowances for work in a difficult seam where working conditions changed almost weekly. After all else had failed the company and the men agreed to go to arbitration and to abide by the award. An experienced arbitrator decided that the allowances offered by the management were reasonable and erred, if at all, in being excessive. The men rejected the award and work stopped. About 4,000 men were idle.

2. Under the National Arbitration Order the strike was illegal and to make matters worse it was backed by local Union Officials. In the Ministry of Labour we felt that the great value of the Order lay in its moral effect. Any quick resort to prosecution could only weaken its authority, we might possibly lose Union support, and the work of the Chief Industrial Commissioner and his staff would be made more difficult. But in coal mining the Mines Department decided on action under the Order and we were only their agents when it came to legal action. The Secretary for Mines, who was himself a former miners' leader, decided on prosecution, and he had Cabinet backing. Reluctantly we set the machinery of the law in motion.

3. The prosecution of 4,000 men seemed a tall order, but as the dispute had started with 1,000 underground workers we decided to concentrate on them. Extra supplies of forms for the serving of summonses were rushed down to the Chief Constable of Kent. Then several Justices of the Peace had to be found willing to sign 1,000 forms in duplicate and extra police were drafted to serve them. After these preliminaries a special hearing was arranged. Charges against 1,000 persons could only be handled satisfactorily if the men pleaded guilty. If each man pleaded 'not guilty' the proceedings might last for months. The Union was asked if they would instruct their members to plead guilty, and accept a decision on a few test cases. The Union obligingly did so.

4. The magistrates met in Canterbury. The news had spread to other coalfields and colliery bands decided to accompany the culprits. Local colliery workers made it an outing for their

families and chartered coaches to take wives and children. The Mines Department authorised the Regional Petroleum Officer to allow petrol for the journeys.

5. Everything on the day was orderly and even festive. Bands played and women and children cheered the procession on its way to the Court. The proceedings in Court went smoothly; everyone pleaded guilty. The three Union officials were sent to prison. The Branch Secretary was sentenced to two months with hard labour; the local President and a member of the local executive each received one month with hard labour. Thirty-five men were fined £3 or one month's imprisonment, and nearly one thousand were fined £1, or fourteen days.

6. Protests came against the severity of the sentences, particularly against the imprisonment of three union officials. Many of the miners in the area were in the Home Guard, and Kent was in the front line. "Was this the way to treat good citizens?" There was talk of sympathetic strikes. But the real trouble was that the only men who could call off the strike were now in gaol. The Secretary for Mines went down to Kent to see them accompanied by Mr Ebby Edwards, then the National President of the Miners' Union. Negotiations were re-opened and five days after the hearing an agreement was signed, in prison, between the colliery management and the Kent Miners' Union. Apart from some face-saving words, it gave the men what they wanted. Then the Secretary for Mines took a deputation to the Home Secretary asking for the immediate release of the three local officials. The men would not start work until their leaders were free. After eleven days in prison they were released. The mine reopened and in the first week the normal output of coal was nearly trebled.

7. In the Ministry of Labour there was gloom and apprehension. Certainly we had shown that it was possible to prosecute on a large scale if everyone co-operated. But even if the remission were necessary for work to start, they were bound to weaken the authority of the Order. Also what would be the effect on the men who had been fined? We were soon to know; for the Clerk to the Justices reported that of the men who had been fined only nine had paid. Before he went to the trouble of preparing nearly a thousand commitment warrants the Clerk asked whether it was proposed to recommend remission. The County gaol could only accommodate a few at a time and it

would take several years to work through the list. He understood that the men had been at work for some weeks, they had made good the lost output and he believed the country needed coal. There might be an outcry if men were sent to prison for not paying the fines, when the original sentences of imprisonment on the leaders had been remitted. He asked for guidance.
8. The company also wanted to avoid further trouble. They asked if they could pay the fines on behalf of the men; the cost to them would be so much less profits tax! They were told on no account to do this. The Court was advised not to enforce the unpaid fines.
9. Of course someone asked: 'What about the nine men who paid their fines? Should they have their money back?' But it was not until 1950 – eight years later – that the National Union of Mineworkers asked formally that the paid fines should be returned. The Union was told, in appropriate official language, to forget it.[37]

In 1942 there was widespread discontent over wages in the coalfields. Wages were still based on price lists plus the district percentage, but the effect of controls on the price of coal and rising prices for other materials was to squeeze the amount available out of the surplus that could go to wages. Miners began to compare their wages with those being paid in munitions and there were serious outbreaks of strikes. The Federation applied for a national minimum wage and substantial increases for all workers. A special Board of Investigation (the Greene Board) was set up and conceded the miners' claims for a national minimum wage and a general increase in wages. The Board also recommended the introduction of district output bonuses but they proved unsuccessful. The most important achievement of the Greene Board was the establishment of conciliation machinery for the industry. This provided for disputes to be classified as national, district or pit issues. A National Board was established consisting of a Joint National Negotiating Committee, on which there was to be equal representation from the Mining Association and the MFGB, and a National Reference Tribunal, composed of independent people, which would make binding awards when the JNNC failed to agree. After nationalisation pit conciliation machinery was established.

In 1944 the National Reference Tribunal, whose chairman was

then Lord Porter, made one of its most famous awards. It provided for the consolidation of the wages of day-wage workers; that is, the basic rate plus the district percentage, plus the Greene award of 1942 plus various other additions. The NRT also consolidated the wages of pieceworkers.

The question of nationalisation was raised during the war but deferred and it was left to the 1945 Labour Government to nationalise the industry in 1947. The main legacy of the war was the conciliation machinery, a national minimum wage and consolidation of various bonuses. Everything else inherited in 1947 was the residue of two hundred years of mining history.

2 The National Coal Board

The coal mines were nationalised because the miners were no longer prepared to work for the private coal-owners. Various reasons could be found to account for the nationalisation of the mines, but it was the miners' attitude that was fundamental. It was also argued that the industry was technologically backward and that only state ownership would guarantee the right amount of investment but that argument presupposed that in the inter-war years the capital market was wrong in directing investment away from the coal industry despite its obvious unprofitability.

Nevertheless, the achievement in 1947 was not all that the miners anticipated and, later, some were to refer to nationalisation as state capitalism – an echo of an earlier criticism of nationalisation. What was achieved in 1947 represented the influence of three strands of thought whose sources could be traced back to the turn of the century. First, there were the miners' views on participation and control which found strong expression in the period from 1900 to 1920. Secondly, certain economic theories began to exert an influence in the inter-war years but their implications were not fully explored until after 1945. Thirdly, there were the ideas derived from Herbert Morrison's experiments with public enterprises.

The various ideological influences on the nationalisation of coal will be considered in the first part of this chapter. The second part will be concerned with the actual operations of the Coal Board and their implications for industrial relations.

WORKERS' CONTROL

Economists distinguish two theories of value by which people make their decisions and organise social activities. One theory – the labour theory of value – suggests that goods exchange on the basis of their labour content so that, for example, one deer is equivalent to two beaver if it takes twice as long to catch a deer as it does a beaver. The other – the utility theory – proposes that commodities exchange on the basis of the utilities (usefulness) at the margin, of goods to prospective buyers. Both theories can be reconciled with each other and both can be thought of as representing two sides of a more general theory of value.[1] Their influence in everyday affairs, however, stems from the emphasis they give to different beliefs about society. Thus a labour theory of value inclines one to the idea that goods might not exchange on the basis of their labour content and that there might be exploitation; a labour theory of value stresses the point of view of the producer and the distribution of income. In contrast, utility theory emphasises the consumer.

Most theories of workers' control have their basis in some labour theory of value. Goods may not exchange on the basis of their labour content, there may be a surplus which labour creates and which is appropriated by the capitalist exploiters of labour. The remedy is the overthrow of the system which permits exploitation and its replacement by some form of workers' control in the form of socialism or communism.[2]

Proposals for, and ideas about, workers' control can be traced far back into the eighteenth century. In the 1870s Shirland Colliery in Derbyshire became a workers' cooperative although the venture foundered in the slump.[3] However, the main period of intellectual ferment came in the last decades of the nineteenth century. The opinions were not peculiar to mining but could also be found in engineering, railways, the post office and building. There was a general movement which was symptomatic of broad underlying causes such as the slackening of the rate of growth of the economy impinging upon workers' expectations. The last decades of the nineteenth century witnessed strikes in all the major industries – coal, cotton, engineering and railways – and there was an attempt, through the events leading up to Taff Vale, to increase the efficiency of labour by a tightening of managerial controls. Mining differed from other industries in the intensity of feeling and the fact that the subject was widely canvassed and received a great deal of support in the reports of the Sankey Commission of 1919. Furthermore, it was possible in mining to distinguish clearly the three strands of thought – syndicalism, industrial unionism and guild socialism.

Syndicalism, the doctrine of workers' control through direct action, emerged appropriately enough in South Wales, which was the weak link in the MFGB. In South Wales syndicalists were opposed to the structure of the South Wales Miners' Federation and its conciliatory policies. They envisaged workers' activities being centralised for the purposes of fighting the employers but wished to retain local autonomy in order that the rank and file could control negotiations. They sought an eight-hour day and a minimum wage of eight shillings a day. At the time the SWMF was badly organised and the South Wales Miners' Reform Committee received a great deal of popular support. Its main achievement was the publication of *The Miners' Next Step* which contained a clear statement of opposition to nationalisation: 'which makes a National Trust with all the force of Government behind it, whose one concern will be to see that the industry is run in such a way as to pay the interest on bonds . . . and to extract as much as possible in order to relieve the taxation of other landlords and capitalists.'[4]

Industrial unionism was proposed by George Harvey, who founded the Northern Counties Mining Industrial Union, and guild socialism was advocated by G. D. H. Cole. The differences between the three groups lay in differences of idealism and implementation. Syndicalism was more revolutionary in expression and espoused the virtues of direct action and the general strike. Industrial unionism – the notion that workers should be organised on industrial lines rather than according to craft – could be construed as fitting into the other philosophies of syndicates and guilds.

In their evidence to the Sankey Commission the Miners' Federation put forward an elaborate scheme of control for the coal industry which was strongly influenced by the guild socialists. All powers were to be vested in a National Mining Council consisting of a Minister of Mines and ten members appointed by the government. Members were to hold office for five years, but were to be eligible for re-election. Below the National Council were to be the district and pit councils and half of the members of these councils were to be representatives of the miners. The Federation also proposed the retention of the right to strike.

The findings of the Commission were, however, inconclusive and in the ensuing recession the industry passed into private hands and the union was concerned to fight a rearguard action against wage cuts, increases in hours and a general attack on the power of the Federation in the coal industry. But despite the change in the economic climate there were weaknesses in the miners' plans. There was no explicit working out of the relations between management and miners at pit level nor of how the legal obligations imposed upon management could be reconciled with the interests of the miners. But these weaknesses merely reflected the fact that the Federation was a federation of pit villages whose purpose was to allow the villages to create their own destinies. There was also no conception of how producers' interests could be reconciled with those of consumers beyond an assumption that the latters' interests would, somehow, be represented by the non-mining members of the council for the industry. And when the doctrine of workers' control was extended to all industries, severe problems were encountered – problems which worried G. D. H. Cole, the leading exponent of guild socialism. For, if each syndicate was interested in maximising the incomes of its members then it might attempt to behave as a monopolist – maximising the incomes of its members by moving to the point on the demand curve where the elasticity of demand was unity – and it was not easy to accept a trade union state that was a state of monopolies in which the actions of each syndicate resulted in a contraction of total incomes and output. Furthermore, the rate of capital accumulation would be lower than in a capitalist economy because each worker would, in the absence of a capital market, be tempted to consume the whole of his income and not allow any revenue to be ploughed back lest he lose the benefits of accumulation should he leave the syndicate. Paradoxically, the lesson of the debate was that it is the capitalist firm which is the socialist firm because it allows a worker the chance to diversify his assets and permits the greatest rate of capital accumulation.[5] What was wrong with the capitalist system was the distribution of income and wealth and the absence of social controls which would check the concentration of wealth through the operations of genes, inheritance, marriage and luck.

GENERAL EQUILIBRIUM AND SOCIALIST ECONOMICS

The difficulties of producing an efficient alternative to a capitalist economy received a great deal of discussion in the inter-war years.[6] Although the protagonists did not explicitly take account of workers' participation and control, they did concentrate on the problems of the interdependence of economic activity. The socialist debate is important not merely because it demonstrated that a socialist economy was possible but because some of the ideas that emerged became embodied in subsequent thinking about nationalised industries and, because many of the issues have not been resolved, we shall survey the controversy from the inter-war years to the present and indicate the contemporary issues.

In the debate of the twenties and thirties it was alleged that a socialist economy would be inefficient because the planners would face insuperable difficulties in processing the vast amounts of information required to allocate resources efficiently. The task could be done more efficiently by the market which was, in effect, a gigantic computer. The fact that the market was often in disequilibrium and appeared chaotic merely reflected the fact that we observe an incomplete sequence of computations which can never be completed because new information is continually being fed into the computer. But the chaos would be less than might be created by a planning system.

In reply, the defenders of socialism pointed out that it was perfectly reasonable to assume that a socialist economy might be decentralised to the extent that planners could use shadow prices to allocate resources, and that prices could be adjusted so as to reconcile demands and supplies. Where a socialist economy would differ from a capitalist economy would be in the distribution of income and the maintenance of full employment.[7]

The outcome of the debate was the establishment of a set of ground rules for the operation of any economy.[8] An optimum, usually referred to as a Pareto optimum, was defined as a situation from which it was impossible to make anyone better off without making anyone worse off. There could be as many optima as there were conceivable distributions of income and from the set of optima the members of a society would pick one which reflected their views on what constituted a fair distribution of income.

The achievement of any optimum depended upon the fulfilment of certain conditions, sometimes called marginal conditions. Briefly, these conditions specified that in the various activities of production and distribution it should be impossible to increase the output of one good without having to reduce the output of another good or to rearrange the distribution of goods between individuals without making someone worse off. One of these conditions was embodied in the principle of *marginal cost pricing* which stated that the price consumers paid for a good should measure the cost of supplying them with the last unit of that good. Since costs represented opportunity costs—the highest value which could be placed on the resources used in producing that last unit if they were transferred to some other use – and since price measured the valuation at the margin which consumers placed on the good they acquired, then marginal cost pricing simply said that prices based on marginal costs would yield the best use of resources.

There was, however, a difficulty in the marginal cost pricing principle, the implications of which were not fully understood in the inter-war years. In some activities it might be that production could not be carried out on a small scale which permitted duplication. Indivisibilities might exist; a bridge once built could be used by one or a hundred. Indivisibilities create opportunity for externalities because the bridge built by one person could be used by others who need not pay for the privilege. And where such indivisibilities exist the marginal cost would be below average cost with the result that overheads would not be recovered and prices would be no guide to replacement or net investment, if a marginal cost pricing policy was pursued. The problem was, of course, not a new one. In the nineteenth century the canals and the railways had introduced indivisibilities and the Victorian solution to the railway was to insist upon some trains being run at a penny a mile each day in order to prevent the companies restricting output and raising prices in order to cover total costs. The 'penny a mile' rule extracted some of the monopolist's profits. In the 1840s the great French economist, Dupuit, had advocated discriminatory pricing which could be used to extract some of the surplus which consumers might get from a marginal cost pricing policy.[9] The general solution suggested in the inter-war years, however, was that deficits should be met out of taxation.

Taxation can either be on incomes or on spending and it was initially assumed that taxes on spending were inferior to taxes on incomes because they imposed an excess burden. All taxes impose a burden in the sense that they take resources away from households but it was argued that taxes on spending imposed an additional burden because they altered relative prices and spending patterns. However, this conclusion was subsequently found to rest upon the assumption that income taxes did not affect the supply of labour. Since income taxes could alter the relative prices of work and leisure such an assumption appeared to be unwarranted – although the fact that income and substitution effects of an income tax could pull in opposite directions rendered any *a priori* judgement impossible.

The problem of financing industries in the public sector which pursued marginal cost pricing policies was also complicated by the fact that the marginal conditions might not be satisfied elsewhere in the economy. Thus if a nationalised coal industry was selling coal to a monopolistic iron and steel industry then it should make the ratio between its price and marginal cost the same as that of the iron and steel industry in order not to increase distortions and if there were more than one monopoly then the general rule would be that a public enterprise should set a marginal cost/price ratio which was a weighed average of the ratios in the economy.

Emphasising the allocational aspects of nationalised industries should not, however, result in a neglect of the equity problems. There are many activities, such as defence, health and education, for which it might be deemed desirable to set zero prices in order to encourage their consumption by the poor. Hence, prices might be set with regard to their effects on the distribution of wealth as well as the allocation of resources. Indeed, this was an underlying theme in the nationalisation of the coal industry because it was argued that only public ownership could guarantee decent wages to the miners as well as cheap coal to consumers – tasks which suggested that the National Coal Board was a branch of the Department of Social Security. But these problems raise again the issues of how the industry should be financed.

The problem of financing deficits has led to numerous solutions, some of which have been mentioned. Deficits can be covered by tapping consumers' surpluses, taxing goods which are inelastic in supply or taxing all activities in such a way as to leave individuals no inducement to alter the pattern of their activities – for example, a tax on ice cream would be a tax on leisure which might be imposed at the same time as a tax on work.[10] Another possibility is to recognise that all actions involve distortions and the simplest thing would be to reduce the amount of distortion by reducing the extent of state activity to a minimum. There would still be a financing problem but it would be minimised. The trouble with this point of view is that it too readily assumes that state activity is bad compared with private activity. It rejects the Pareto criterion, because that criterion accepts the possibility that state activity might be more efficient than private activity, and substitutes a Liberal criterion that only private market arrangements should be used. Yet there may be instances where people believe that the only way to achieve laudable objectives is through the state and are only prepared to finance such activities if undertaken by the state. The trouble with the Liberal criterion is that at best it is founded upon the untested assumption that there is no substitute for private action or at worst it is based upon a value judgement that the state is an evil whose actions must be severely curtailed.

The examples of financing mentioned in the previous paragraph highlight the problems created by the need to finance state activities by extracting resources from the private sector. If society were ever reconstructed by means of a revolution its members would probably find it easier to vest the ownership of resources in the state and allow individuals to lease them by bidding for their use in competitive auctions. The revenue derived from the leases could then be used to finance state activities, such as defence and the prevention of poverty. Such a system was implicit in the Tudor and Stuart practice of creating statutory monopolies and allowing the revenues to support the monarch. Whilst the system was abused, it did have greater potential when the era of parliamentary democracy emerged. Unfortunately, economic development took the form of allowing private individuals to annex resources and neglecting the social problems which that intensified. When the problems of poverty were mentioned the solution was thrust back to the local government units – a task for which they were ill-equipped and for which they should not have been equipped as long as the issues were national and not parochial. The general solution, however, posed the problem of how the state was to acquire the resources from the private sector. In the case of the post-war nationalised industries it was done by buying them from their owners. Since the purchase price was based upon the stock market valuations which took into account the future earnings of those industries it was difficult to see what benefit would accrue to the community. What socialism with compensation did was to transfer the management of industries to the public domain without transferring the income from the assets – which was the criticism of nationalisation made by the South Wales Miners' Reform Committee. If the state has to undertake certain activities then the long-term solution must be to acquire assets which can finance those activities and those assets must be obtained through the generation of budget surpluses.

The main controversy in socialist economics has now been surveyed. There are, however, two other issues which have received less attention. In his *Economics of Socialism*, Lange introduced two other points. First, he envisaged the introduction of a social dividend which was to be a payment to each citizen in the form of a lump sum so as to avoid distorting relative prices. Secondly, Lange thought that investment policy would make use of a social rate of time preference which would be reflected by the market. Both these ideas have been considered in the post-war period and both have aroused some interest. The social dividend or negative income tax raises the question of whether collective bargaining can be retained as an instrument of income distribution. The social discount rate raises the problem of how it can be determined.

MORRISONIAN SOCIALISM

We are now in a position to appreciate the third strand of thought that went into nationalisation. In the inter-war years there emerged an alternative to workers' control. This alternative had its antecedents in nineteenth-century experiments in municipal socialism; what is sometimes called 'gas and water socialism'. There was an emphasis upon the public interest and a rejection of workers' control – 'the dust does not belong to the dustmen'. There was an emphasis upon managerial efficiency and there was a belief that the public interest could be reconciled with commercial efficiency. There was also the acceptance of the idea that industries should be acquired through purchase.

Morrisonian socialism came into conflict with the doctrines of workers' control in the inter-war years but came to be accepted as Labour Party policy. Its success was due to a variety of causes. First, there was the decline of influence of some unions in policy-making within the party – the last vestiges of the conflict can be found in the TUC's report on post-war industrial reconstruction in 1944. Secondly, there was the apparent success of Morrisonián socialism in the thirties in London. This success was due in part to the fact that many of the services were due to fall into public hands as a result of decisions made in the nineteenth century and which excluded compensation. Secondly, some industries were new ones, such as motor transport, which the market had not had time to evaluate, and the return on which was to grow. Thirdly, any deficits could be covered by the taxable surplus yielded by the monopoly site of London.

NATIONAL COAL BOARD

The Coal Industry (Nationalisation) Act of 1946 embodied many of the principles of Morrisonian socialism. Compensation was paid to the former coal-owners. The industry was required to break even over a period of years although no rules were laid down as to the circumstances in which losses could be incurred. Parliamentary control was to be exercised through a minister but the day-to-day operations were excluded from parliamentary questions in an endeavour to separate commercial considerations from the public interest.

The organisation and structure of the coal industry was as follows. The line of command was from the National Coal Board through the divisional boards and area managers to collieries. At all levels there were functional specialists and the geographical and functional structures were linked by the principle of line and staff. The structure of the industry appeared to be authoritarian and reflected the ideas and experiences of Morrisonian socialism and wartime planning.

During the late forties and early fifties the organisation and structure of the industry were severely criticised, particularly by members of the Conservative Party. It was argued that the industry suffered from excessive centralisation and that the only solution was to decentralise the industry and allow the coalfields to compete against each other. Some slight concessions were made to the critics in 1948 and 1953 but the tide was stemmed by the report of the Fleck Committee in 1955.[11] What the Fleck Committee did was to point out that mining was the same job wherever it was performed and that coal produced anywhere could be sold anywhere. Hence the common problems of production and marketing permitted central control. The Committee criticised the Board for failing to understand what centralisation meant and for failing to ensure that orders were carried out. The Board accepted virtually all the Committee's recommendations.

Looking back it is possible to discern wider influences shaping the structure and behaviour of the industry. The Coal Board did not pursue a marginal cost pricing policy: it set the price of coal below the free market price and created a situation of excess demand. This policy dictated a very simple production and marketing strategy which fitted in easily with the bureaucratic model. There was no marketing problem because all the coal could be sold at the prevailing price.

The first phase of organisational behaviour stretched from 1947 to 1957, and we can now examine its implications for industrial relations. First, there was the rejection of workers' control. This did not imply that the interests of workers were ignored but it did serve to influence the manner in which those interests were accommodated. The importance of industrial relations was emphasised by the fact that the director of industrial relations had a seat on the Board. But because workers' control was rejected the trade unions were not directly represented. What happened was that those industrial relations specialists who were appointed and drawn from the unions, resigned from the unions. Apart from the opposition of politicians to workers' control there was a reluctance by the unions to have members on the Board who might find themselves pulled in conflicting directions. The second feature which followed from the rejection of workers' control was the acceptance of the distinction between collective bargaining and joint consultation, between wages and non-wage issues. However, the distinction was not always sharply drawn and many issues, such as pensions and redundancy payments, became the subject of collective bargaining. The third feature was the determination to have a system of orderly industrial relations and this was to be achieved by determining the unions to be recognised and the purposes of collective bargaining – even to the extent of recognising and having negotiating machinery for managerial staffs. Fourthly, there was a high degree of commitment to industrial relations on the part of management at all levels. Indeed, the major difficulties in industrial relations in the early period stemmed from ministerial intervention to keep miners' wages down in order to keep the cost of living down.

The Fleck recommendations had only a brief period of usage before the industry's environment changed. From 1957 onwards the demand for coal fell, there was a rise in mechanisation, many pits were closed and there was a huge cutback in production and employment. These changes increased the importance of marketing and the need to increase flexibility in the response of the industry to the varying circumstances. An initial decision was taken to by-pass the layers of command by the creation of conferences; the longer-term response was to alter the formal structure. In 1966 the Board eliminated the divisions and altered both the size and importance of the areas as a decision unit. Experience had shown that it was possible to control about 20 pits.

The changes in the organisational structure were also accompanied by changes in the goals and in the techniques of achieving those goals. In the period before 1957 the concept of public interest was broadly interpreted; prices were set below free market prices. After 1957 the interpretation of public interest altered. There was a greater emphasis upon marginal cost as a determinant of price; investment and financial criteria were introduced and specific subsidies were given to cover redundancies and closures. But the problems of ministerial intervention and confusion still persisted. The increasing emphasis upon the long-term plans of the industry raised the question of how society's preferences between present and future consumption were to be divined. After the 1972 energy crisis the problem became more acute.

JOINT CONSULTATION

The Nationalisation Act drew the time-honoured distinction between collective bargaining and joint consultation, and consultative machinery was set up at national, divisional, area and pit levels. The early reports of the Coal Board reveal great enthusiasm for joint consultation which was seen as a means of promoting unity, a method of tapping the knowledge and experience of the labour force and a channel for communications.

But this enthusiasm began to wane in the mid-fifties. From the point of view of the miners joint consultation meant consultation only, there was no reason for management to accept their views. This meant that controversial issues disappeared from agendas: controversial issues had to be approached through collective bargaining. From the point of view of management joint consultation proved unreliable as a means of imposing discipline and coping with absenteeism. At many pits union representatives refused to discuss absenteeism. Joint consultation, therefore, came to be preoccupied with the past rather than the future.

After 1957 management found substitutes for joint consultation. Coalface conferences by-passed the cumbersome consultative machinery and were used to introduce power loading. On the more general level there emerged 'Coal News', 'Management News' and Staff College. Throughout the sixties management continuously expanded the channels of communication and improved the quantity and quality of information flowing along all channels.

Since 1966 the usefulness of joint consultation and the means by which consultation takes place has come in for further questioning. The introduction of time-rates and the slackening of the increase in productivity have led to a search for new methods of raising productivity. Furthermore, there was the widespread upsurge of interest in workers' participation in the late sixties which had repercussions in the coal industry. At the most elementary level the questioning has taken the form of attempts to reform the present structure of consultation by integrating the face conferences and other committeess into the older structure of pit committees. At the deeper level the issue is whether any changes can be made to improve participation in an industry which already has a higher degree of commitment to participation than most industries and an industry in which the unions have secured their major objective of security of collective bargaining rights.

Participation is, any case, a matter of attitudes. At some pits the machinery for consultation is moribund yet participation is lively and vigorous. At other pits the machinery works in a highly professional manner and yet there is no impression of participation. What is difficult to fathom is what the rank and file expect from participation as opposed to the full-time officials. The disappearance of piece-rates resulted in the loss of the most effective lever for getting management to listen and the easiest method of discussing working conditions and manning requirements. And across the coalfields the issues which give rise to conflict seem to vary. Nor does it seem that any lessons can be gained from European experience. The only evidence in favour of co-determination is that in the German coal industry it prevented strikes against redundancy in the sixties. But there were no strikes against redundancy in Britain. And the German system did not prevent the great strike waves of 1968 to 1970 which were led by works councillors and which have resulted in the unions seeking to produce something like the British shop steward system. Any developments of the British system must derive from what the unions, want, which is the subject we must turn to next.

3 The Unions

The problems of the efficient organisation of the coal industry, the central issue of the previous chapter, were left unresolved. They depended on an analysis of the unions. In this chapter we shall, therefore, look at the structure and behaviour of the unions and the effects of nationalisation upon them. But because nationalisation created a new union of managerial workers, particular attention will be paid to it and to the general development of white-collar unions.

NATIONAL UNION OF MINEWORKERS

The National Union of Mineworkers was formed in 1944 when it replaced the Miners' Federation. Despite its success legally and politically, the Federation, as we have seen, always tended to be weak industrially. There were differences between the domestic and inland coalfields and between the high-cost and low-cost coalfields. In the inter-war years these differences had pulled the Federation apart and had led to the emergence of rival unions in the Midlands, South Wales and Scotland. The creation of the NUM was, therefore, an attempt to overcome difficulties which would have existed even in the absence of nationalisation. What the 1944 administrative reforms did was to establish a new relationship between the national union and the former country unions. The country unions were renamed 'areas' and to these were added units to cover cokemen; two power groups comprising workers who had dual membership with either the Transport and General Workers' Union or the National Union of General and Municipal Workers; craft groups, such as the Scottish Enginemen and Durham Mechanics; and clerical workers who were organised by the Colliery Staffs and Officials Area (COSA). This arrangement yielded 21 area unions which, in some cases, contained constituent associations. The constitution of the NUM also provided for the election of a president and general secretary by a ballot of the membership. Both the president and the general secretary were to be full-time officials and were to hold office 'at the pleasure of the union'. The post of vice-president was to be part-time and filled biennially at the annual Conference. The president, general secretary and vice-president were to be *ex officio* members of the National Executive Committee and the remaining places on the NEC were to be filled by the areas, who usually elected their general secretaries, although provision was made for lay representatives. The structure of area councils varied according to local practices. Below the areas as constituent associations lay the branches.

The formation of the new union did not, however, bring about any radical changes for a long period. This was because power still lay in the coalfields. Many areas had considerable financial reserves, paid benefits and, above all, as long as wages were negotiated locally, the president and the general secretary had to go 'cap in hand' to the areas. The tendency was, therefore, for the union to remain a federation of trade unions, even a federation of pit villages, with an untidy organisational structure and overlapping and competing unions. In 1971 it was revealed that of the weekly paid industrial staff, 604 were in COSA, 761 were in NUM Areas, 131 were in Power Group 1 and 213 were in Power Group 2. In 1966 COSA complained that the Midlands Area was poaching members and in 1971 South Derbyshire accused Power Group 1 of poaching. There have, of course, been attempts to rationalise the Union's structure and the NEC can recommend mergers – but such advice need not be taken. In 1966 recommendations were made for the mergers between South Derbyshire and Leicestershire, between Durham enginemen and Durham mechanics and between Lancashire area and Lancashire tradesmen but nothing happened. Such changes as have taken place have usually been the result of accidents, retirements, deaths and bitter struggles. Thus, the decision of the National Union of Enginemen, an affiliate of the Transport and General Workers' Union, to seek closer links with the TGWU allowed the transfer of members with dual membership to Power Group 1. In 1971 the NUM and NACODS agreed on spheres of influence which allowed all overmen and deputies to become members of the latter union and thereby ended jurisdictional disputes in Scotland and the North East. In 1969 the Yorkshire area finally managed to integrate colliery winding-enginemen after a struggle which had lasted several decades and had involved, on occasions, state intervention.[1] Most problems arose because of the existence of organisations prior to nationalisation. In the case of electricians and fitters the NUM and NCB were able to control developments because the main increase in mechanisation came after nationalisation. But there still remain problems of the relationship of the NUM to the white-collar unions in the industry between the various constituents of the NUM.

The persistence of sectionalism has been partly a result of nationalisation, for what public ownership did was to give union security. The NUM, which organises about 90 per cent of the labour force, was given quasi-closed-shop rights by the Board and an automatic deduction of subscriptions from wages. From a position of insecurity in the inter-war years the union moved to one of comparative security and this allowed it to indulge in a high degree of membership participation in decision-making. In contests for the posts of president and general secretary the high level of regional autonomy produced a pool of candidates of about the same ability and experience from which the membership could choose. The presence of many full-time officials in the areas provided an automatic check on the powers of the national president and general secretary. Thus, Sam Watson, the former general secretary of the Durham area, never contested the national posts despite his outstanding ability. The elections for the posts of president and general secretary have always been closely contested and the pithead ballot and system of transferable votes provided a sensitive interpretation of members' wishes. In the sixties there appeared to be a dearth of good candidates, but with the decline in the number of parliamentary seats going to miners and the upsurge of industrial militancy there would appear to be no shortage of future candidates.

The existence of comparative security has also allowed an incipient party system to develop.[2] Nationalisation gave the NUM a monopoly position and factionalism has tended to be superimposed upon regionalism. South Wales, Scotland and Kent have generally been dominated by communists. In the case of South Wales the explanation of a communist presence may lie in the tendency of those areas to have low wages. In the case of Kent the reasons may lie in the migration of disenchanted miners in the twenties and thirties from other coalfields – an explanation which may also fit South Yorkshire, although a communist influence in South Yorkshire only began to emerge in the fifties, and then fitfully.

But despite the fact that South Wales and Scotland are numerically large areas and provide communist candidates for national posts, it is doubtful whether the candidates they sponsor would get into office without support from other areas. There is, in fact, a high degree of cross-voting. Many miners prefer communist, or marxist, candidates because of their records of militancy. And in the case of Arthur Horner and Will Paynter, former general secretaries both from South Wales, there was a tacit acknowledgement that their communism was something different from that presented by the Press. Hence, in 1945, both Northumberland and Durham – two traditional right-wing areas – did not oppose Horner. And communist areas have supported non-communists, such as Alwyn Machin (Yorkshire) for the presidency in 1958 and Lawrence Daly (Scotland) who had left the Communist Party after the Hungarian Civil War in 1956.

In addition to the high degree of participation created by public ownership, regionalism and factionalism, considerable strength is exerted by the pit and the village. In 1977 the average vote in pit elections for branch positions in Yorkshire was about 60 per cent. At pit level simple majority voting is used, all posts are periodically contested and any official who wishes to contest another post must resign from his own office. Pit voting behaviour differs from that used for the national posts and is more akin to that used by the former craft unions, such as the Amalgamated Union of Engineering Workers. Paradoxically, an attempt to introduce periodic elections for the national posts was defeated by the votes of South Wales and Scotland. To the high degree of voting in pit elections should be added the extra-constitutional pressures exerted at pit level. In 1962 miners at Denaby Main struck in an attempt to have their manager removed and when they got no support from their county officials the pit turned non-union for six months, refused to meet county officials and ostracised the manager and his family. And the record of unofficial strikes called by branches in the fifties attests to the strength of the rank and file, as does the strike wave during the years 1969 to 1974.

Yet, despite the record of vigorous participation nourished by the public ownership, nationalisation and violent changes in the demand for coal in the sixties have created problems. Like all good radicals, the NUM did not seek to change the world but to prevent the world changing it. Unfortunately, the union has not always been successful. The original structure of divisions and areas created by the Board fitted easily into the union's structure in most coalfields. Thus, the East Midlands Division had areas which mirrored the spheres of influence of the North Derbyshire and Nottinghamshire areas of the NUM. On the other hand, the Yorkshire Miners had no structure which matched that of the eight areas into which the North-Eastern Division was divided, and the resulting stresses and strains led to the emergence of unofficial area panels and, ultimately, to the creation of area agents, although the panels still persisted. By the end of the fifties the formal structure of unionism in Yorkshire came to resemble the national structures of Scotland and South Wales, both of which had agents covering groups of pits – unlike the traditional English coalfields which had no intermediaries between the full-time county officials and the branches.

The second problem has arisen from the switch to a national system of time rates. As long as wages were negotiated locally the NEC was relatively innocuous; it could be linked to a meeting of feudal barons with King John although the power of the barons was severely limited by the ability of pit officials to negotiate wages. The introduction of time-rates has taken away power from the areas and the pits without giving the local officials any other functions. Compensation work, another important field for establishing reputations, may soon become routine if common law actions are replaced by statutory automatic income payments. Safety work, pit inspections and joint consultations are hardly subjects to arouse enthusiasm, although being relatively unexplored they could prove to be useful avenues for the ambitious member. Indeed, in the light of the changes in the scope for decision-making at pit level the high degree of participation at pit level is all the more remarkable.

The shift to time-rates has been superimposed upon a contraction of the industry whose location over the country has called into question the composition of the NEC and the geographical structure of the union. The NEC attempts to reflect the structure of areas and constituent associations but what this now means is that the big coalfields, such as Yorkshire, find themselves relatively under-represented. Hence the conflicts of the seventies have been marked by divisions between the big and small areas which mirror, to some extent, the conflicts between the Right and Left and which are often resolved by rank-and-file pressures in the larger coalfields pushing the right wing members of the NEC to the left. One solution to this problem would be to leave the geographical structure of the NEC unchanged on the grounds that it provides a useful qualitative element in the union's decision-making, but to refer more major issues to pithead ballots. Failing such a solution the alternative would be to reconstitute the NEC along lines which reflected the numerical strength of its constituents – although that policy would have repercussions if it gave greater weight to the votes of the white-collar members.

UNITED MINEWORKERS OF AMERICA

Despite current problems the existence of strong decision-making procedures in the NUM stands in strong contrast to their absence until comparatively recently in the United Mineworkers of America, although the similar achievements of the two unions might suggest that the problems of the UMWA might overtake the NUM. The contrasts and comparisons are, therefore, worth examining.

In the nineteenth century the American coal industry exhibited the same characteristics as the British. There were separate coalfields with different cost structures which served different markets. These forces gave rise to attempts to form a national union although it was not until the 1890s that an effective industrial union was formed. This union, the UMWA, was a highly decentralised organisation in which the locals and districts had considerable autonomy. What gradually happened was that district autonomy was reduced and power was centralised. Economics dictated some attempt to deal with competition between the coalfields created by wage disparities. In 1898 the union succeeded in establishing more or less uniform wage rates in the central coalfield but was unable to secure a similar agreement with employers in the new and expanding coalfields of West Virginia, Kentucky and Tennessee.

The problems of competition were also tackled by constitutional changes. The president was given the power to appoint or discharge members of the executive and gradually this right was extended to cover district and local officials. In addition, the right to strike was taken away from branches and districts. The reasoning behind these moves was no doubt laudable since it reduced the drain on funds for futile and unofficial strikes and it enabled the union to present a solid front to the employers. There were also forces within American society propelling the union towards centralisation. The huge influx of immigrants and the dynamism of American society created the need for some kind of organisation which would provide stability. In society at large this meeting point was provided in the big cities by urban machine politics which delivered in an apparently efficient manner what the citizens wanted in return for their votes. The heterogeneity and mobility of the population created the political machine which had its counterpart in the union machine. The corruption and racketeering which were to be noted in American unions and politics had their antecedents in the turmoil of American society at the turn of the century. And whereas the mobility of unskilled labour in Britain had given rise to the full-time official, the cultural homogeneity of the labour force tended to dampen the kind of adverse effects that were to appear in America.[3]

The tendencies towards centralisation which existed in the UMWA around the turn of the century were given further impetus by the rise to the presidency of John L. Lewis. At the turn of the century the UMWA was the largest union in America but during the twenties its membership fell drastically as excess capacity emerged in the industry. Non-union coalfields expanded at the expense of those which were unionised and substitute fuels were developed. What Lewis did was brilliantly to exploit the National Industrial Recovery Act passed by Roosevelt in 1933. The Act gave unions legal protection and hundreds of organisers poured into the coalfields shouting: 'The president of the union wants you to join the union'. Lewis's entrepreneurial flair, coupled with a willingness to use violent methods, beat down the non-unionism of the coal operators.

Lewis was an industrial tycoon, comparable with Carnegie and Rockefeller. He took his union out of the American Federation of Labour and created and financed the Congress for Industrial Organisation to unionise the mass production industries, such as cars and rubber. He then took his union out of the CIO and became independent. He quarrelled with Roosevelt and led strikes during the war. He emphasised efficiency, pushed up wages to dramatic heights and accepted mechanisation even if it meant the displacement of labour. He suspended and sacked district officials and replaced them with his own protégés, and he even ran locals from the national office. But such was the magnetism of his personality that a survey of members' attitudes in the fifties could find no fault with him.[4] In 1960, when Lewis retired, the union comprised 30 districts of which only seven were autonomous, three had semi-autonomous status which gave the members the right to appoint all the district's governing body except the secretary, treasurer and president, and in the remaining districts all officers were appointed by the parent body.

The history of the union following Lewis's retirement appears to have been one of increasing centralisation, corruption and inefficiency. Lewis was succeeded by vice-president Kennedy who was then 73 years of age and the International Executive Board appointed W. A. (Tony) Boyle as Kennedy's successor. When Kennedy retired he was automatically succeeded by Boyle and the membership had no say in his appointment.

Boyle's downfall was brought about by the union's failure to concern itself with safety and by the murder of Jock Yablonski who stood against Boyle in the 1969 election. One result of the stagnation of the industry in the fifties and sixties was that the welfare and retirement fund, which Lewis created, encountered financial difficulties. The fund was financed by the royalty payment based on output rather than on productivity and when output and employment fell the fund received a smaller cash inflow. At various times benefits were cut and conditions for eligibility revised. But what intensified the problem was the union's apparent indifference to safety. In the sixties a semi-official movement, the Black Lung Movement, emerged and it was this association that provided the opposition to Boyle. In 1969 Yablonski was murdered, the murderers were caught and Boyle was implicated. In 1971 Boyle was defeated by Arnold Miller, a miner who had never held office above local level. The change in leadership brought a return to something approaching primitive democracy. In 1974 the union bargaining team contained 40 rank-and-file members.

BRITISH ASSOCIATION OF COLLIERY MANAGEMENT

Before nationalisation unionism among officials was weak. Colliery managers strongly identified themselves with their employers and this tie was particularly strong when there were kinship bonds. The individualistic, pro-employer orientation was reinforced by the geographical spread of the industry and the small size and heterogeneous nature of the managerial unit at pit level. Some groups, such as deputies and clerks, organised but the resistance of the coal-owners prevented any extensive development of unionism. In West Yorkshire, for example, there was a staff mutual provident fund operated by the coal-owners and the National Association of Colliery Managers was a technical body concerned with the promotion and dissemination of knowledge; it repeatedly stressed that it was not a trade union.

What nationalisation did was to alter the employment relationship for managers; instead of many employers there was now one. Nationalisation brought about a change in ownership and a centralisation of authority. These distinct, although interrelated, changes had a profound effect on colliery staffs. Whereas managers had previously been important figures in the local communities, they were now reduced to discussing only 'mothers' meetings' and 'socials' with the Press and barred from participation in local government. And a further change was a wages policy for managers. The Coal Industry Nationalisation Act required the Board to negotiate with associations representative of the various groups of employees.

At the onset of nationalisation the only significant union of managerial workers was the Yorkshire Association of Colliery Officials (later known as the British Association of Colliery Officials and Staffs). The origins of YACOS are obscure. Just before nationalisation the South Yorkshire coal-owners apparently became alarmed about the welfare of their staffs and helped them to form a trade union to protect their interest. It rapidly recruited members in South Yorkshire, Durham and South Wales in occupations ranging from deputy to clerk and agent to manager. By 1947 it had a membership of 6,000. But its successes were limited and it was strongly criticised by the NUM on the grounds that it was organising groups which were in the NUM's sphere of influence. Similar criticisms were made by the National Association of Colliery Overmen, Deputies and Shotfirers and the clerical workers' unions. There was a general feeling that BACOS was an attempt by the coal-owners to sabotage the nationalised industry and in the end the Board refused to recognise it despite strike threats from its members. The resulting vacuum was filled by the National Association of Colliery Managers, the Institute of Mining Surveyors and other professional bodies sponsoring a new union, the British Association of Colliery Management. BACM quickly gained the support of professional and managerial grades and eventually the Board recognised BACM'S right to negotiate on behalf of managerial grades.

In 1952 the Board intervened in the affairs of BACM by granting recognition to the Labour Staffs Association. This latter union was organised because it was felt that labour officers should not be members of an organisation with which they had to negotiate on behalf of the Board. Some such organisation would, however, have had to be created, given the constant clashes between the production and labour departments. Most labour officials felt that BACM was dominated by production men and most production men felt that they were being pushed around by the long arm of the NUM from whose ranks most of the labour officials were recruited. However, by 1966 changes in the wages systems for both groups of workers and staffs had removed many of the sources of conflict and the labour Staffs Association merged with BACM. The Labour Staffs Association had been a product of piece-rates.

BACM is a trade union but it has been reluctant to acquire the other characteristics by which British trade unions are recognised. In 1972 it registered under the Industrial Relations Act despite the widespread hostility of the trade unions to the Act. The move was, however, necessary in order for the union to retain a considerable portion of its membership when the Coal Board established two holding companies and thereby relinquished any claim to be the employer. This implied that any union could seek to organise the workers and BACM applied for and obtained an Agency Shop Agreement with the two holding companies. In 1977 BACM became affiliated to the TUC in order to protect its members against the encroachment of other unions but it is not affiliated to the Labour Party. In collective bargaining BACM tends to wait upon the Board's settlements with the NUM. This should not be taken to imply a lack of bargaining power. When miners at Denaby Main went on strike in an attempt to have their manager removed the impression was conveyed that if the Board agreed to such a move then BACM would black all pits in Yorkshire.

NATIONAL ASSOCIATION OF COLLIERY OVERMEN, DEPUTIES AND SHOTFIRERS

A national union of deputies, the General Federation of Colliery Firemen, later to become the National Association of Colliery Overmen, Deputies and Shotfirers, was formed in York in 1910. The cause of the meeting seems to have been the effect of the Eight Hours Act upon the work of under-officials, although the reports from the districts indicated that there had been organisations in some coalfields for a considerable period and that Northumberland and Durham had the greatest number of deputies organised. The variation in the degree of unionisation, which persisted for thirty years, reflected the hostility of the coal-owners and the miners' unions in some areas. Thus in Yorkshire attempts were made to destroy the union by the creation of benefits schemes which the employees were compelled to join. In 1912 the Scottish and Northumberland miners tried to retain deputies in their ranks – a policy which was not surprising given the recruitment of under-officials from the ranks of miners, the instinctive tendency of any union to follow the line of advancement of its members and the ideological impetus of industrial unionism and syndicalism. In 1920 there was a proposal to become affiliated to the MFGB but it was rejected and hostility between the deputies' union and some sections of the MFGB continued throughout the inter-war years. It was only in 1973 that the NUM agreed to recognise NACODS' sphere of influence although that did not imply any diminution in the NUM's desire for industrial unionism or concerted policies strikes. In the early years the deputies sought to strengthen their position by getting themselves classified as agents of the Mines Inspectorate. In 1919 there was an application from a Federation of Colliery Under-managers to join the deputies and in 1922 there was an approach from the shopworkers and clerical workers. Had either of these two overtures been pursued then managerial or white-collar unionism in the coal industry might have been developed before the upsurge of unionism in the sixties.

Within the coal industry NACODS has suffered the general problems affecting foremen in industry. Successive wage increases, reductions in hours and the possibilities of overtime, as well as pensions, have tended to erode the benefits of being a foreman. NACODS members have also been affected by changes in the degree of mechanisation, the alterations in payments systems and methods of work organisation. In the fifties when the characteristic method of working was machine-cut/hand-filled longwall and piece-rates were prevalent, the deputy's job was less strenuous in the sense that he was primarily responsible for safety and supplies. With the change-over to power loading and time-rates the deputy was required to supervise in a much more intensive work situation. This found vent in the expression that many miners' backs were being burned by the glare from their deputies' lamps. But the problem of supervision is one that affects not merely the relationship between the miner and the deputy but also the deputy's relationship to under-managers and other officials who now exist in mechanised mining. Any attempt to define the role of the various groups involves not merely issues of status but also the respective jurisdictions of the NUM and BACM as well as NACODS. These interrelationships could be disturbed by any movement back to incentive wage systems.

ASSOCIATION OF PROFESSIONAL, EXECUTIVE, CLERICAL AND COMPUTER STAFF

The final union to be considered in the coal industry is the Association of Professional, Executive, Clerical and Computer Staff (APEX). Some colliery clerks were organised around the turn of the century by clerical workers' unions and at nationalisation the Clerical and Administrative Workers' Union from which APEX was descended, claimed all clerical and administrative staffs. The claim was resented by COSA, the NUM's white-collar affiliate, and for several years the establishment of salary scales for clerical workers was delayed until spheres of influence were resolved. Eventually, the CAWU was given recognition for those clerks it had organised, mainly at area level. During the disputes of 1972 and 1974 APEX and the NUM came into conflict because the former refused to call its members out on strike. The attitude of clerical workers in the NUM was, however, lukewarm, and it appears that some clerks left the NUM as a result of experiences in those years. The conflicts between the two unions are, however, only relevant to the coal industry and in 1977 various sections of the NUM joined in the picketing of the Grunwick plant which APEX was trying to organise.

WHITE-COLLAR UNIONISM

A description of unionism in the coal industry invites some comment on the development of white-collar unionism in general.[5] Various reasons have been put forward for the slow development of unionism among clerical workers and for their uneven incidence. The first evidence of unionism occurs in the last decades of the nineteenth century and seems to be associated with the general expansion of unionism to embrace unskilled workers and clerks and teachers. The late development of such unionism has sometimes been accounted for by lack of employment concentration, ease of promotion, scarcity of skills, the presence or absence of other groups of workers who were organised and employers' attitudes.

The trouble with many of these explanations is that it is always possible to provide counter-examples and the truth probably lies in some judicious mixture of reasons applied to particular cases. Thus, lack of employment concentration did not prevent pattern-makers organising in the nineteenth century. And the emergence of unionism in the cotton industry seems to have coincided with the period of greatest expansion of opportunities for vertical mobility. It is also suggested that the development of white-collar unionism is crucially dependent upon employers' attitudes and that sympathetic attitudes are strongest in the public sector. On this assertion several observations can be made. First, employers' attitudes to unionism may be influenced by the amount of militancy exerted by workers. What would have happened if, for example, BACOS had struck? The problem is one of resolving a simultaneous equation and not a single equation. Thus, employers' resistance to manual workers' unions was determined, in part, by the degree of militancy of those unions. The second point to bear in mind is that employment in the public sector does not, of itself, readily establish white-collar unions. If it did there would have been unions in the nineteenth century. The absence of profit motive has been too readily construed as implying that the employers' utility functions contained a liking for unionism. But that need not be the case and would have to be demonstrated; just because profit-constrained managers may develop a liking for appointing pretty secretaries does not mean that they would appoint ones who are trade unionists.

The expansion of the public sector in Britain has been closely influenced by the expansion of the manual workers' unions and the Labour Party. It may reflect a more fundamental desire of people for goods and services that cannot be supplied by the market, but its form has been strongly influenced by the unions and the Labour Party. White-collar unions, of course, existed in the coal industry before nationalisation but were opposed by both employers and unions and so it may be useful to consider what part the intellectual wing of the Labour Party played in the development of white-collar unions. Morrisonian socialism exalted managerial efficiency and that was created and preserved in the new unions, themselves a buttress against the manual workers' notions of industrial unionism and syndicalism and against the lack of public service mentality enshrined in private capitalist management.

But why were the manual workers' unions unable to resist the impact of elitism and sectionalism? For the miners it would have been as natural to organise some groups of white-collar workers as it would have been to exclude them. Following the natural line of promotion all the supervisory grades would have been suitable for organising and clerical jobs would have been suitable for disabled and elderly miners. And, in part, the NUM has followed these paths, but the nature of job markets has created tensions. The clashes between the NUM and APEX are paralleled by conflicts within the NUM between the coalface workers and the members of COSA. For what constitutes membership of COSA is the method of wage payment—daily or monthly—and the dividing line has been drawn at daily pay with all day wage workers being members of the area unions. But that means that weekly-paid inspectors as well as clerical workers are members of COSA. Now most colliers regard weekly-paid inspectors as miners since they have often worked at the coalface. In contrast, the clerical members of COSA frequently work at area level away from the pits, do not pay the political levy, and exercise a disproportionate effect on the outcomes of ballots on strike action. The average miner does not see any point in having clerical workers in the union because he can exert sufficient bargaining power without them and he no longer sees clerical jobs as jobs for the disabled and elderly. The reluctance to organise explains multi-unionism; it was grounded in the realities of the labour market. Ideally, the miner would prefer the other groups not to be organised.

INDUSTRIAL DEMOCRACY

The starting point of our discussion was the question: what industrial organisation would the miners prefer to see in the coal industry.? Nationalisation gave them security of collective bargaining rights and as long as wages were negotiated locally that right was guaranteed. It even survived the catastrophic decline in the demand for coal after 1957. The change in attitudes has been caused by the shift in the locus of power away from the pit. The NUM's preferred solution to that problem has been a return to the ideas embodied in their evidence to the Sankey Commission but that has been resisted – notably in BACM. The Board's own suggestion, and one which has some following by the union, has been to offer incentive wage systems again – but that has been opposed by those groups who see in the National Power Loading Agreement the realisation of solidarity. What have not been resolved are the interrelations of national and local pressures. The Bullock Report's proposals for industrial democracy provide no assistance to an industry which has already gone further along the road of participation, whilst Friedman's proposal to denationalise the industry by offering it to the miners is not likely to be accepted.[6]

4 Wages

Nationalisation created a wages problem. Before nationalisation the structure of wages might be defended as the outcome of the distribution of labour and capital. Highly mechanised and highly productive pits in the East Midlands could give higher wages than the more labour-intensive, low-productive pits of South Wales, Scotland and Lancashire. And it could also be argued it was necessary to maintain these differences so as to encourage an expansion of the industry in Nottinghamshire and Yorkshire and a contraction elsewhere. Hence many of the apparent irrationalities and anomalies which led to differences of earnings for workers doing a similar job or different jobs could be rationalised. After nationalisation such arguments carried less conviction. The common ownership of all capital and the common employment of all miners suggested a more egalitarian sharing of income, and wage differences had to be defended as fair as well as efficient. Furthermore, the very workings of the market were themselves subjected to attack. Economic forces were slow to generate change. Successive governments had intervened in determination of wages in the industry. The wage system was seen as the historical record of layers of wage settlements in which particular payments lay unconformably on top of one another. Even before nationalisation the industry had been urged to modernise its wage system.

From 1947 to 1966 the industry attempted to produce a rational wages structure which would command acceptance on grounds of fairness as well as efficiency. The period from 1950 to 1955 was particularly fruitful and creative. In that period the Board and the unions agreed wage structures for managerial and technical staffs and for the bulk of surface and haulage workers. Missing from the catalogue of achievements were the coalface workers. The history of the attempts to introduce a satisfactory wage structure for piece-workers forms one of the most fascinating endeavours in industrial relations in the post-war period. It involved a consideration of the relative merits of piece-work and time-work and, as such, formed part of the widespread debate on methods of wage payment which has continually beset British industry. But before methods of wage payment could be determined the nature of jobs had to be analysed and the Coal Board conducted some of the most extensive job evaluation programmes attempted by any industry. Finally, the Board had to determine the relationship between the levels of wages yielded by its wages structures and those paid in other industries.

THE 1955 DAY WAGE STRUCTURE

The 1955 Day Wage Agreement represented one of the most comprehensive attempts to reconstruct the wages of time-workers who formed 57 per cent of the industry's labour force and who were mainly engaged on the surface and on haulage work (Table 4.1). Their wages had been composed of a basic time-rate determined at pit level and a percentage determined by a district ascertainment of proceeds. During the Second World War the percentage was frozen and subsequent increases took the form of additions based upon changes in the cost of living. The other

TABLE 4.1 Effective adult manual workers (including craftsmen), 1955

	Number of jobs		*Number of men*	
			Day-wagemen	*Piece-workers*
Coal face . . .	44	136	39,235	194,357
Elsewhere underground . . .	92		141,626	39,252
Surface . . .	125		108,483	1,617
Central workshop . . .	96		5,451	Not known
Total . . .	357		294,795	235,226

Note: These figures exclude youths under 21, numbering about 64,000 effectives, and, of course, weekly-paid industrial staff, including under-officials, of whom there are about 40,000 effectives.
Source: NCB, *Reports and Accounts* (1955).

major factors introduced during the war were the establishment of a national minimum weekly wage in 1942 and an age-wage scale in 1942.

The effect of the wartime flat rate increases was to narrow wage differentials and the process of narrowing was continued between 1947 and 1955 by six national flat-rate increases which lifted minimum rates and limited increases to the higher paid workers. But though some compression of differentials took place the changes in wages did not produce a rational wage structure in the sense that workers doing the same job were paid similar wages. What did occur, apart from the compression of differentials, was a tendency for many workers to be paid minimum rates because the virtual freezing of local wage determination meant that national wage increases tended to 'catch up' with local rates. But the existence of anomalies presented the NUM with a source of arguments for wage increases and created for the Board the problems of trying to maintain stability of wage costs.

In the mid-fifties, therefore, the Board began to consider the possibility of rationalising the wage structure for time-workers. The first step was to collect a list of job names and job descriptions. The number of jobs apparently exceeded 6,500, though the number concealed two important points. On the one hand, the figure was inflated by the existence of innumerable local names for similar jobs; in the end they were compressed into 350 job names. On the other hand, the workforce was extremely uneven in its distribution between the jobs. Some 85 per cent of the labour force were located in less than a quarter of the jobs and, at the other extreme, 3 per cent of the men were scattered over half of the jobs. The most populous jobs were haulage hands and general workers elsewhere underground and on the surface. At the other end of the scale there were six jobs each of which were filled by only one man.

The 350 job names were assimilated into 13 occupational grades by a process of job evaluation. The task of job evaluation was carried through by examining the total job rather than by splitting jobs into their components and then awarding points to each component. A points evaluation scheme in which points are awarded for such things as 'skill', 'responsibility' and so forth always runs into the difficulty of determining the basis upon which the various quantitative factors should be aggregated. What the Board did was to look at the 'total job' and make some decision about the rankings of 'total job'. This appears to be a crude procedure but since the Board also invited the union to discuss job rankings it allowed for a market determination of the ranking of jobs. The outcome of the bargaining process was that 350 job titles were placed into 13 job grades of which five were surface grades, five were underground and three were craft grades.

The next step was to examine the frequency distribution of wages – defined as all payments excluding the Five Day Week Bonus.[2] These distributions tended to be Pareto-like in form as compared with the more normal distributions for piece-workers. They, therefore, raised an academic point of interest which might have practical relevance. Frequency distributions of earned incomes usually follow a form which tends to be lognormal for low and medium earnings and Pareto for high earnings, which suggests that different forces are operating on different parts of the earnings spectrum. However, the mining evidence suggested that the method of wage payment might also have an influence on the distribution of earnings since a hierarchical structure is most easily achieved with time-rates.

The other feature revealed by the frequency distributions was the existence of overlap in the earnings of different grades. There was, in fact, no obvious pattern of wage differentials other than that indicated by the mode and the tendency of the mode to be located near the minimum of each grade as a result of the successive flat rate increases that had been granted previously.

The absence of recognisable differentials suggested, therefore, that national wage differentials could be introduced. Had recognisable differentials existed then the Board and the Union would have had to settle for a wage structure based on, say, regional wage differentials. But no obvious regional wage differentials existed. Thus although Nottinghamshire NUM argued for a distinct wage structure based on their higher earnings and productivity, there were no obvious Nottinghamshire differentials. Most Nottinghamshire pits had wage structures based on pit bargaining which had given rise to its own haphazard set of differentials. Spencerism had not produced any unique arrangement.

The outcome, therefore, was the creation of a national wage structure of standard rates, not minima, for each grade. Most miners obtained an increase as a result of this decision but those above the grade rates were placed upon a personal rate which lapsed when the person concerned left the Coal Board's employment. The scheme cost £14 million to implement and was carried through with little disturbance, though some personal rates seemed to last a long time.

PIECE-WORK WAGES

The 1955 National Day Wage Agreement seemed to solve many of the problems created by the common employment of time-workers, but left unresolved the difficulties in establishing some form of wage system for the industry's piece-workers, who comprised about 45 per cent of the labour force as compared with 39 per cent in manufacturing industry. The Day Wage Agreement need not have led to a revision of piece-rates, since the industry possessed no obvious link between time-rates and piece-rates, but because the Day Wage Agreement contained fall-back rates for workers whose own work was not normally available, an implicit relationship had been attempted. Moreover, there was the alternative feedback – not of time-rates on piece-rates, but of piece-rates on time-rates. As long as piece-rates were determined at pit level the Day Wage Structure might be vulnerable to forces outside the control of the Coal Board.

Investigations had, of course, been going on into the problems of piece-rates since the early fifties. The 1944 Porter Award[1] had suggested that the industry should rationalise its wage structure, especially for piece-workers and the 1946 Miners' Chapter contained, as one of its aims, the abolition of piece-rates. In 1951 the second wage increase to miners issued the following directive:

> The Board and the Union shall appoint a joint committee with the following terms of reference.
> 'To consider the existing wage structure of the industry with particular reference to piecework and to submit a report to the Joint National Negotiating Committee on the procedure which would be most suitable for the future regulation of the wages and conditions of such wokers so as to achieve a more rational wage structure with greater uniformity in wages and endowments for similar work and effort.'[3]

In 1952 the 24th Porter Award considered the revision of piece-rates to be a matter of vital importance and the 1953 wage agreement indicated that the work was continuing. In 1955 the Day Wage Agreement was concluded and from then on the problem of piece-rates became the most important issue.

THE STRUCTURE OF PIECE-WORK WAGES

In the mid-fifties the majority (about 80 per cent) of the industry's piece-workers were employed at the coalface and the remainder were employed elsewhere underground. At the coalface the piece-workers were colliers, cuttermen, conveyor movers, rippers, borers, packers and power loaders. Elsewhere, underground back rippers and hard-ground men were employed on piece-rates. This concentration of piece-work owed its origins to the problems of management control in difficult working conditions and had led to a system of self-control at the coalface and joint control of the quality of output through the presence of a check-weighman at a point away from the coalface.

PRICE LISTS

Piece-work contracts were extensively devised in the nineteenth century following the abandonment of the big butty system, though contracts did exist in the North East from the eighteenth century. In their coverage, contracts could take a variety of forms. A contract could be established for each particular job, and the set of such contracts would then form a price list which would be the subject of negotiation, and agreement between management and individuals or groups or sections of men. Alternatively, a contract could be 'all-in', by which the wage was based upon coal output in the shift and no attempt was made to measure and pay for individual operations connected with coal-getting or setting props. Piece-work contracts were fixed at pit level for seams, districts and faces. Revisions might be made as a result of changes in such factors as the price of coal, or changes in the wages of other groups of workers, though contracts could, on occasions, show a high degree of rigidity. Some contracts operating in Yorkshire in the fifties had actually been drawn up after the 1926 strike.

The distinction between individual, sectional and all-in contracts reflected the compromise between the quest for incentives and the prevailing geology and technology. On longwall faces individual contracts could prove to be an anachronism if the pace of work was strongly influenced by the attitudes of other workers and the nature of its task. On the other hand, sectional and all-in contracts could result in shirking by some members of a group. Sectional contracts were most prevalent in the East Midlands (about 80 per cent of all contracts), while 70 per cent of all contracts in South Wales were individual contracts. All-in contracts tended to be common in the West Midlands. Welsh payment systems may have been due to the smaller size of pits and intense individualism. The better conditions and bigger pits of the East Midlands may have fostered sectional contracts, though similar conditions in Yorkshire did not produce a tendency to sectional contracts.

PIECE-RATE ADDITIONS AND FLAT-RATE INCREASES

On top of the basic price list earnings came the percentage addition which was determined in the inter-war years by the revenues earned in particular regions. This pooling system represented a shift from the nineteenth-century system of varying the percentage according to the price of coal. During the Second World War the percentage addition was frozen and there was introduced a wide variety of flat-rate additions to compensate for changes in the cost of living. Flat-rate increases had, of course, been paid in the First World War but they had been merged into the base rate in the inter-war years. In the fifties, however, there were several flat-rate payments which had not been merged. First, there was the 1944 'skilled shilling'. Secondly, flat-rate increases were made in 1950 and in 1951. The former had its origins in the 1940 War Additions to Wages Agreement. The 1951 increase, however, was unique in that it represented the only occasion after nationalisation when piece-workers obtained a general wage increase by national agreement and it was paid in return for a general freeze on piece-rates for one year.

Flat-rate increases formed an interesting element in piece-workers' wages because they were national wage rates and because they were not an incentive payment but a time-rate. Their importance varied over time. In the late forties they formed about 12 per cent of average wages, but by the late fifties they had fallen to under 10 per cent as a result of the rise in piece-rates.

MONETARY ALLOWANCES

The third component of piece-workers' earnings was monetary allowances, which also took the form of flat-rate payments. Allowances were paid for a variety of reasons. First, there were the allowances paid for such items as carrying powder, tools and first aid equipment. Secondly, there were payments for problems caused by changes in the environment or breakdowns in organisation. The existence of faults, variations in seam thickness and dirt bands are examples of severe environmental conditions, while organisational problems might comprise being required to do extra work, being required to do alternative work or being required to wait while repairs were carried out. Problems involving alternative work could be divided into two categories: those which involved a transfer to other work even though a miner's own work was available, and those occurring when a man's work was not available.

How important these allowances were was often difficult to discover. Moreover, the inability to discover why payments were made often meant that allowances were being paid to avoid revising prices.

FIVE DAY WEEK BONUS

The fourth category of payment was the Five Day Week Bonus which arose out of the 1947 Five Day Week Agreement. Until 1957 the bonus tended to be paid only if all five shifts were worked and the payment took the form of an extra shift payment; that is, six shifts instead of five. Because it was difficult to establish reasonable absence, for example, at funerals, the qualifications governing its payment were modified and the bonus was paid on a shift basis. Since the bonus was paid as a percentage (16 per cent) of piece-worker's earnings it formed a sizeable proportion of take-home pay.

GUARANTEED WAGE

The fifth element in earnings was the guaranteed wage paid when men presented themselves for work, but when, for a variety of reasons, they were unable to carry out their normal work. The guaranteed wage was a time-rate which was lower than the average piece-worker's earnings. It tended, however, to form only a small proportion of piece-workers' earnings.

HOLIDAY PAY

Holiday pay formed another part of earnings, and was determined by the wage bill in the previous year.

PAYMENTS IN KIND

Another component of earnings comprised allowances in kind, of which free or concessionary coal and a free house, or rent allowance in lieu, were the most important. The rent allowance tended to be confined to Northumberland and Durham. Free or concessionary coal agreements existed in various coalfields, and different agreements existed for their regulation. Over time there was a tendency for the number of participants to increase. Thus, in some areas, pensioners, widows of men who had died while at work, and widows of men who had died of natural causes, were eligible. Furthermore, difficulties arose after 1958 when output fell and the number of claimants increased.

OVERTIME PAY

The final element was overtime pay, which was paid at the rate of time and a half for ordinary overtime and double time for weekend work. Overtime payments were calculated either on individual earnings or the average earnings of piece-workers at the pit or in the district.

THE STRUCTURE OF PIECE-WORKERS' EARNINGS

From what has been said it is apparent that piece-workers'

earnings comprised a variety of payments, each of which varied in importance. The main contribution came from price lists, which were responsible for about 60 per cent of earnings. But even with the price list component there could be enormous variation between workers in the importance of allowances. Apart from allowances, the Five Day Week Bonus (about 10 per cent) and overtime (about 10 per cent) were important contributions to take-home pay.

THE REVISION OF PIECE-WORKERS' EARNINGS

From 1955 to 1958 the Industrial Relations Department of the Board attempted to produce a rational wage structure for piece-workers. The method adopted was similar to that used for time-workers, but incorporated many novel features because of the need to recognise explicitly the relationship between tasks and earnings. Colliery managers supplied information on each piece-work job and face. From this information were derived frequency distributions of tasks (for example, cubic feet of coal filled per shift) and earnings. The averages of these distributions were then used as proximate norms of tasks and earnings – a rough guide to the notion of a fair day's wage for a fair day's work. However, the basic concept was a ratio derived from two absolute values which could be manipulated to yield any desired ratio. Thus, if it was ultimately decided that actual earnings were too low, then pay could be raised and, if necessary, tasks raised to maintain a given ratio. Alternatively, tasks could be set at any one level and wage costs kept constant by varying pay. The frequency distribution could be linked in a variety of ways.

The next step was to consider whether the deviations from the norms could be explained in any systematic and rational manner. This involved an analysis of a variety of factors which were grouped as follows:

1. Geological
   - seam section
   - gradient
   - dirt
   - density of coal
   - roof and floor conditions

2. Physiological
   - temperature
   - water
3. Method of extraction
   - handgot
   - mechanical pick
   - machine cut
   - power loading
4. Social organisation
   - method of wage payment
   - size of work group

Given these work factors, it was then possible to discover whether there were linear or non-linear relationships between the factors and tasks. Thus, seam thickness did not show much influence on extraction over some ranges, for example, 4 feet to 4 feet 6 inches. On the other hand, below 3 feet extraction became progressively more difficult. It was, therefore, possible to establish general tendencies for many factors, though not for some, such as method of payment. It was, however, possible sometimes to infer relationships because of the existence of complementarity between factors, such as geology and payments.

The analysis of the general effects of various factors on tasks permitted the creation of schedules indicating the amount by which tasks should be increased or decreased below the task norm. Thus, thin seams could justify a reduction in task below the norm, while thick seams could justify an increase in the task above the norm.

The creation of task norms implied a change in the nature of collective bargaining and an extension of managerial control. The earnings and task norms and the task schedules (deviations from the task norm) were to be the subject of national negotiations and could not be altered by local bargaining. Furthermore, the earnings norm could be linked to the day wage grade rates for face and underground workers, thereby establishing fall-back rates and guaranteed minimum earnings, and creating an effective link between time-workers and piece-workers. At pit level, management and workers would determine the nature of the tasks and which values in the national task schedules corresponded to the actual tasks. Slight difficulties in implementing tasks would be dealt with by making small variations in the norms at local level.

Large-scale modifications would, however, require arbitration or national agreement. The emphasis of the proposals lay in the attempt to maintain the effectiveness of incentives and central norms rather than permitting the wage structure to be undermined by the payment of allowances at pit level.

The establishment of norms and task schedules implied an attempt to equalise efficiency earnings. They also implied a redistribution of income from those who were relatively overpaid to those who were relatively underpaid. It was on this issue that the similarities between the Day Wage Agreement and the attempted revision of piece-rates became apparent. For it was suggested that one method of overcoming resistance to change would be to place those who were overpaid on personal rates, and when they left the industry to replace them with workers paid according to the national norms and task schedules. The costs of implementing such a scheme would then depend upon the norms adopted, since that would determine the amount to be paid to the underpaid. The problem of implementation was one which involved a variety of strategies. A once-and-for-all approach would have been the most expensive, whereas a phased approach, in which the new wage structure was applied only to new faces, leaving old ones to die out, would have been the least expensive, although it would have taken many years to accomplish.

In terms of the regional impact the proposed earnings/tasks scheme would have produced some interesting results. Many miners in Scotland would have gained, because their existing tasks were high while their earnings were low. Miners in the East Midlands would have gained because, though their wages were high, they were relatively underpaid in relation to their tasks. On the other hand, many miners in Northumberland, Durham and Lancashire would have suffered a reduction in wages because their tasks were low. In other coalfields the gains and losses would have been evenly divided. Of course, losses could have been temporarily concealed by the use of personal rates. In the long run, however, the use of task schedules would have brought about a substantial transformation of the pattern of earnings.

Task schedules were opposed because production engineers preferred tasks to be determined by method study. But method study had weaknesses. It assumed the existence of sufficient method-study engineers to undertake the work. The Board possessed only a few, and it would have taken many years to train more. The other criticism of method study was that its proponents believed that it was scientific and could produce rational and consistent results; defendants of task schedules were able to show that where method study had been applied, it gave inconsistent results. While method-study engineers could assume that they were merely concerned with efficient methods of work, workers would be interested in prospective rates of pay and hence there was an implicit effort bargain. Indeed it was admitted that mines in Yorkshire and South Wales might oppose method study. Finally, it was often the case that the discrepancies of method study resulted from the tendency of method-study engineers to be overwhelmed by trivial details.

Production engineers were also concerned about the effect on inter-regional and inter-pit standards, and some felt the high productivity pits might allow productivity to slip towards the national norms. And this fear reinforced the demands of those who argued for regional tasks and regional pay norms. Whether productivity would decline would, however, have depended upon the strength of the incentive built upon the earnings norm. It would have been possible for workers to earn more than the norm for extra effort. And the disadvantage of regional norms would have been their tendency to create pressures by the county unions to eliminate them.

The introduction of a national piece-work structure was also criticised by the Board's Finance Department on the grounds of cost. This conclusion needed to be put into the context of the alternatives. In 1957, wage drift was responsible for an increase of about £15 millions in piece-workers' wages and, though not all of this amount could be eliminated through a revision of piece-rates, it was hoped to obtain a substantial reduction in the upward movement of earnings. Furthermore, cost had to be judged in terms of the time scale over which revisions would be achieved.

The introduction of task schedules was finally rejected, and the decision was made to proceed by the application of method study, commencing with power-loaded faces. The decision was the outcome of a variety of factors. It was felt that task schedules were complicated, and there were doubts as to whether managers and workers could understand them and implement them. In 1958 W. H. Sales, the Board member responsible for the introduction of the 1955 Day Wage Agreement, was appointed Chairman of the North Eastern Division. His move left no one with the drive and ability to push through task schedules and his successor, J. Crawford, former President of the National Union of Boot and Shoe Operatives, was a proponent of method study. In 1958 Jim Bowman, the NUM vice-president was appointed chairman of the National Coal Board and it was natural that a chairman with experience in industrial relations should wish to take a more direct interest in wage determination. Finally, there were the changing circumstances after 1957. The reduction in the demand for coal meant that pit closures and redundancies became the central problems of industrial relations, and the fall in the demand for coal acted as a restraining influence on piece-workers' earnings.

Although the problem of revising piece-workers' earnings was one for both the Coal Board and the union, the NUM was never allowed to see the results of the Board's investigations and the task schedules. The Board made certain assumptions about the union's attitude and feared showing its executive any of the findings. But the union's attitude was not clear cut. The Miners' Charter proposed the abolition of piece-work, but there was never any strong pressure for that action. Writing in 1956 in *The Miner*, the official journal of the South Wales miners, Will Paynter noted that 'the clamour is for the extension of piece-work and not for its abolition'. Paynter found this element puzzling in view of the fact that the 1955 Day Wage Agreement had provided a springboard for the abolition of piece-work and the tendency of national agreements to exclude piece-workers had narrowed the piece-workers' differential. In 1957, at the union's annual conference, D. D. Evans proposed the establishment of a national piece-work structure, and his resolution received overwhelming support.

1957 TO 1966

From 1957 onwards the Board sought to apply method study to power-loaded faces and tried, wherever possible, to link the earnings of workers on conventional faces to those on power loading. Agreements covering power loading had, of course, existed since the early fifties, when Huwood Loaders and Gloster Getters were introduced, but it was not until the sixties that mechanisation began to be extensively applied and the need for new wage agreements became urgent. But in seeking to apply method study and to establish contracts, no uniform policy with respect to method of wage payment was formulated. Scotland and Durham had agreements which provided for day wage payment whereas South Wales and the inland coalfields retained piece-work. The Yorkshire Agreement of 1958 allowed workers to choose one of two methods of wage payment:

1. A *contractual method* which provided for
   a) a basic task to be agreed locally) for which 60s 0d per manshift would be paid.
   b) a payment (to be agreed locally) for performance in excess of the basic task.
   c) an abnormality rate of 64s 0d per manshift when the agreement could not operate because of adverse conditions.
2. A *day wage rate** for a fixed performance (to be agreed locally) as follows:
   a) either 75s 10d (A rate) or 74s 10d (B rate) per manshift for a task which was fixed;† plus
   b) a completion of task bonus of 4s 6d per manshift if the agreed task was completed before the men left the face.

* This particular method of wage payment for power-loading operatives was referred to as the 'Mecco Moore' after the machines it was applied to first.

† Men employed filling out coal in the stable hole, cable men and spillage cleaners were paid at the lower rate.

Whichever method was adopted, it was intended that similar effort should receive similar reward; that is, that two strips per shift on contract should give no higher earnings than would be given on the day wage. The agreement, of cource, contained weaknesses. First, it encouraged men on the Mecco Moore provisions to press for overtime working because the completion of task bonus was too small an incentive to work harder. And the problem of overtime was one shared by the Board, anxious to reduce wage costs, and the union, anxious to reduce hours of work. The second weakness was that the Mecco Moore system contained an annual compensatory uplift clause whereby the shift rates of men on Mecco Moore faces were to be related to the previous years' average earnings of men of the contractual provisions. And this primary drift could set up a secondary drift, as those on piece-work insisted that their fall-back rate should be not less than the Mecco Moore rate. This could open up a gap between the abnormality rate and the actual fall-back rate, and so perpetuate the allowance system that had plagued the Yorkshire coalfield in the fifties.

On the other hand, the system could have been defended on the grounds that it worked. It did not result in any severe stresses and strains. The options system allowed workers to choose the method of payment they preferred. Industrial unrest had declined since 1957, and that might be attributed to the system of options. It also allowed managers to choose between running machines on a cyclic or non-cyclic basis. Furthermore, the amount of drift created by the compensatory uplift clause was small, as Table 4.2 indicates.

TABLE 4.2 Yorkshire Agreement: Annual Increases in Base Rates to Mecco Moore Agreement

	Increase		*Base rate*	
	s	d	s	d
1958	4	0	62	4
1959	3	4	65	8
1960	2	3	67	11
1961	1	2	69	1
1962	2	2	71	3
1963	1	5	73	8
1964	2	2	75	10
1965	1	9	77	7

Source: R. Hepworth *et al.*, 'The Effects of Technological Change in the Yorkshire Coalfield', in D. M. Kelly and D. J. C. Forsythe (eds.), *Studies in the Coal Industry* (Pergamon, London, 1969).

The Yorkshire Agreement represented a compromise of two methods of wage payment. Elsewhere there was a polarisation into either time rates or piece rates though there was no apparent conflict or discord. And on the faces that were still being mined by machine-cut/handgot methods the revision of price lists was proceeding and consolidation of allowances was being achieved so as to give higher base rates and a smaller, but more effective, incentive.

THE INTRODUCTION OF A DAY-WAGE SYSTEM FOR FACEWORKERS

THE THEORY OF MANAGEMENT CONTROL

After 1957 the demand for coal fell and the urgent need was to increase the competitiveness of the industry. Although increased mechanisation, through power loading, was seen as an important element in the campaign for improved efficiency, the main thrust was seen to necessitate an increase in the general competitiveness of pits by making them compete against each other. This strategy required the removal of the administrative structure established in the period of excess demand. Hence, the powerful Divisions had to be removed, and managements at area level had to be given more discretion. But a move towards greater decentralisation could be taken to imply that competitive pressures would fall on wages. Spencerism threatened to emerge, and when Robens became Chairman of the Board there were fears that the industry would return to the inter-coalfield wage-cutting policies of the inter-war years.

In the light of these fears the prospect of a national time rate for all faceworkers must have appeared as a means of overcoming the suspicions of the NUM. Furthermore, a national wage, in association with power loading, would give even greater control over wages, remove the need for local initiative concerning the pace of work by the individual worker and place it on management and the speed of the machine, and remove the causes of local disputes. Taken in conjunction, the administrative reorganisation and the national time rate would bring about greater central control. By removing the powerful Divisions the Board could confront a large number of area Boards which might find it less easy to collude and resist pressures from above. At the same time a national time rate would render the NUM impotent at national and local level. At local level there would be nothing to negotiate about and at national level the union leadership would be severely controlled by the competition from other fuels.

But if the idea of a national time-rate appealed to the NCB, it had still to be sold to the NUM. As we have seen, there existed no strong pressures within the union. The traditional piece rate coalfields seemed to be content with the revisions made in the late fifties and early sixties. There was, however, a body of opinion within the NUM – common to some members of both the left and right wings – which regarded a national wage, whether based on piece- or time-rates, as the solution to many of the union's internal weaknesses. A national wage would mean that the total wage bill could be shared equally among all miners, irrespective of working conditions. No longer would some miners earn more than others because of favourable geological conditions. A national time rate would represent the culmination of the reforms begun in 1955.

But were the facts underlying the theory of management control well founded? The American coal industry had introduced time-rates in the forties and there had been a noticeable decline in big strikes. But the industry was experiencing the competition of oil, and the fall in the demand for coal might have been expected to lead to a fall in strike activity. There were, however, large numbers of unofficial, wildcat strikes, and these may have suggested that the removal of local bargaining increased the numbers of strikes against centralisation. So a national time-rate might not lead to a fall in strikes but might increase them, either by increasing the number of small-scale strikes, as in America, or by forcing the union into large-scale strikes to increase the national wage. And might not organisational strikes be much more difficult to solve under a time-rate system? In Britain, strike activity had declined since 1957, so the need for a change in the wage structure seemed to have disappeared. Which leads us to the question: were wages out of control? We shall examine the behaviour of wages from 1947 to 1966 and we shall divide the discussion into two periods, one coinciding with the boom, 1947 to 1957, and the other with the slump, 1957 to 1968.

1947–1957

The first phase of nationalisation, which ran from 1947 to 1957, was a decade of acute coal shortage not merely in the UK but also throughout Europe. Cheap oil imports were something that lay far off in the future, and fuel-using techniques tended to be inefficient. Mining was still essentially a muscular activity, and coal production depended upon more men being employed and men working harder. Throughout the period the shortage of coal was intensified by price controls. The world price of coal, as measured by the free market price of American coal sold in Europe, was about £1 a ton higher than the UK price. And the effects of the cheap coal policy were to increase the demand for coal, to necessitate the use of rationing and the use of high intensive coal-using sources of heat, such as electric fires, which were uncontrolled. Furthermore, the absence of a free market system made Coal Board planning difficult and disguised the extent to which investment in the production of substitute fuels and fuel-using techniques was taking place. Thus, the Board's 1950 *Plan for Coal* estimated that the total demand for coal between 1961 and 1965 would be about 240 million tons and that to produce that tonnage would require the expenditure of £635 million (at 1949 prices) between 1950 and 1956 on the opening of new collieries and the modernisation of existing pits. It was also estimated that the industry would employ 80,000 fewer in 1965.

However, difficulties were encountered in attempting to fulfil the *Plan*. It rested on highly dubious assumptions concerning productivity in the coalfields where labour was freely available and in those coalfields where labour was scarce. The productive regions tended to be those where labour was scarce, and they were also those in which productivity was likely to be checked by the need to deploy labour on expansion and modernisation. In 1956 the Board published its review and reappraisal, *Investing in Coal*. The fulfilment of the *Plan*'s projected 240 million tons was pushed back to the end of the period 1961–5, and the required investment expenditure was increased to £1,350 million at current prices.

During this period Arthur Horner, then General Secretary of the NUM, stated that the miners could have had the moon if they had demanded it. Yet the miners never asked for the moon. Miners' wages increased relative to those of other groups, but not appreciably so and certainly less than they might have done under private enterprise. What has to be explained, therefore, is the apparent lack of militancy of the NUM and the lack of willingness of the NCB to raise wages in order to increase manpower.

LABOUR SUPPLY

The behaviour of wages cannot be understood without reference to the behaviour of labour supply. In the first instance, labour supply was dependent upon wastage and recruitment. Annual wastage tended to be high because of deaths, retirements, dismissals and movements to other industries. And wastage of new recruits was exceptionally high except for schooleavers, who had no experience of conditions in other industries. Wastage was also high in boom periods. Indeed, the Board tended to regard the general level of unemployment in the economy as exercising a much more important influence on recruitment and wastage than the wages it paid relative to those in other industries. Finally, recruitment was strongly influenced by the distance men had to travel to work. Roughly speaking, most miners lived within 2 miles of their pits, and field studies showed that some pits, such as Rossington near Doncaster, had great difficulty in expanding their labour forces because of poor transport facilities.

COAL BOARD WAGE POLICY

Faced with an excess demand for coal and a rising supply curve of labour, the Coal Board responded with policies of discrimination in an endeavour to keep wage costs down. But whereas such policies are often a prelude to a long-run rise in wages in competitive firms, the Board persisted with discriminatory policies throughout the fifties. It lowered hiring standards in periods of tight labour markets, and raised them when other markets were slack, and varied its internal standards by accelerating upgradings. In addition, the Board engaged in extensive welfare schemes including housing.

In emphasising the Board's manpower policies with respect to the various dimensions of recruitment and wastage, we are inevitably drawn to a consideration of the Board's policies for the overall level of wages. The pursuit of a break-even policy for coal leads to an emphasis on discriminating policies of recruitment in an endeavour to stay within the rules laid down by a break-even policy. The notion that the Board should break even was, of course, an interpretation of the Nationalisation Act, though since the charter did not specify over what period the Board was expected to break-even it was always possible for the Board to make profits or to raise prices and wages in an endeavour to expand supply and break-even at a new price level. Fears of the effects of increases in the prices of coal upon the prices of other goods and hence upon the cost of living and the volume of exports, were often expressed though Little thought that the fears were much exaggerated.[3] There were also fears of the effect of raising the price of coal on miners' wages which could, however, have been nullified by the acceptance of Sir Arthur Lewis's suggestion that an excise tax be placed on coal.[4] This proposal harked back to the policy adopted after the First World War. Domestic prices were regulated by the government, and surplus profits went to the Exchequer. Then the government was interested in a free market in coal and, therefore, favoured price increases.

But though the government and the Board favoured a break-even policy in the fifties, it is possible that a higher break-even point would have expanded coal output. Alexander suggested that the Board was apparently mistaken in its views as to the effects of wage increases upon recruitment, wastage and absenteeism. His analysis of the effects of wage increases indicated a tendency for recruitment to rise and for wastage to fall, while the impact of wage increases upon absenteeism seemed to be ambiguous.[5] Furthermore, the coal industry did not appear to be a wage leader, so there seemed to be no problem of miners' wages forcing up wages elsewhere.

NUM WAGE POLICY

If the Board's policies were explicable, though possibly confused, those of the NUM were no less enigmatic. Having achieved public ownership of the coal industry the union felt that it had to defend it even though it meant exercising wage restraint. The leadership tended to be concerned with the wider issues of economic stability, and Lawther, the President of the NUM, along with Deakin (T&GWU) and Williamson (G&MWU) formed the backbone of trade union support for the Labour government's policies of wage restraint and wage freeze in the late forties and early fifties, and late into the sixties; even with Conservative governments, this restraint persisted. Having accepted restraint and the settlement of differences through the use of conciliation machinery, the union tended to acquiesce in the movement of wages being governed by changes in the cost of living.

But the influence of the leadership was strongest on the wages of time-workers because they tended, increasingly, to be determined at the national level whereas piece-workers' wages were determined at pit level. What then determined the movement of piece-workers' wages, and was there no impact of changes in piece-workers' wages upon wages of time-workers? To answer these questions we must now examine the behaviour of piece-workers' earnings.

Between 1947 and 1957 the earnings per manshift of piece-workers doubled from 36/7d to 72/7d. But this increase did not take place at an even rate. There were variations in the rate of increase of wages which could be ascribed to a variety of factors, including,

1. changes in productivity;
2. overtime working and absenteeism;
3. external factors such as cost of living and wages in other industries;
4. newness of the bargaining machinery and the miners' attitudes to nationalisation; and
5. internal differences between various occupational groups within the piece-work labour force.

Some of these influences were relatively unimportant. Productivity did increase between 1947 and 1957, but most of the increase occurred between 1947 and 1951, and thereafter productivity tended to stagnate. Over the whole period productivity rose by about 18 per cent, an increase that seems too small to account for the large rise in earnings. Absenteeism also tended to remain constant throughout the period, and though there was an increase in overtime working, its effect was not all that great. Productivity, absenteeism and overtime working seemed to have played little part in the rise in earnings.

The influence of factors 3 to 5 can best be understood by analysis of the movement of piece-workers' earnings. From 1947 to the middle of 1948 there was a rise in earnings. Between the middle of 1948 and the end of 1950 there was a slowing down of the rate of increase. Between 1950 and 1952 the rate of increase was about the same as that which occurred in 1947. The rate of increase then slowed until about 1954. Thereafter, the rate of increase quickened and rose rapidly in 1955 and 1956.

The variations in the rate of increase of earnings bear a strong relationship to changes in general economic activity, changes in the cost of living and changes in government economic policy. Retail prices rose about 7 per cent per annum between 1946 and 1948, slowed to 3 per cent between 1948 and 1950, and then rose to 7 per cent during the Korean War boom. After the Korean inflation, prices fell back during the general world recession and did not rise again until the beginning of the boom of 1955–6. These movements of prices coincide with movements in earnings even to the extent of including thc impact of thc government's wage freeze of 1948 to 1950, which seems to have been accepted, to some extent, at grass roots level.

Movements of retail prices do not, however, provide the sole explanation of the behaviour of piece-workers' earnings. They can explain variations in the rate of increase of earnings. But piece-workers' earnings doubled between 1947 and 1957, whereas retail prices increased by only 59 per cent. Some other explanations must be sought for the divergence of earnings and prices. Two possible sources of explanation exist. Miners' wages stood at the top of the wage league table for most of the period and, therefore, there is no need to propose wages in other industries as the cause of movements in miners' wages. But differentials between different groups of piece-workers could provide a source of discontent and pressure for wage adjustments, particularly where discontent over occupational wage groups allied itself to geographical wage differentials. Studies of mining in the fifties suggested that there were strong differences in the status rankings of various occupational groups, and that these groups exhibited different patterns of behaviour. Typically, fillers had low status, whereas rippers and cuttermen had high status. However, wage surveys indicated no obvious ranking of face jobs. While average earnings of conveyor movers tended to be highest, and those of packers tended to be lowest, there was no consistency between coalfields or pits. Some part of the explanation may have lain in the need to have monetary compensations for the differences in the nature of jobs, but the blurring of occupational wage differentials suggests that a more probable explanation lay in the struggles of various groups to attain ascendancy or wage parity.

Thus small groups, such as rippers and cuttermen, might easily gain increases, which would then lead to the larger groups having to exert tremendous pressure to keep in step.

The pressures to keep in step were reinforced by the Board's own policy of break-even. The break-even implied that there was no strong pressure on individual pits to be efficient. Under private ownership each pit had to be efficient in order to survive. Any variations in efficiency were reflected partly in the prices charged to consumers and partly in the wages paid to workers. High productivity pits cut prices in order to expand their share of the market and raised wages in order to attract more labour. Low productivity pits tended to charge relatively higher prices and paid lower dividends to owners and lower wages to workers. Nationalisation abolished this process by compelling the efficient pits to subsidise the least efficient, in order that all consumers should be charged an average price which avoided giving any person or group unreasonable preference or advantage. The notion that consumers should all be charged a similar price became imperceptibly extended to the notion that all workers should receive a similar wage. There thus grew up the concept of an earnings norm and though differentials might persist and be defended there was an attempt to reduce them. And, more important, the 'average wage system' broke the link between wages and tasks and resulted in the perpetual motion of wages because someone was always below the average.

The pressures to keep in step seem to have developed without any necessity to invoke the unofficial strike weapon. In an earlier paper Hughes had suggested that the Board did try to maintain the average price policy and inter-regional efficiency by keeping wages in line with productivity, but that this policy was continually broken by strikes in the less profitable areas creating revisions of wages and causing price increases.[6] The shortage of coal forced the price of coal up, not by demand acting directly on price but acting directly through wages by means of strikes. Thus did market forces break through. But apart from the strong evidence for such a strike process at work in the Yorkshire coalfield in 1955 and 1956, where strikes led to wholesale revisions of contracts and an increase in the price of coal by £2 a ton there is insufficient evidence to support Hughes's hypothesis. Abstracting from the strikes of winding-enginemen in Yorkshire and Lancashire in 1949 and again in Yorkshire in 1952, deputies in

Nottinghamshire in 1956 and day-wage workers in Lancashire, the coalfields with the highest strike records were Scotland, South Wales and Yorkshire. Of these coalfields only Scotland and Yorkshire show any correlation between strikes and productivity, whereas South Wales had lower than average earnings despite large tonnage losses through strikes. Furthermore, productivity was also static in Durham and the West Midlands, and yet in both wages rose faster than the national average. In the case of the West Midlands high wages in other industries could have pulled up wages but the same explanation would not fit Durham. Militancy does not seem to be a strong explanation despite the fact that the high productivity coalfields of the East Midlands, Northumberland and Cumberland had high wages and few strikes as compared with the low productivity, low wages and many strikes of coalfields such as Scotland and South Wales. There were too many exceptions.

The differential between piece-workers and time-workers was strongly influenced by the differing institutional methods of wage payment. Throughout the period it was very difficult for time-workers to obtain wage increases at pit level except by the possible device of regrading. On the other hand, piece-workers could obtain local increases, but their awareness of bargaining power was something which only increased with time. To appreciate what happened to the differential between piece-workers and time-workers we need to look at some of the changes that took place in that differential before nationalisation, and how the establishment of collective bargaining machinery at pit level, on nationalisation, subsequently influenced the movement of the differential.

Before nationalisation, piece-workers' price lists were determined at pit level and, generally speaking, their alteration was tightly controlled by the private coal-owners. Changes in price lists were usually brought about by substantial changes in methods of working or the opening of new seams. And on to the basis was added the district percentage. During the war, as we have seen, flat-rate increases were substituted for percentage additions. In 1944, however, all but one of the flat-rate increases was consolidated into the basis. The intention of the 1944 Revision of Wages Agreement was to create a better incentive by consolidation of flat-rate additions but to bring about little change in overall earnings. Furthermore, the agreement prohibited all alterations in wage for a period of 3½ years. The effect of the agreement, was, however, different from its intention and an enormous gap was opened up between the earnings of piece-workers and time-workers. Roughly speaking, piece-workers got increases of about 5s 0d a shift whereas timeworkers got about 6d a shift. This disparity was to be a source of embarrassment to the union and, despite subsequent attempts to close the gap, it widened after nationalisation.

Between 1944 and 1947 there were changes in the industry's machinery for collective bargaining. In 1946 the national and district conciliation procedure was established. This involved, among other things, the voluntary renunciation of the strike weapon by the NUM. In 1947 the machinery was extended down to pit level. From June 1947, after the expiration of the 1944 agreement, it became possible for piece-workers to press for wage increases at national or local level. They chose the latter, though there was a lag in response due to the uncertainties surrounding the nature of the new machinery.

An impetus to the revision of price lists came from the introduction of the Five Day Week Agreement which called for a reassessment of tasks. The agreement resulted in widespread stoppages, notably the Grimethorpe stint strike, but there is no doubt that its ultimate effect was to bring about an increase in wages. Thereafter, piece-workers' wages increased partly as a result of external factors and partly as a result of internal tensions. Between 1947 and 1957 the earnings of piece-workers per man-shift rose by about 99 per cent, whereas the underground minimum – the link to time-workers – rose by about 90 per cent. And in terms of absolute differences the increase was about £1-10s-0d per shift. The differentials did not, of course, widen at a constant rate. Time-workers received their increases at discrete intervals and a see-saw relationship developed whereby, on occasions, time-workers tended to close the gap only to find piece-workers had subsequently reopened it. In a period of inflation, however, early wage increases are better than those which arrive later.

The account of differentials given here differs from those presented by Turner, Alexander and Searle-Barnes.[7] Over the period from 1945 to 1950 Turner observed a widening of the differential between the weekly earnings of face-workers (a proxy for face piece-workers) and the underground minimum weekly wage. The underground minimum rose from £5 to £5-15s., while average weekly earnings of face-workers increased from £5-19s. to £9-2s-7d. Taking the period 1945 to 1955, Alexander also found a widening of differentials, but believed that most of the widening had occurred before nationalisation and that some narrowing had occurred between 1947 and 1950. Searle-Barnes criticised both Turner and Alexander for neglecting to note that the Five Day Week Agreement increased earnings but did not affect the minimum rate, and that the agreement gave bigger increases to time-workers than to piece-workers. He also pointed out that more overtime would tend to have been worked by surface and haulage workers. By taking the earnings of piece-workers we have sought to avoid some of the problems created by the use of a proxy—face-workers' weekly earnings—and by the incidence of overtime. Furthermore, we have attempted to estimate the influence of productivity, overtime and absenteeism. When these differences are taken into account, some of the differences in interpretation are resolved. First, there was a widening of the differential after nationalisation, *pace* Alexander, because of the effects of the Five Day Week agreement and the use of the new conciliation machinery. Secondly, the use of earnings per man-shift stresses the point that however time-workers tried to reduce the differential by more regular attendance and relatively more overtime, they would have to forfeit leisure. Thirdly, and this applies with special force to Searle-Barnes, although the differential did on occasions narrow and there was a long-run attempt for the differential to remain constant these attempts at constancy required conscious effort and much time-consuming negotiation by the Board and the union. There was a sort of dynamic equilibrium created out of the leap-frogging process but it was not something which national negotiators could view with satisfaction.

1957–1968

In 1957 the sellers' market for coal collapsed. The availability of cheap oil, increased fuel efficiency, the contraction of major coal-using industries (such as the railways), a few mild winters and, later, the Clean Air Act of 1965, conspired to bring about an unexpected and sharp decline to the demand for coal. During the period 1947–57 the demand for coal by the electricity supply industry had outweighed the falls in demand from railways and other industries. But from 1957 onwards, the demands by electricity supply were insufficient to mask the general fall in the demand for coal. Indeed, the relative importance of electricity supply aggravated the problem, because power stations, being able to burn anything, yielded lower profits. Sales fell from 207.3 million tons in 1958 to 193.7 million tons in 1959. Undistributed stocks rose from 27.4 million tons in 1957 to 50.0 million tons in 1959.

From 1957 to 1961 the industry was in fundamental disequilibrium; supply greatly exceeded demand. But in 1962 the industry began to achieve a rough balance between consumption and production, and though there were further falls in demand none was comparable with that of 1957. There were, however, still problems. The sixties saw a sharp increase in the degree of mechanisation. The proportion of coal power-loaded rose from 23 per cent in 1957 to 37 per cent in 1960, 75 per cent in 1964 and 92 per cent in 1968. And there were parallel developments in haulage and surface handling, so that while the industry had to adjust to a fall in the demand for labour brought about by changes in the demand for the product, it was now faced with significant reductions in the demand for labour as a result of mechanisation. But whereas product market changes were to a large extent outside the Board's control, the pace and extent of mechanisation were controllable.

Just how significant mechanisation was can be gleaned from two sources. In the 1960 *Annual Report* the Board stated that: 'In 1960, 151 manshifts were needed, on average, to win a thousand tons of coal from mechanised faces of all types. By comparison, 251 manshifts were needed where coal was hand-filled'. A second crude estimate can be obtained by discovering how many men would have been needed to produce the 1968 output had productivity remained at the 1957 level. In 1968 approximately 365,000 men were needed whereas 552,000 men would have had to be employed if productivity had remained at the 1957 level. Mechanisation would, therefore, have appeared to have resulted in the loss of 187,000 jobs. But these estimates are still crude, and fail to distinguish between the effects of mechanisation, closures and concentration of output on productive faces within pits; that is, the effects of shifts of the average product curve due to technical change as distinct from movements along a given average product curve. It was also usual for the most productive handfilled faces and seams to be mechanised first. For the period 1958 to 1961, Sealey estimated that mechanisation accounted for 25 per cent of the increase in output, closures accounted for 12 per cent and concentration for 12 per cent.[8] Sealey's analysis, however, took place before the great increase in mechanisation; 187,000 lost jobs may therefore be a crude but a confident estimate of the effect of mechanisation.

The immediate response of the Board to reduced demand was to regard it as temporary. Therefore there was no policy, only a series of expedients. Hours of work were reduced by stopping Saturday work and curtailing overtime; the former saved about 10 million tons. There were restrictions on recruitment, and net wastage rose from 9.2 per cent in 1957 to 15.5 per cent in 1960. Coal was stockpiled at a cost of £27 million, and open coalmining was cut back even though it was extremely profitable. By this series of expedients the closure of seams and pits was delayed until 1959.

The optimistic view of the future found expression in the Board's *Revised Plan for Coal, 1959*. The demand for coal was expected to be between 200 and 215 million tons in 1965. Productivity was expected to rise by 22 per cent, and the industry was envisaged as requiring some 587,000 to 626,000 men. Opencast output was to be cut, and some 200 pits were to be closed. The gap between optimism and realisation is shown in Table 4.3. All the Board's estimates were considerably wide of the mark, particularly the failure to forecast the rise in productivity and the implications for the size of the labour force.

By the beginning of the sixties there was a change of opinion and the fall in demand came to be regarded as permanent. But though the Board accepted some reduction in the size of the industry it strove for a national fuel policy with a guaranteed share for coal. In pursuit of this policy the Board was supported by the NUM, and in the early sixties the Board acquiesced in the NUM's attempts to obtain safeguards for the industry. For despite the rumblings of industrial action the union adopted a political stance. It was a policy forced on the NUM by its weak bargaining position, though favoured by those who still believed that in a nationalised industry solutions should be sought through political change. Hence the union sought and obtained the support of

TABLE 4.3 Manpower, 1959–65

Division	*Actual 1956*	*Estimate 1965 (thousands)*	*Actual 1965*
Scotland	79	68–76	49.6
Northumberland	43	36–9	93.5
Durham	95	79–83	
North East (Yorkshire)	131	123–9	106.0
North West	51	39–43	36.9
East Midlands	100	98–102	82.9
West Midlands	52	49–54	34.2
South West	94	90–4	69.2
South East	7	5–6	5.0
G.B.	652	587–626	477.3

Source: NCB *Annual Reports* and *Revised Plan for Coal* (1959).

the TUC and the Labour Party. It pressed for a national fuel policy and it stressed the political dangers of too much reliance on Middle East oil. It proposed bans on the use of oil by power stations, the complete cessation of opencast mining and the creation of a buffer stock scheme. In 1966 the union urged the underwriting of the industry's losses; the financing by government of stocks; the government financing of the social costs involved in redundancy and redeployment; a tax on fuel oil; and a promise that North Sea oil should not be used to replace coal.

But protection on any large scale was denied by successive governments, both Conservative and Labour. Conservative governments took the view that there should be a free market in fuels and that the consumer should be allowed to exercise his sovereignty. And Labour governments, though they tended to qualify the doctrine of laissez faire, did not disagree. Both the 1965 *White Paper on Fuel Policy* and the *National Plan* envisaged that the industry would employ 160,000 men in 1975 to produce 149 million tons and that by 1980 the industry would employ about 65,000 men. The actuality of 1975 was that 246,000 men produced 114.99 million tons.

Policy as laid down in 1965 stipulated that: oil imports were not to be a burden on the balance of payments; indigenous fuel supplies were to be conserved and fostered; there were to be limits to the contraction of the coal industry; a ban was to be placed on coal imports; and a duty was to be levied on fuel imports. The 1967 White Paper proposed a reduction in the use of oil by power stations; the allocation of new industries to the coalfields; and more generous compensation for redundancy and redeployment. Limited protection was to be the rule.

REDUNDANCY AND REDEPLOYMENT

Given the attitudes of successive governments, the Coal Board had to find ways of running down the labour force. To a large extent the problem was eased by the great amount of wastage the industry incurred each year.

Merely by not replacing workers wastage rose from 9.2 per cent in 1957 to 15.5 per cent in 1960. However, such a policy has its dangers. In the first place wastage was considerably influenced by voluntary leavers, who tended to comprise the young. Hence, for an industry which was heavily dependent upon the services of able-bodied young men, the age distribution of the labour force could be adversely affected. Thus, between 1957 and 1964 the average age of miners rose from 41.3 to 42.7 and the Board was forced to ease the ban on recruitment. Secondly, voluntary wastage tended to be highest in those areas where jobs were plentiful and where coal was most profitably mined. Thirdly, voluntary wastage was considerably affected by fluctuations in the general level of demand for labour and, since these fluctuations lay outside the control of the Board, wastage could not be planned. Fourthly, from the community's point of view, wastage without recruitment tends to raise unemployment in local labour markets, especially for school-leavers.

Despite these reservations, wastage did assist in overcoming the problems of a labour surplus; some 228,326 jobs were removed through wastage, leaving 89,774 jobs to be removed through redundancies, redeployment and dismissals.

The removal of about 8,000 jobs a year presented the Board with a formidable task, and the second line of approach to the labour surplus was through redundancies and redeployment. Provisions for redundancy had existed in the forties and were revised in 1959. These provided that miners were to receive compensation based upon two-thirds of the national minimum wage plus the state pension. These provisions were subsequently found to be inadequate and were revised, notably after the enactment of the Redundancy Payments Act in 1965.

Policy, as it emerged in the late fifties, was that men over 65 were to be laid off and given a lump sum compensation; men over 60 were to be given the option of retirement and lump sum compensation; juveniles were to be retained; and all other workers were to be given the option of transfer to another pit in the same coalfield or another coalfield. But a noticeable feature of these agreements was that the Board had the right to decide which pits were to be closed and how many men were to be made redundant. The NUM did obtain the right to be consulted but it never seemed to challenge the Board's prerogative.

Pit closures – the most significant and socially traumatic form of redundancy – tended to be concentrated in Scotland, Northumberland and Durham, and Lancashire. And for miners in these coalfields the major solution was redeployment, either locally or in other coalfields. Most miners were, in fact, redeployed locally. Thus, of the 1,987 miners affected by closures in the Houghton-le-Spring district of Durham, 1,384 were transferred to other pits and 99 per cent of that number were found jobs within an eleven-mile radius.[9]

Some coalfields – Yorkshire, the East and West Midlands and South Wales – were seriously short of labour, and to alleviate their problems two transfer schemes were devised. In 1962 the Board introduced an inter-divisional transfer scheme, whereby workers in Scotland, Northumberland and Durham, and the North West could transfer to areas of labour shortage. And in 1964 the Board introduced a long-distance re-entrants scheme, whereby workers who had left the industry in either Scotland or Northumberland and Durham could re-enter the industry in one of the expanding coalfields. With generous housing and travelling allowances for miners and their families, between 1963 and 1967 these schemes transferred about 9,000 men, the majority being inter-divisional transfers. Apart from solving the Board's difficulties, these schemes served to reduce the level of unemployment in the labour surplus areas.

Most miners transferred went to the West Midlands (31 per cent of those transferred between 1963 and 1965), with Yorkshire (11.5 per cent) and the East Midlands (10.2 per cent) being the other favoured coalfields. The popularity of the West Midlands stemmed from the availability of housing, the possibilities of piece-work and the general prosperity of the area. Since most men were married, wastage rates among transferees were strongly influenced by the availability of housing.

The third group affected by closures comprised those who found jobs in other industries. In Scotland many went into the car industry; construction and local government were also popular. Most men went into semi-skilled and unskilled jobs and received a drop in pay. Few went to government training centres; indeed few seemed aware of their existence. In some instances a reluctance to re-train was influenced by the fear of affecting the amount of compensation received.

Finally, there were those who became permanently unemployed. In the main they consisted of older men who had been employed on the surface, were often disabled, and were 'left stranded by the onrush of industrial change and technical progress and who presented the nation with a social and economic problem'.[10]

By all objective standards the coal industry's redundancy programme was one of the biggest undertaken by an employer or industry. The removal of 8,000 jobs a year for a decade dwarfed the average of 75 jobs per firm in the sixties and overshadowed the closures of railway workshops, the mass lay-offs of the car industry and the general 'shake-outs' of the sixties. It also took place in a period when the burden of dependency was being increased by a rise in the percentage of elderly people in the population. And judged against this background it was more considerate and humane. It was also more successful than the haphazard arrangements of the twenties and thirties.

Yet the success must be qualified. The run-down of the coal industry took place in a period when the general demand for labour was appreciably higher than in the inter-war years, and this served to ease the burden of adjustment for those displaced from the coal industry and for those school-leavers who were diverted elsewhere. It was also assisted by the existence of one employer and of one union which, though it had to endure the displacement effects of mechanisation, seemed more able to cope with diversification effects than craft unions would. But the adjustment process was protracted, and a more vigorous run down of the industry might have resulted in an earlier stabilisation of the industry's labour force. As it was the contraction was spread out over a decade and this meant that wages were depressed for a long time. Furthermore, the characteristics of labour mobility and immobility revealed in the inter-war years remained much in evidence. Miners tended to move to other mining jobs because their skills were specific. These problems – immobility and a protracted adjustment – were aggravated by certain aspects of government manpower policy. In the mid-sixties governments passed the Redundancy Payments Act and the Industrial Training Act. Both, however, presented problems for the Coal Board's redundancy programme.

The Redundancy Payments Act provided that workers who were made redundant through reasons other than misconduct were to receive a lump sum payment based upon length of service. As such it was criticised because it represented a negative action and did nothing to encourage workers to move into new jobs. It could only, therefore, be defended on grounds of equity – 'if directors received golden handshakes then so should workers.' The Act, however, did provide that no payments need be made if an employer offered suitable alternative employment. 'Suitable employment' tended to be interpreted widely by the Industrial Tribunals, as in the case of *Sheppard v National Coal Board* where an offer of employment which involved a longer journey to and from work and the loss of overtime was interpreted as suitable employment and a claim for redundancy pay was rejected. But the concept of 'suitable employment' could not be extended to jobs in other coalfields and it was on this score that the Act was criticised by the Chairman of the NCB, Lord Robens:

> The Act was supposed to make it easier for workers to move to new jobs. In fact, by 1968, it had reduced the flow of transferring miners to a trickle. Whatever the good intentions behind the Act may have been, the hard fact was that a sizeable redundancy payment was a much more attractive proposition for many people than continuity of employment. Miners at closing pits would not go near our employment vans for fear of being offered 'suitable employment' and thereby losing their redundancy payment.
>
> In fact we would never have tried to withhold a redundancy payment on the ground that we could offer jobs in another coalfield, but you simply could not get this over to the miners. Often we were put in the strange position of making a redundancy payment, keeping track of the recipient until he

> had spent it, and then offering him the transfer to another coalfield he would not even look at in the first place . . . . . In my opinion the Government would have spent less money to much better effect if they had concentrated on improving transfer allowances for moving workers to other jobs. This is precisely what we had to do in an effort to counteract the incentive which the Redundancy Payments Act offered redundant workers to stay where they were.[11]

The Act encouraged workers to demand redundancy pay even to the point of striking, as at Cefn Coed in 1962 when miners staged a sit-in, not as a protest against the closure of the pit, but in order to ensure that they got redundancy pay.

The Industrial Training Act was intended to increase the amount of training by imposing a levy on firms which did not train labour and subsidising those which did. As such it was criticised because it assumed that workers did not pay for their training and therefore produced a misallocation of resources. But its main weakness, from the point of view of redundant workers, was that the training boards tended to concentrate on school-leavers and apprenticeships. There was a notable lack of coordination of redundancy, training and redeployment programmes in an economy whose main source of labour supply lay in its ability to transfer workers from contracting to expanding industries.

WESTERN EUROPE

The effects of the decline in the demand for coal in Western Europe were no less dramatic than in the United Kingdom, though the implications were more intriguing because of the clash between nationalism and economic union within the European Economic Community.[12] The EEC was established to achieve political ends but required economic means. At the end of the Second World War Europe was devastated and divided. There was the threat of communist infiltration and invasion. And, if the communist threat was averted, there was the problem of a resurgence of German nationalism once Allied control of the coal, iron and steel industries ceased. The French solution to the German problem was a plan, put forward by Monnet and Schuman, for the internationalisation of the ownership of coal, iron and steel by the creation of a common market. The idea proved acceptable to Germany, Belgium, Holland, Luxembourg, Italy and France, but not to the UK, and by the Treaty of Paris, signed in 1951, the European Coal and Steel Community was established. In 1957 the union was enlarged to embrace other goods and the UK joined in 1968.

The basic idea of a common market, or customs union, is the removal of all tariffs and subsidies by member countries, in order to create a situation of free trade between members, and the erection of uniform tariffs on goods imported from non-members. Such a common market exists within the UK since, in principle, there are no obstacles to trade, other than transport costs, between all the regions of the UK, whilst imports from foreign countries pay the same tariff rates regardless of whether the goods are required by the inhabitants of London, Glasgow or Sheffield. The creation of a customs union involves, therefore, the belief that the gains from trade creation between the members outweigh the losses from trade diversification as regions are forced to buy from each other rather than from some cheaper external source. The concept of a customs union also involves the assumption that balance of payments problems between members will be solved, not by the erection of tariffs or subsidies or monetary devaluation or appreciation of currencies, but by monetary deflation and inflation and the migration of factors of production or the provision of financial assistance by the supreme authority of the customs union. Thus, to take the UK as an example, the exchange rate between Yorkshire and other parts of the UK is fixed at par unity; one Yorkshire pound is equal to one Derbyshire pound, and so on. Now a fall in the exports of coal from Yorkshire with imports into Yorkshire remaining initially unchanged would lead to a fall in bank balances in Yorkshire and a rise in balances elsewhere. Thus, monetary flows would be automatic and quick, since there exists complete monetary integration. The monetary flow would lead to a reduction of spending in Yorkshire and a rise in spending elsewhere. The fall in spending in Yorkshire would cause a fall in costs and prices and a fall in imports. The cut in costs and prices would induce some resources to migrate to more prosperous regions whilst those that remain would find employment as the reduction in prices induced greater purchases by those in the more prosperous areas. Should there be any obstacle to falling costs or migration then unemployment and poverty could occur and the national authority would have to render assistance – but in such a way as not to seriously impair the benefits derived from economic union. The UK has achieved full economic union in the sense that there is monetary union. The Common Market countries have not, however, achieved such a union, though that is their ultimate goal.

In the years preceding the fall in the demand for coal the coal industries of France, Belgium, Holland and West Germany attempted to expand capacity and increase output. Oil was imported to supplement energy supplies but after 1955 there was a steep rise in importing coking coal from America. In 1956, 45 million tonnes of coal were imported. When the fall in demand for coal occurred there was a rise in stocks and a conflict of policy between the coal producers and the non-coal consumers, both within and between member countries. The Treaty of Paris forbade direct financial assistance by producer countries and instead placed emphasis upon assistance from the European Social Fund. But the centralised policy embodied in the Paris Treaty conflicted with the belief and impulses of member countries. In 1959 the Council of Ministers attempted to reassert the powers of the Community by attempting to declare 'a state of manifest crisis' but this was rejected by France and Germany who objected to supranational control. From 1959 onwards the views of the supranational authority were forced into line with those of the coal producers. Community regional policy came to be accepted as a complement of, and not a substitute for, 'national' regional policies. The coal crisis was, therefore, the first occasion on which the members' willingness to accept the implications of a common market was put to the test and represented a severe setback to the hopes of monetary union.

All the coal producers took steps to lessen the impact of the fall in the demand for coal. In Belgium, government aid was extended

TABLE 4.4 Hard Coal Production, Western Europe, 1957–65

	1957	*1959*	*1962*	*1965*
Belgium	29.2	22.8	21.2	19.8
France	56.8	57.6	52.4	51.3
W. Germany	149.7	141.8	141.4	135.1

Source: Eurostat: *Energy Statistics*.

to 679 communes containing 35.5 per cent of the population and 25 per cent of the territory. Aid comprised employment subsidies, rebates and grants to new firms entering the coalfields. Licences were imposed on coal imports in 1958 and two years later a 5 per cent tax was imposed on coal imports and a tax on fuel oil was imposed. The government also gave assistance to the miners' pension funds.[13] In West Germany oil quotas were placed on imports from Eastern Europe. In 1963 the coal industry was nationalised and a cartel agency, Ruhrkohle, was established with a £133 million fund.

But restrictions on the import and use of oil and financial assistance were not sufficient and contractions in the industries and increasing mechanisation, which was also employment-reducing, had to be accepted after 1965.

FRANCE

The French coal industry experienced similar problems to those of the UK. The industry, which was nationalised in 1946, comprised three centres of production – the Nord-Pas-de-Calais region, the Lorraine and the Centre-et-Midi coalfields. From 1946 to 1958 the industry was encouraged to expand and, starting from an output of 50 million tonnes in 1946, it was planned to produce 65 million tonnes in 1950 and 70 million tonnes in 1955. These plans proved difficult to attain, partly because of the strikes of 1947 and 1948 which resulted in large losses of production and partly because of the relative backwardness of the industry and difficult geological conditions.

There was a sharp fall in the demand for coal after 1958 and the pattern of coal consumption was similar to that of the UK with heavy falls in demand by railways, gas and manufacturing industries (Table 4.5). The Jeanneny Plan of 1960 envisaged a cut-back in output of 5.75 million tons by 1965, mainly in the Centre-et-Midi, but the coal crisis created a climate of fear among miners which led to a five-week strike in 1963. The strike was ended by convening a round-table conference of government ministers, directors of the Charbonnages de France and delegates of the unions which led to the creation of a government economic and social policy to cover the adjustment process. In 1968 the coal industry minister, M. Bettencourt, compared the 37 per cent

TABLE 4.5 Basic Statistics of the French Coal Industry, 1947–73

	1947	*1958*	*1973*
Deep-mined coal output 000m tonnes			
Nord-Pas-de-Calais	25,509	28,858	10,404
Lorraine	7,432	14,971	10,111
Centre-et-Midi	12,594	15,068	6,621
Total nationalised industry	45,435	58,897	27,136
Non-nationalised	1,874	1,142	1,310
Total deep mined	47,309	60,039	28,457
Opcn cast output	640	1,182	2,100
Productivity (Kilogrammes per man)			
Nationalised industry			
Employment			
Nord Pas-de-Calais	196,390	113,633	39,407
Lorraine	41,389	37,769	17,328
Centre-et-Midi	82,301	51,699	15,010
	320,080	203,101	71,745
Other	10,179	1,649	218
	330,259	204,749	71,963

Source: Charbonnages de France, *Statistique Annuelle* (1965 and 1975).

decline in output between 1955 and 1967 in France with that of 50 per cent in West Germany, Holland and the UK and 65 per cent in Belgium. He proposed a series of medium-term measures which comprised a fall in output of 3 million tonnes a year to reach a target of 25 million tonnes in 1975; financial assistance by the government and the Community, the introduction of a greater variety of uses for coal and diversification of the coal regions. The emphasis upon financial assistance and industrial diversification stemmed from the experiences of 1953 and 1963. In the early fifties there was a crisis in the Centre-et-Midi (Aquitaine, Cevennes and Provence) as a result of competition from electricity and imported coal. In 1953 there was a request for aid in order to reduce the labour force by 5,000 over three years. It was envisaged that many miners would be re-employed in the

Lorraine and lump sum grants, including travelling expenses, were paid to those prepared to travel. But the plan proved to be a failure: there was a lack of collaboration between the despatching and receiving regions, a lack of housing, strong differences in culture and protests from local shopkeepers at the fall in incomes and a failure to compensate them.[14] In 1963 there were strikes.

In the Nord-Pas-de-Calais region output fell from 28,858 million tonnes in 1958 to 10,404 million tonnes in 1973. Employment fell by 18,299. The decline was achieved by migration, redeployment and financial assistance. Between 1962 and 1968, 49,000 people migrated from the region and there was a reduction in the number of migrant workers employed in the coalfields.[15] New roads were constructed and new industries, particularly cars and electronics, were established in the region. The Lorraine coalfield, which has over the long run come to produce an increasing proportion of French coal output, as a result of political stability and increasingly effective use of low-quality coals, experienced fluctuations. Between 1950 and 1960 its population rose, mainly by natural increase. But after 1962 the population rose only slightly – a natural increase of 19,058 between 1962 and 1968 being offset by a migration of 13,018. Some miners migrated to the relatively prosperous Saar mines. The smaller coalfields of the Centre-et-Midi have also undergone contraction, migration and diversification.

WEST GERMANY

At the end of the war German coal production was 38.9 million tonnes, which was a quarter of pre-war output. As a result of foreign aid and intensive investment production was raised to 125 million tonnes in 1950. In 1951 Germany joined the ECSC and as a result output was considerably expanded until the pre-war peak of 151 million tonnes was reached in 1956. The following year the Saarland mines were returned from French control.

After 1957, however, oil came to be the primary source of energy. Refineries were built and pipelines were laid across Federal territory. Oil and gas came to supply the needs of most manufacturing industries and electricity became coal's principal customer. The effects of the fall in demand were sharply felt despite the considerable amount of aid given to the coal industry.

The atomic programme was delayed and tax concessions were granted. But between 1957 and 1965 coal output fell by 65 per cent. In the Ruhr, which was the main coalfield, employment fell by 60 per cent between 1955 and 1970. Total employment in the area fell by 25 per cent – a much smaller decline due to an inflow of new industries, such as cars and chemicals and the migration of one and quarter of a million people. In 1957 coalmining accounted for 40 per cent of all jobs but by 1970 it had fallen to 25 per cent. Some towns, however, such as Bottrop, still have over 60 per cent of their labour force in mining and during the mid-sixties there was considerable unemployment in the coal towns. Within the coal industry there was a considerable number of closures and mergers largely brought about by the cartel, Ruhrkohle. The effect of the closures was to shift the axis of production northwards and the Ruhr Valley, which had given the name to the region, joined Wigan and Barnsley as an historical monument to a past coal industry. The Saar coalfield, which remained nationalised, when returned to Germany in 1957, was not so severely affected by closures and the coalfield managed to retain a considerable hold on the steel and power markets in the border areas of France and Germany.

TABLE 4.6 Coal Production in West Germany 1945–1970 (m. tonnes)

	Ruhr	*Saar*	*Aachen*	*Lower Saxony*	*Total*
1945	33.3	3.4	0.8	1.2	38.7
1956	124.6	16.9*	4.2	2.5	148.2
1964	117.4	14.6	7.7	2.2	141.9
1966	102.9	13.6	7.4	1.9	123.8
1970	91.0	10.5	6.8	2.7	110.0

*Under French Control

BELGIUM

The problems of the Belgian coal industry, and of the Belgian economy, commenced before the general decline in the demand for coal in 1957. They began with the formation of the European Coal and Steel Community. An early post-war boom was followed by domestic inflation and in 1951 Belgium was a high-cost economy. In the coal industry, which employed some 10 per

TABLE 4.7 Basic Statistics of the Ruhr Coalfield

	1957	*1961*	*1970*
No. of pits	141	–	56
No. of small mines	127	–	3
Output (million tonnes)	123.2	–	91.1
Productivity (kilogrammes per man)	1.614	–	3.843
Power loading (per cent)	16.4	–	91.9
Employment in coal	472,500	–	192,300
Employment in all industries	1,007,500	–	755,500
Total population (million)	4.7	4.91	4.86
Migration			259,000
Coal contribution to regional income (%)	65		58

Source: *La reconversion des charbonnages dans les bassins allemands – Ruhr* (Brussels, 1972).

cent of the labour force, productivity was about 40 per cent below the average of the rest of the Community. The result was severe balance of payments problems vis-à-vis other members of the Community as well as with non-members. Unlike Holland, which successfully used incomes policies, Belgium relied heavily on deflationary measures and, in the case of the coal industry, aid from the government and the ECSC High Authority. Between 1952 and 1958 the High Authority paid over to the Belgian government about 150 million pounds, financed from a levy raised from German and Dutch mines, to be used for modernisation. The programme of reconstruction was not, however, successful, mainly because of the fall in demand after 1957, and the later slump resulted in a great deal of discontent within the coalfields. But change did occur. There was a run-down of manpower, a closure of pits and a migration of labour from the coalfields. From 1960 there was an influx of new industries, though this tended to aggravate the intense conflict between Flanders and the Walloons because the investment was mainly in the low-wage area of Flanders.

AMERICA

The coal crisis in America began a decade earlier than in Europe. The conversion of the railroads to diesel wiped out an important market for coal as a motive force and the introduction of the welded steel pipeline permitted intercontinental transportation of oil and gas and reduced the use of coal in domestic heating. At the same time there was an increase in fuel efficiency. The response of the United Mineworkers was to press for an intensive mechanisation programme. And between 1949 and 1959 there was an 85 per cent increase in output per man-hour which was twice as great as in the total private economy and three times as great as in the non-farm sector. The labour force fell by three-fifths to less than 150,000. Furthermore, there was a change in the job structure with relatively more miners being employed in administration, supervision and maintenance.

The major effects of increased mechanisation on mines were to permit very large increases in wages, severe unemployment problems and a reduction in accidents. Between 1949 and 1959 average hourly earnings rose by 90 per cent and in 1959 hourly earnings were 50 per cent greater than average hourly earnings in manufacturing, weekly earnings were 33 per cent higher and annual earnings were 10 per cent higher than in manufacturing. The unemployment effects were, however, extremely severe. In 1957 the unemployment rate among bituminous coal miners was two-thirds greater than that for workers in all industries and 50 per cent greater than the average for all mining industries. In West Virginia the unemployment rate was 20 per cent higher than the average for all other industries in the State. A favourable effect of mechanisation was that the fatal and non-fatal injury rates in mining between 1947 and 1959 were reduced by a quarter.

As in Europe, migration eased some of the troubles, but this was difficult and voluntary switches of jobs caused problems due to lack of skills. In the mid-sixties various Federal and State schemes were introduced to train displaced miners and relocate them in new jobs and new surroundings.

The various responses to the contraction of the coal industry in Western Europe and America throw some light upon debates concerning demand-deficiency and structural unemployment. In the post-war period it has been suggested that the rise in the general level of unemployment, particularly in America, reflected a rise in structural unemployment, due to automation, which could not be removed by merely increasing aggregate money demand. Yet the relative ease of adjustment, especially in Britain, was often attributed to the prevailing high level of demand which marked the difference between the comparative calm of the sixties and the strife of the twenties. Now, undoubtedly, the high level of demand did absorb some of the displaced labour, but it is important to realise that the absorption was mainly of the young and single persons and that for others different methods including grants to cover retraining and relocation had to be introduced. Furthermore, the success of redeployment within the Common Market was strongly affected by the rise of American investment in Europe during the sixties. And, finally, despite the various counter-measures to ease adjustment, in most countries the wages of miners fell relative to those of other groups – some part of the adjustment was borne by immobile miners.

WAGE EFFECTS

An understanding of the causes of the fall in the demand for coal and the impact of mechanisation are prerequisites for an analysis of wages. The fall in the demand for miners arose because of the emergence of competing fuels, etc., and because of mechanisation. Both causes created a *displacement effect* which would have served to bring about a fall in wages. On the other hand, mechanisation created an increase in the demand for certain types of labour – a *diversification effect* – which would have tended to pull wages up. The actual behaviour of wages would be the resultant of these two sets of forces.

The movement of hourly wages can be explained as a result of the numerous causes underlying contraction and mechanisation. In 1957 the geographical distribution of wages reflected the productivity and profitability of the various coalfields. Those coalfields which had high productivity tended to pay high wages; the notable exception was Kent, where transport costs gave an otherwise unprofitable coalfield a privileged position. In 1966 the geographical rankings remained much the same as in 1957. The geographical distribution showed a remarkable stability. But between 1957 and 1966 there were considerable changes in the relative importance of the various coalfields. As a result of closures and the movement of labour, the more productive and profitable coalfields increased their share of the labour. Furthermore, the relatively unprofitable coalfields closed some of the gap as a result of the closure of unprofitable pits. What occurred between 1957 and 1966 was that NCB, a multi-plant firm, behaved as if it was a competitive industry or economy.[16] Those pits where productivity and profitability was increasing attracted labour – and the unproductive and unprofitable plants contracted until they could pay wages comparable (though not identical) with those paid elsewhere. The correlation between changes in output per man-shift and earnings was low. And those coalfields which had the greatest run-down in labour, such as Scotland and the North West, also experienced the fastest increase in productivity and wages. Thus, the coal industry passed on some of the advantages of increased productivity in the form of low prices and higher wages (as indicated by the low correlation of productivity change and wage change). The difference between the coal industry and a competitive industry lay in the speed, rather than the direction, of change. Mindful of the social obligations the Coal Board ran the industry down slowly.

TABLE 4.8 Structure of the Labour Force 1957–66 (Occupational Groups as a Percentage of the Total Labour Force)

	1957	*1966*
Underground	80.0	82.9
Underofficials	5.8	6.8
Face workers	40.0	33.6
Engineering	4.0	7.3
Development and reconstruction	4.5	3.6
Haulage, etc.	25.0	27.6
Surface	20.0	17.1
Foremen	0.5	1.0
Maintenance	4.5	5.4
Others	15.0	14.7
Totals	100.0	100.0
No. of men (000s)	704	414

Source: NCB, *Reports and Accounts*

So far we have concentrated on the adjustment of the coal industry without paying attention to the impact of mechanisation. Apart from its displacement effect, mechanisation created a diversification effect. The nature of the diversification effect can be seen from a study of Table 4.8. The industry's labour force fell from around 704,000 to about 414,000. But this fall in the labour force concealed a change in the relative importance of different occupational groups. As a proportion of the labour force those working on the surface fell while those underground rose. This would tend to push wages up. However, faceworkers, as a percentage of the underground labour force, fell, and the percentage on haulage rose. Both these influences would tend to depress wages. On the other hand, the proportions of craftsmen and officials rose.

Mechanisation brought an increase in the demand for craftsmen and electricians, and required skills which had previously not been demanded in the industry but which were closely comparable with those used outside mining. This served to keep craftsmens' wages up. Furthermore, craftsmen tended to do considerable amounts of overtime, especially at weekends.

Once craftsmen are abstracted from the labour force we are left with the traditional distinction between pieceworkers and time-workers. What Tables 4.9 and 4.10 reveal is the close similarity of movements of their wages over the period. There are, of course, variations in the rate of increase in particular periods and there is a big increase — a catching-up increase — for time-workers in

TABLE 4.9 Weekly Earnings of Face Piece-workers (ex Overtime), Underground Day Wage Minimum and Retail Price Index 1957–66

	Face piece-workers (1)	*Underground minimum* (2)	*Absolute difference* (1 *minus* 2)	*Retail price index*
1957	£16.88	£9.00	£7.88	100.0
1958	17.86	9.50	8.36	103.5
1959	18.33	9.85	8.48	105.7
1960	18.70	9.85	8.85	105.3
1961	19.35	10.55	8.80	107.6
1962	20.28	10.55	9.73	112.6
1963	20.76	10.90	9.86	115.6
1964	21.76	11.35	10.41	117.8
1965	22.64	11.85	10.79	123.3
1966	23.48	12.65	10.83	124.3

Source: R. G. Searle-Barnes, *Pay and Productivity Bargaining* (Manchester University Press, 1969).

1960. But the striking feature of Tables 4.9 and 4.10 is the fact that the wages of both piece-workers and time-workers tend to move in line with changes in the cost of living – a proxy for the supply price of labour in general. Despite the fact that piece-workers could still negotiate wage changes at pit level—and there would have been 'bribes' to workers to accept the new machines and methods of working—the Coal Board seems to have been able to control the movement of piece-workers' earnings.

TABLE 4.10 Percentage Change in Earnings of Face Piece-workers (ex Overtime) and Underground Day Wage Minimum

	Face piece-workers	*Day wage*	*Cost of living*	*Face productivity*	*Change in mechanisation*
1957–8	+5.8	+5.6	+3.5	+2.0	+5.8
1958–9	+2.6	+3.7	+2.1	+6.1	+3.5
1959–60	+2.0	–	+1.8	+6.0	+6.2
1960–1	+3.5	+7.1	+2.2	+5.0	+10.2
1961–2	+4.8	+4.1	+1.9	+6.7	+7.2
1964–5	+4.0	+4.4	+4.6	+4.5	+6.6
1965–6	+3.7	+6.8	+3.9	+7.1	+5.7
1957–66	+39.1	+40.6	+29.3	+62.0	+62.5

Source: derived from Table 4.10

Our analysis of wage movements shows that piece-workers' wages pulled away from those of time-workers in the boom period 1947–57 but in the recession period the differential tended to remain constant. And the process of wage determination was reversed in the sense that changes in time-workers' wage rates tended to determine piece-workers' wages because the time-rate was influenced by wages in other industries. The time-rate represented the minimum supply price.

But what has been said about the relative movements of piece-rates and time-rates applied also to their behaviour in other industries. Over the post-war period students have observed and analysed the phenomenon of 'wage drift' – the tendency of earnings to rise faster than rates. Some part of this drift was due to the fact that the wage rate index was a base-weighted index (by the distribution of employment) whereas the earnings index was a current weighted index. Hence drift could occur because, over time, there would be a movement from low wage industries – a redistribution of labour. There would also be variations in the amount of overtime and short-time working. But over and above these factors there would occur a residual – pure drift net of overtime and changes in the distribution of labour. This drift was attributed to local wage bargaining by piece-workers arising out of: (i) changes in new materials and methods of working; (ii) learning effects; (iii) state of demand in both product and factor markets and bargaining strength. The effect of rises in piece-workers' earnings was to create pressures for time-workers' wages to be revised. Wage drift tended to be at a maximum during the mid-sixties. Its subsequent decline may be due to changes in the factors mentioned above and to the tendency for time rates to supersede piece rates in many industries and to the general move towards local negotiations reducing the disparities between rates and earnings. The subsequent rise in drift in the seventies may have been due to the extreme inflationary pressures which tended to destroy the remnants and relevance of national wage bargains (Table 4.11).

TABLE 4.11. Wage Drift: Manual Workers 1949–73

	Per cent per annum over 4-year business cycles		
October	*Average hourly earnings overtime* (1)	*Average hourly wage rates* (2)	*Difference* (1) *minus* (2)
1949–53	6.3	6.0	0.3
1953–7	7.3	6.3	1.0
1957–61	5.1	14.2	0.9
1961–5	6.4	4.9	1.5
1965–9	6.6	5.8	0.8
1969–73	14.5	13.5	1.0

Source: Department of Employment *Gazette* (1975).

The conclusion from our analysis must be a question. Given the apparent stability of the differential between piece-workers and time-workers in the sixties, why did the Board pursue the goal of time-rates for face-workers? There was no obvious reason to believe that wages were out of control. The only answers that

TABLE 4.12 Occupational Differentials 1961–6 (Average earnings per manshift)

	Scotland	*North*	*Durham*	*Yorks.*	*N.W.*	*East Midlands*	*West Midlands*	*S.W.*	*S.E.*
					Surface/Face earnings				
1961	0.58	0.57	0.63	0.56	0.59	0.53	0.57	0.70	0.53
1962/3	0.59	0.57	0.63	0.56	0.57	0.53	0.57	0.69	0.54
1963/4	0.61	0.63		0.57	0.58	0.53	0.57	0.68	0.53
1964/5	0.60	0.64		0.57	0.58	0.54	0.58	0.68	0.56
1965/6	0.61	0.65		0.58	0.56	0.54	0.59	0.69	0.56
					All underground/face earnings				
1961	0.87	0.84	0.87	0.85	0.84	0.82	0.84	0.92	0.82
1962	0.87	0.84	0.87	0.85	0.82	0.82	0.84	0.92	0.86
1962/3					not available				
1963/4									
1964/5	0.88	0.87		0.84	0.82	0.82	0.84	0.92	0.83
1965/6	0.89	0.89		0.85	0.83	0.91	0.85	0.91	0.84

Source: NCB *Reports and Accounts*

seem to emerge are that the Board wished to bring about administrative simplicity even though there might be no cost savings, that the Board feared a return to the conditions of the fifties, though that seemed most unlikely, or that the case for change rested on other considerations.

It is, however, possible that the Board's concern over the wages of piece-workers was based on the regional variation of their earnings and their relationship to those of day-wage workers in those regions. That is, the disparities in productivity increases in different coalfields were tending to create anomalies within those coalfields and threatening the entire day-wage structure. The obvious case would be Nottinghamshire, where high rates of productivity advance were associated with a piece-rate structure which could create a much bigger gap between face-workers' and day-wage workers' earnings in that coalfield than elsewhere. In order to test this conjecture we need to look at the intra-regional wage differentials between piece-workers and time-workers. Unfortunately, this is not easy to establish. The Coal Board's reports and accounts give information on face-workers, and discrepancies can arise because of the presence of day-wage men working at the coalface. However, if their numbers are considered to be small then the available data can be used as a proxy. Table 4.12 seems to suggest that though the differential between the face-worker and surface-worker was wider in Nottingham than elsewhere, it did not exhibit any tendency to widen further.

THE NATIONAL POWER LOADING AGREEMENT 1966

The National Power Loading Agreement, sometimes known as the Second Day Wage Agreement, was signed on 6 June 1966, and applied to new power-loading faces. The Agreement introduced a uniform national wage rate for power loading operators but the uniform rate was not to be achieved immediately. Because of the variations in wages paid in the different coalfields it was decided that uniformity was to be attained over a five-year period, at the end of which all coalfields were to be brought into line with the level of earnings in Nottinghamshire. Of course, miners in Nottinghamshire were not to be forced to stand still for five years, but were to receive increases proportionally smaller than those paid to others. Miners in Kent earned higher wages than those in

Nottingham, but because of their small number they were not regarded as the norm (Table 4.13). There was, however, an immediate levelling up for miners in the lowest-paid districts, who were lifted up to £3.75 per shift.

The NPLA was applied to faceworkers, including rippers and craftsmen who worked on the coalface during production shifts. As a result these craftsmen obtained considerable increases in their pay, and this created a sizeable differential between craftsmen on production shifts and those on maintenance and repair work. On the other hand, craftsmen did not enjoy the benefits of overtime pay based upon the NPLA rate, nor did they enjoy the benefits of a fall-back rate at the NPLA rate as did non-craft workers. Instead, their rates were based on the day-wage rates. The agreement did not include these anomalies but they were to be subsequently covered by the Third Day Wage Agreement of 1972, which was the final step in the abolition of piece-rates and task-rates.

The NPL Agreement stressed the interchangeability of workers on power-loaded faces. Thus, all labour was regarded as homogeneous. The Agreement also specified that jobs were to be determined by method study. And the acceptance of method study by the NUM areas could be regarded as the sole justification for the introduction of the Agreement. Unfortunately, there was no indication in the Agreement on how method study was to be implemented.

THE EFFECTS OF NPLA

The effects of 1966 National Power Loading Agreement have to be considered in the context of a changing demand for coal from 1966. Between 1966 and 1978 the trend in the demand for coal was a continuation of the trend observed between 1957 and 1966. The demand for coal and employment continued to fall. The demand by power stations rose, but it was insufficient to offset the fall in consumption by other users. From 1972, however, there was a temporary halt to the rate of decline, as a result of the decision of the Arab oil producers to cut back supplies and to raise the price of oil. The halt was temporary, in the sense that though there have been statements suggesting that coal would be a more important source of energy supplies in the future, there have been no signs of

TABLE 4.13 District Power Loading Rates and Changes 1966–72

Wages district	*June 1966 Rate*	*Increase*										*1972 Rates*
		Nov 67		*Nov 68*		*Nov 69*		*Nov 70*		*Dec 71 (Parity)*		
	£	£	%	£	%	£	%	£	%	£	%	£
Scotland												
Durham												
Cumberland	22.50	0.55	2.4	0.60	2.6	1.20	5.1	2.37½	9.6	2.77½	10.2	30.00
N. Wales												
S. Wales												
S. Staffs & Shropshire	22.50	1.10	4.9	0.75	3.2	1.20	4.9	2.37½	9.3	2.07½	7.4	30.00
N. Staffs	23.07½	0.82½	3.6	0.75	3.1	1.20	4.9	2.37½	9.2	1.77½	6.3	30.00
Cannock	23.85	0.50	2.1	0.50	2.1	1.20	4.8	2.37½	9.1	1.57½	5.5	30.00
Northumberland	24.30	0.42½	1.7	0.42½	1.7	1.20	4.8	2.37½	9.0	1.27½	4.4	30.00
Leicestershire	23.77½	0.90	3.8	0.75	3.0	1.20	4.7	2.37½	8.9	1.00	3.4	30.00
Yorkshire	24.75	0.40	1.6	0.40	1.6	1.20	4.7	2.37½	8.9	0.87½	3.0	30.00
Warwickshire	24.95	0.40	1.6	0.40	1.6	1.20	4.7	2.37½	8.8	0.67½	2.3	30.00
S. Derbyshire	24.92½	0.42½	1.7	0.42½	1.7	1.20	4.7	2.37½	8.8	0.65	2.2	30.00
Lancs & N. Derbyshire	25.32½	0.35	1.4	0.35	1.4	1.20	4.6	2.37½	8.7	0.40	1.4	30.00
Notts	26.02½	0.30	1.2	0.30	1.1	1.00	3.8	2.37½	8.6	–	–	30.00
Kent	26.82½	0.17½	0.7	0.17½	0.6	0.45	1.7	2.37½	8.6	–	–	30.00

a shift to coal by fuel users. The strikes of 1969 to 1974, and the subsequent big uplift in miners wages, have reduced coal's advantage over other fuels, created uncertainty and increased the potential inroads to be made by North Sea gas and oil.

Productivity and Supervision

The NPL Agreement implied a considerable change in methods of work and supervision and a consolidation of the changes in management control which had begun to take place in the early sixties. The Board had begun to introduce the principles of management by objectives, and had established long- and short-run plans for areas and pits. The NPL Agreement could be construed as simplifying planning by eliminating the uncertainties surrounding the impact of local bargaining on wage costs. Henceforth with the wage given, the only variable was effort and this could be controlled by method study and interchangeability of the work force and by an increase in the supervisory rates which could be achieved with the run-down of the labour force. So the Agreement implied a shift of control to management.

What was anticipated was not often realised. The most striking feature of the period following the Agreement was the decline in the rate of productivity advance and, in some instances, an absolute fall in productivity. The slowing down of productivity advance could be associated with the virtual completion of the mechanisation programme. But some of the decline seems to have been due to the introduction of time-rates. With the removal of piece-rates there was no incentive to increase or maintain effort; there was no incentive to seek out maintenance men when machines broke down. The slackening of effort was most pronounced in the most productive coalfields, such as Nottinghamshire and Yorkshire. The slackening of effort was reinforced by the redistribution of income that the NPL Agreement introduced. In effect, the high-wage areas had to stand still while the low-wage areas caught up, and the fall in relative wages was heightened by the prevailing inflationary conditions.

The NUM

The Agreement implied a transfer of job control from the coalface and the NUM areas to the NCB and the National Executive Committee of the NUM. At pit level, local negotiations, except over tasks, meant a reduction in the importance of the branch. It also meant that the area unions were to become administrative unions. But paradoxically, since the agreement was a national agreement, it required a closer link between the pits and the National Executive Committee — a link which could by-pass the area unions and resurrect, in areas such as Yorkshire, the power of unofficial groups. With the extension of national wage agreements the need for the National Executive Committee to respond to branches became more urgent.

The shift in power implied a change in the nature of the union's policies, particularly at pit level. Henceforward, the disappearance of the issue of wages implied a need to increase attention on methods of work. If wages were no longer a local issue then safety – an important consideration in methods of working – could become the basis upon which rank-and-file workers could exert some influence upon the management decision-making. The agreement suggested the possibility of an upsurge of interest in participation, but without the focal point that wages formerly provided it was difficult to see such a development taking place.

The Agreement implied an increase in the power of the NEC – something which presidents and general secretaries had enjoyed in the past. This increase in power might have been illusory but for the change in the industry's fortunes and the change in the composition of the NEC. The rise in oil prices gave coal a reprieve, and gave the NEC some leverage in negotiations with the NCB. Had that change in relative prices not occurred, the NCB would have continued to grant wage increases of amounts similar to those throughout the sixties. The added factor was the change in the composition of the NEC. In the late sixties there was a noticeable shift to the left in the attitudes of all unions, and this shift occurred in the NUM. As a result the NEC was able to dictate the methods of collective bargaining – overtime bans, strikes, etc. Had piece-rates prevailed, power would have been diffused and the big strikes of 1972 and 1974 might have been averted.

THE NEED FOR INCENTIVES

Over the period 1966 to 1978 several factors accounted for a revival of interest in incentives and a questioning of the day-wage structure. First, there was the failure of output and productivity to rise. Secondly, there was the increase in oil prices which gave the promise of a revival in the coal industry's fortunes. And thirdly, there was the effect of wage increases on the industry's costs, which threatened to eliminate the price advantage of coal over other fuels.

In their evidence to the Wilberforce Court of Inquiry in 1972, the Board envisaged the industry taking a more important part in providing the country's full requirements. But to increase output would need increasing amounts of labour, capital and new ideas. In the short run new ideas could not be increased. The major phase of mechanisation had taken place in the sixties and while new drift pits might increase productivity there were no obvious ideas to be exploited. The problem of increasing output therefore turned upon increasing the labour supply. The big wage increases of 1972 and 1974 stimulated some movement of labour into the industry though some of the effects were cancelled by imitative wage increases in other industries. But general wage increases, with given levels of productivity, may not be the most efficient method of increasing output if wage increases lead to price increases which reduce the demand for coal. Furthermore, in the short run the main intake of labour would be school-leavers and re-entrants, and they would constitute only a small source of supply.

So the obvious method of increasing labour supply would be to increase the amount of effort from the existing labour force by means of payment-by-results schemes. In 1973 the Board proposed an incentive scheme for each coalface in which face-workers and other workers could share. To the union's objections that such a scheme would create differences in earnings which would reflect differences in seam conditions, the Board responded by suggesting different norms for different faces with norms based on method study. But there were objections from some areas to the use of method study. The scheme was rejected by the NUM Executive.

There were, of course, other reasons why the Union would object to an incentive scheme based on individual performances. The introduction of the NPL Agreement saw a reduction in pit stoppages and conflicts between workers in pits and their county officials. It permitted a centralisation of strikes and gave an appearance of a redistribution of power from the rank and file to the full-time officials which the latter were not anxious to relinquish. Under the day-wage structures the 26–man Executive gained an appearance of authority and control. Furthermore, the day-wage structure established the nature of the wage differentials between the various groups, and any return to piece-rates would have disturbed those differentials. The opposition to change was therefore not merely from some piece-workers but also haulage workers, surface workers and white-collar workers. Within the NUM faceworkers now form a smaller percentage of the labour force, and resistance to change must have reflected the opinions of other groups. Among faceworkers opposition was based not only upon a dislike of piece-rates but also upon a fear that their introduction would provide the Board with an excuse to close pits whose productivity was deemed to be low. These various factors were strengthened by the fuel shortage. For, given the monopoly position of the miners, it was not obvious why the NUM should switch from piece-rates to time-rates. Increases in wages could be brought about by national wage bargains. And even if wage increases had unemployment effects, then those unemployment effects would be borne by the non-militant areas.

COMPARISONS WITH OTHER INDUSTRIES

Table 4.14 throws some light upon the trends in methods of wage payment in all industries. During the Second World War there was a big expansion of incentives. After the war there was some decline in their use, although the most notable features of table 4.14 are the rise in the numbers of male workers on incentives, the fall in the numbers of women and the absence of

TABLE 4.14 Percentage of Wage-earners Paid under Systems of Payment by Results, All Industries, 1938–74

Date	*Men*	*Women*	*Youths*	*Girls*
1938	18	46	21	27
1947	24	39	20	35
1951	28	44	22	38
1961	30	41	22	43
1974	41	34	23	11

Sources: Ministry of Labour *Gazette*, New Earnings Survey, and Department of Employment

any dramatic change in the total numbers on incentives. These results seem surprising in view of the criticisms of incentives that were made in the fifties. Then they were attacked because it was argued that there was no connection between effort and output and between wages and effort.

A defence of the critics can be constructed from the disaggregated data. Change has come about as a result of contrasting tendencies. Some industries have retained their use of incentives but because of a fall in numbers employed they have reduced their contribution to the aggregate. For example, employment has fallen in the traditional piece-work industries of textiles and clothing. Somc industries, such as coal, abandoned piece-rates from 1966 to 1978 and also suffered a reduction in numbers employed. Others, such as engineering, have retained a constant labour force but have reduced their use of incentives. Finally, some industries, such as construction, have switched from time-rates to piece-rates and other forms of bonuses. These differences also contrast strongly with American experience, where virtually all workers have been paid on time-rates since the early fifties.[17]

COMPARISONS WITH OTHER COAL INDUSTRIES

In the small coal industries of France, Belgium, Western Germany and Japan, mechanisation did not bring a shift to time-rates and productivity bonuses persisted. In Australia incentive schemes also persisted. The American coal industry moved to time-rates in 1945 and by 1967 only 5 per cent of the labour force was on incentives. There is no uniform time-rate but the range of differentials is extremely narrow. In 1962 some 70 per cent of underground workers earned between $3 and $ 3.50 an hour.

SUMMARY

Since nationalisation the coal industry has reformed its wages structure and between 1966 and 1978 it abandoned piece-rates. The arguments for the change to time-rates were not well-founded and from 1972 onwards the Coal Board attempted to bring back incentives. Until the end of 1977 those efforts foundered on the resistance of the miners. Indeed there was a great deal of irony in the fact that coalfields, such as Yorkshire, which had voted against time-rates were the most vociferous in their opposition to the re-introduction of piece-rates. There was an awareness after the strikes of 1972 and 1974 that the national time-rate had united the NUM. The sudden and dramatic change to piece-rates at the end of 1977 is dealt with in the final chapter where it forms part of our conclusions on the development of industrial relations in the coal industry.

In other countries mechanisation did not bring about a switch to time-rates, which suggests that technology may not be a crucial determinant of the method of wage payment. In other British industries there were diverse trends. In manufacturing there was a decline in the importance of piece-work but in non-manufacturing industries there was innovation in and extension of the use of incentives.

5 Absenteeism, Accidents, Strikes and Labour Turnover

Absenteeism, accidents, strikes and labour turnover may be regarded as the outcomes of economic activity and may be intended or unintended in the sense that the amount of, say, absenteeism may be optimal because there is no tendency for either employers or workers to want to change the amount of absenteeism. The notion that the number of absences or their severity is optimal seems, at first sight, to be bizarre, but a moment's reflection suggests that the idea makes sense if consideration is paid to the costs of reducing absenteeism.

The proposition expressed in the previous paragraph is illustrated in Figure 5.1. Along the horizontal axis is measured the output of absenteeism (or accidents or strikes or labour turnover). Along the vertical axis are measured the costs and benefits incurred by individual *I* as a result of his absences. The marginal valuation curve, ${}^{I}MV_a$, is simply individual *I*'s demand curve for absences; the superscript *I* refers to the individual concerned and the subscript *a* to absence.[1] In the negative portion of the diagram are measured the external diseconomies incurred by *II* as a result of *I*'s absences. Now *I* will equate the marginal benefits and costs of absence and assuming, for simplicity, that marginal costs are constant, he will produce *OP* absences; that is, if the costs of absences (which can be measured by the wage foregone) were *OC* then he would be absent for *OP* hours or days. But *OP* absence will result in costs of *PY* to *II* and since *PY* is greater than PR, which is the wage paid to *I*, then *II* will seek to reduce *I*'s absences by raising the value of the wage foregone or threatening to dismiss him. If negotiations are possible then an equilibrium will be attained with *ON* absences. At *ON* individual *I* will equate the marginal benefits of absence with the new, higher marginal costs,

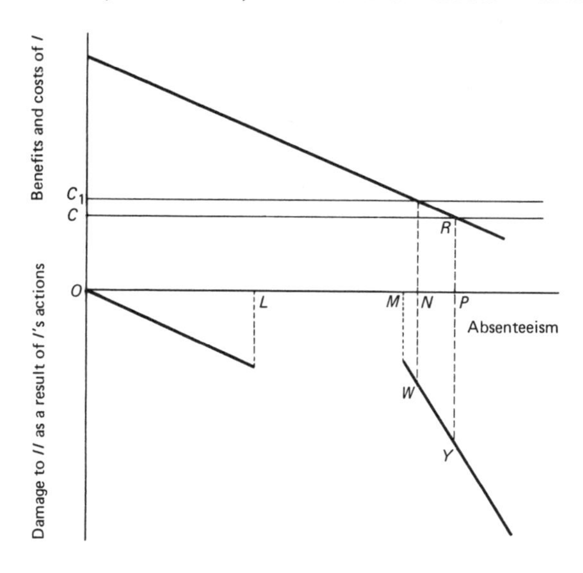

FIGURE 5.1

OC_1 and OC_1 is equal to *NW*, the marginal externality imposed on *II*. The output of absences, *ON*, is therefore Pareto optimal in the sense that it is impossible for both parties to gain by an increase or decrease in absenteeism.

Figure 5.1 also indicates two other possible outputs which deserve attention. The output *OL* constitutes an externality from the point of view of *II* but it is not Pareto relevant because there is no amount of compensation which would induce *I* to reduce his output below *ON* and still leave *II* no worse off. The second case consists of the range of outputs between *OL* and *OM*. These outputs can be considered to generate irrelevant diseconomies (strictly speaking, infra-marginal external diseconomies) for *II* in the sense that *I*'s output of absences will cause no change in *II*'s marginal valuation. Hence, over the range LM, *II*'s marginal valuation curve follows the horizontal indicating zero marginal valuation. What this indicates is the possibility of satiation. Irrelevant diseconomies are likely to occur when there are small changes in *I*'s output of absences, but if *II* attaches some significance to the absolute amount of absenteeism and, therefore, to his own total valuation curve, then he will seek to change *I*'s behaviour. 'Magic numbers', such as one million unemployed, can give rise to a sudden change in government policy as compared with that which occurred when unemployment varied between eight and nine hundred thousand. The interesting case of irrelevant marginal external diseconomies is indicated in Figure 5.2 where *I*'s marginal valuation curve moves about without causing any change in *II*'s behaviour.

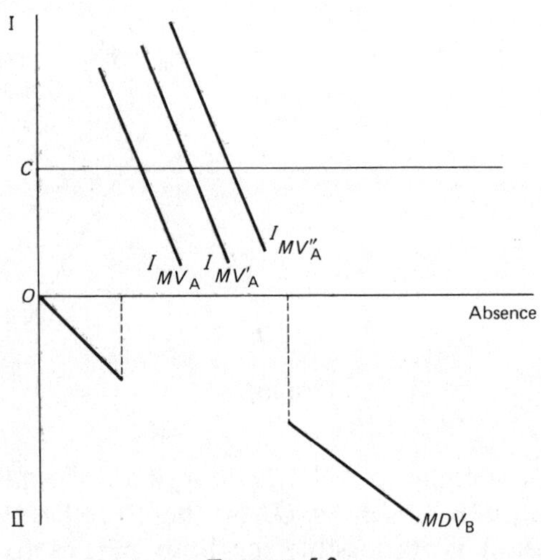

FIGURE 5.2

Finally, we need to take account of income effects. The marginal valuation curve is a demand curve which incorporates substitution effects but not income effects. Now in the case of an increase in the wage offered to a worker the cost of absenteeism would rise and there would be a substitution of work for leisure. But since the worker receives a higher wage for each hour that he works there is an income effect which may induce him to greater absence because he can obtain a given weekly income for less hours of work at the new, higher, hourly wage rate. On the other hand, the income effect may induce him to work more in order to acquire a higher standard of living. The income effect may, therefore, work in the same direction or in the opposite direction to the substitution effect and the total effect will depend upon the strength and direction of the income effect in relation to the substitution effect. In terms of the diagrams the substitution effect involves a movement along the marginal valuation curve whilst the income effect leads to a shift of the curve either to the right or to the left. Perverse income effects can, of course, influence the type of policy pursued to reduce absenteeism, accidents and strikes.

PRONENESS TO ABSENTEEISM, ACCIDENTS, STRIKES AND LABOUR TURNOVER

The view that absence, accidents, strikes and labour turnover can be thought of as outputs from a production process can be linked to another concept – proneness. Absence-, accident-, strike- and labour turnover- proneness may be taken to indicate an opinion about the magnitude of the Pareto optimal amounts of absenteeism, accidents, strikes and labour turnover and that the magnitudes differ between firms and industries. Thus, as in Figure 5.3, industry *B* may be considered to be more absence-prone than industry *A* because its absence rate is greater as well as being Pareto optimal.

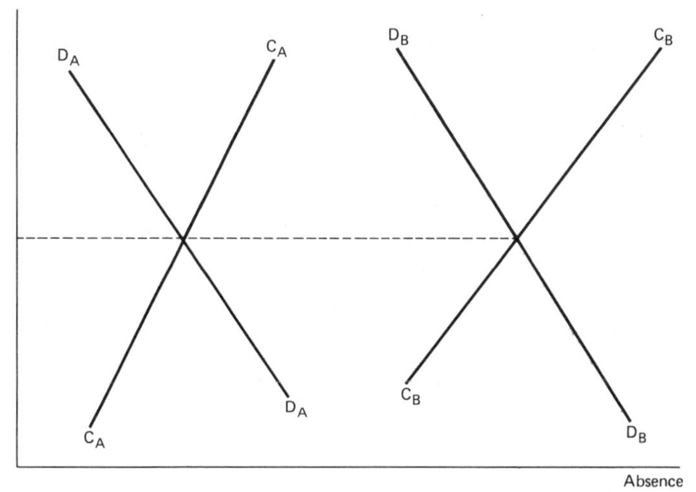

FIGURE 5.3 *D*, Demand for absences; *C*, Cost of absences

However, 'proneness' seems to carry many meanings. In the first place it may simply mean a tendency for there to be a lot of something, strikes, etc., without implying any causation. The frequency distributions of absenteeism, etc., would result from random factors in the sense that any attempt to reduce absenteeism by removing those who had high absence rates would be futile because random processes would throw up another and different group of offenders in a subsequent period. This explanation rests upon an assumption of the homogeneity of individuals. A second interpretation denies this assumption and postulates *unequal liabilities*. Thus, if an urn contains more black balls than white balls the probability of a black ball being selected is greater than if equal numbers of black and white balls existed. Some individuals, factories or industries may possess characteristics which make them more susceptible to absenteeism, accidents or strikes than others. The third explanation of proneness assumes that all individuals might start with the same characteristics but an individual who by chance had one absence might in consequence have his probability of a further absence increased or decreased. Hence, there would be *contagion* or *biased distribution* in the sense in which the drawing of a black ball from an urn dictates that it must not be replaced or that it must be replaced by two or more black balls.

Of the three interpretations of proneness put forward in the previous paragraph, it is the second which attracts the most attention. Thus, Yorkshire miners are supposed to be more strike-prone than Derbyshire miners because of differences in temperament. But the third explanation might be found masquerading as the second because, after a period of time, a contagious distribution would give rise to an unequal number of black and white balls in an urn. Finally, we may note another connection between contagion and unequal liabilities arising out of group solidarity. A strike at one factory may prompt a strike at another. In this case the concept of unequal liabilities would need to be based upon the group of factories rather than an individual plant.

ABSENTEEISM

TRENDS

Published statistics of absenteeism in the coal industry over a long period do exist. In addition to those compiled by the Coal Board, there are figures for the period 1922–45 published in the Ministry of Power *Statistical Digest*. Before 1922 there are fragments for the nineteenth century in various government reports. For no other industry are such records available and it is their existence which has contributed to the belief that mining is characterised by a lot of absenteeism.

The available statistics do, however, vary in quality and reliability and are often affected by changes in collectively agreed hours of work and definitions of absenteeism. Before 1954 the absence rate was expressed as a percentage of man-shifts thought 'possible' by management. Hence, the absence rate would vary according to the arbitrary definition of possible shifts. For example, if work was available for four shifts and a man worked four shifts then his absence rate was zero. But if work became available for six shifts and he worked five then his absence rate would increase to 16.7 per cent even though his attendance rose by 25 per cent. This statistical problem possibly accounts for the tendency for absenteeism to rise when earnings rise. Earnings would rise when the number of shifts rose, and so would absenteeism. It is possible to observe parallel movements in attendance and absenteeism in the 1920s. During the Second World War absenteeism was high even though attendance was high. And it is highly likely that most nineteenth-century accounts of absenteeism ignore the problem.

Even in the period since nationalisation it is possible to find evidence of the statistical illusion. Thus, absenteeism fell between 1946 and 1948 and attendance also fell. This result seems to have been brought about by the 1947 Five Day Week Agreement which reduced the length of the normal working week to five days and thereby reduced the number of possible shifts from which a man could be absent. With the continuing coal shortage regular overtime working was introduced and produced anomalies. In some areas Saturday working was included in the number of possible shifts although Northumberland and Durham miners opted for a longer shift rather than Saturday working and in one coalfield the introduction of overtime working was delayed until 1951 and then produced a rise in both the national attendance and absence figures.

After 1954 the method of calculating absenteeism was changed and based on appearances from Monday to Friday. No account was taken of overtime, particularly weekend work, which continued up to 1958, nor of its possible effect on attendance during the week despite overtime being included in the attendance figures. As a result, attendance and absence figures became less closely related. In 1973 the definition of absenteeism was again revised to eliminate anomalies surrounding the treatment of attendances on statutory holidays and rest days. The Board now calculates two measures of labour deployment; one of which corresponds to the published absence figure and the other which takes account also of absence on official business (such as union or local government meetings), holidays and disputes. The effect of taking into account the latter causes of absence is to double the published absence figure. The effect of the changes on the published absence figure was to cause a fall of 0.8 per cent in absence in 1973. The overall effect of the changes was, however, to bring the calculation of absence more into line with the definitions used in the rest of the EEC countries.

If the above qualifications are borne in mind then the post-war data fall into three distant periods (Table 5.1). Up to 1955 absenteeism tended to be fairly stable, being on average 12.3 per cent per annum. Attendance was likewise fairly stable at about 4.75 shifts per week. From 1955 to 1966, however, absenteeism started to rise by about 4 per cent per annum and attendance fell from 4.74 shifts in 1955 to 4.13 shifts per man per week in 1965. Finally, absenteeism continued to rise from 1966 to 1971 and then fell slightly even after allowance is made for the revised definitions.

The major feature of the whole period is the rise in absenteeism from 1955 to about 1971, which has been attributed to a variety of causes. Thus, in 1966, Lord Robens expressed the view that it was due to the existence of social security benefits. 'As a politician,' he said, 'I fought for social services but not for social services to be exploited. It is fair to say in my industry a man with a wife and two children is sometimes better off sick than when he is working.'[2] He believed that it was sometimes more profitable for the low-paid miner to stay at home drawing state benefits than to go to work and he drew attention to the increases in National Insurance benefits in 1961, 1963 and 1965 and the apparently associated rise in absenteeism.

A more thorough investigation was attempted by Handy in 1968.[3] His conclusions may be summarised as follows.

1. The rise in absenteeism was mainly due to pessimism.

TABLE 5.1 Coal Miners' Absence and Attendance, 1946–74

	Average number of shifts per week per wage-earner	*Absence percentage All workers*		
		Voluntary	*Involuntary*	*Total*
1946	4.86	–	–	16.4
1947	4.72	6.5	6.0	12.5
1948	4.74	6.0	5.6	11.6
1949	4.70	5.5	6.9	12.4
1950	4.75	5.1	6.9	12.0
1951	4.84	5.7	6.6	12.3
1952	4.82	5.9	6.2	12.1
1953	4.73	5.0	7.4	12.4
1954	4.77	4.0	8.2	12.2
1955	4.74	4.1	8.4	12.5
1956	4.71	4.3	8.7	13.0
1957	4.68	6.1	7.7	13.8
1958	4.43	6.4	7.7	14.1
1959	4.28	6.0	8.7	14.7
1960	4.31	6.0	8.7	14.7
1961	4.31	6.4	9.0	15.4
1962	4.32	6.3	9.0	15.3
1963	4.30	5.9	10.2	16.1
1964	4.27	5.7	10.1	15.8
1965	4.21	5.8	11.7	17.5
1966	4.13	5.9	11.8	17.7
1967	4.13	5.4	12.4	17.8
1968	4.13	4.7	13.4	18.1
1969	4.09	4.7	13.5	18.2
1970	4.02	4.5	15.3	19.8
1971	4.12	4.4	13.7	18.1
1972	3.68	4.0	12.8	16.6
1973	3.89	4.1	13.9	18.0
1974	3.57	4.1	12.1	16.2

Note: Breaks in the table arise through changes in definitions which do not, however, cause material differences in the trends.
Source: Digest of Energy Statistics

Miners were willing to work, as in the late forties and early fifties, when the industry's future looked secure, but not when its future became uncertain.

2. Social security benefits may have been influential in inducing men to have a day off work, particularly low-paid

surface workers. However, there was no apparent correlation between changes in absenteeism and changes in benefits.

3. There was no apparent correlation between changes in absenteeism and changes in wages, in the sense that a backward sloping supply curve existed. (Handy did not attempt to see whether there was a correlation between changes in absenteeism and changes in miners' wages relative to those of other workers, although some of the pessimism may have been due to this deterioration. The cross-supply price elasticity may have been positive even though thc own-supply pricc clasticity bctwccn mincrs' wages and leisure appeared to be zero.) The supply curve of labour therefore appeared to have shifted to the left.
4. The increase in mechanisation and the rise in the average age of miners may have been contributory factors in explaining absenteeism, but they do not account for the sharp increases between 1957 and 1959, nor for the increases in 1962, 1963 and 1965. These sudden changes Handy attributed to official pronouncements on the future of the industry.
5. The increase in absenteeism was associated with a rise in overtime working and the latter explained the apparent constancy in attendance. Faced with a fall in the demand for their services miners sought to maximise their earnings and establish job security by working fewer shifts and choosing to work only those shifts which gave the highest earnings.
6. Absenteeism was an alternative to strike action as a means of reducing output but with the difference that absenteeism did not lead to a fall in income. In boom periods miners will strike; in slumps they will go absent.

In the mid-fifties voluntary absence started to decline relative to involuntary absenteeism as miners went to see their doctors for ailments which they had previously ignored or treated themselves. Whether the transformation from voluntary to involuntary was a good or a bad thing is one of those questions which is difficult to answer. However, what is also noticeable is that not only was there a transformation but there was also an increase in involuntary absenteeism. And it was not confined to mining. There was a noticeable rise in certificated absenteeism in the late fifties and sixties. Nor was it confined to industrial areas or declining industries. The absence figures for a relatively homogeneous industry, such as the Post Office, show a fall throughout the early fifties followed by a rise in the late fifties and sixties (Figure 5.4). The upward trend was widespread and occasioned comment in industries as diverse as atomic energy, chemicals and engineering.[4] Furthermore, it occurred in the USA, in market and non-market economies.[5] And everywhere it was a rise in minor ailments, such as sprains and strains, slipped discs and neuroses—some of which may have reflected better recording.

In addition to the general rise in absenteeism there was a marked increase in overtime working in the UK although not apparently in the USA and Europe. The magnitude of overtime working occasioned much comment. Opinions were divided as to causes. One school of thought believed that the amount of overtime working was determined by demand and supply; by what both employers and workers wanted. Another school of thought maintained that overtime working reflected managerial inefficiency and union restrictive practices and that the solution lay in 'productivity bargaining' to buy out restrictive practices. But many productivity bargains proved unproductive and the idea collapsed at the end of the sixties when inflation made wage increases inevitable. The significance of productivity bargaining – an old idea whose forerunners included the 1947 Five Day Week Agreement – lay in the fact that it forced employers to consult unions and it led to a relaxation of managerial prerogatives.

In retrospect the forces at work creating absenteeism and overtime were complex. There was a slow rate of growth of the labour force as a result of variations in the birth rate, the raising of the school leaving age and the rise in the numbers retiring. Britain became an over-dependent economy – too many young people and too many old people not in the labour market. This dependency affected savings, investment and the growth rate. In Europe and the USA the burden of dependency was eased by the run-down of surplus labour in agriculture and through immigration. But in Britain there was no surplus of labour in agriculture and the surplus that existed in stagnant industries, such as mining, docks and shipbuilding, did not appear to be so easily transferable to other industries. It seems highly likely that the transfer of labour out of agriculture is more easily achieved than between urban industries because it is reinforced by the

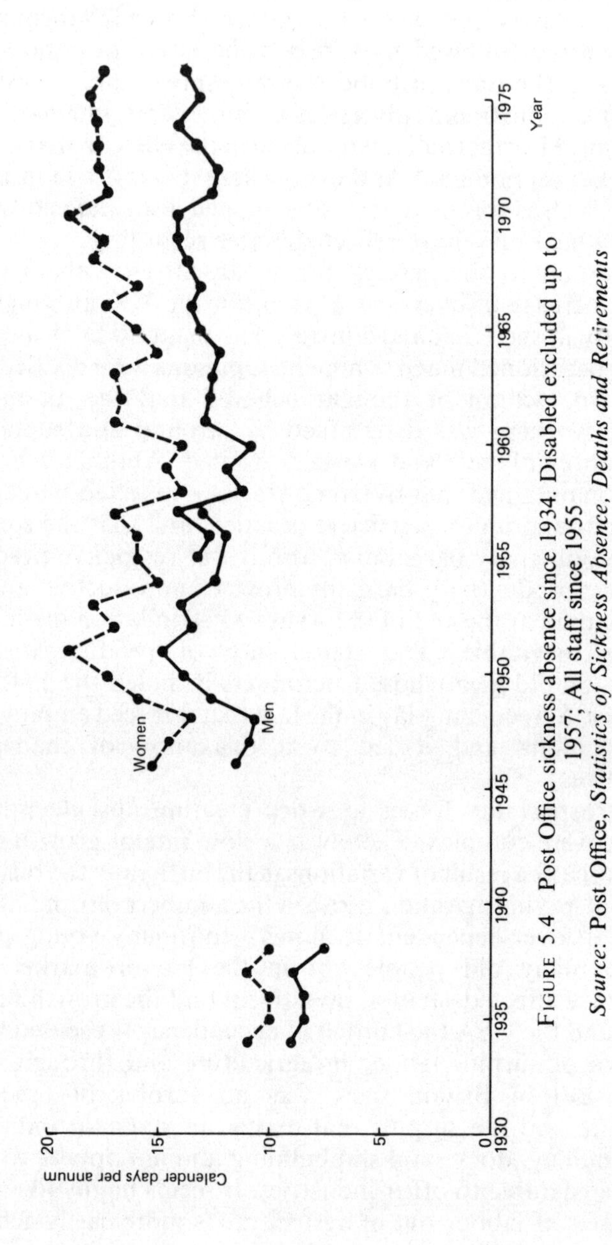

FIGURE 5.4 Post Office sickness absence since 1934. Disabled excluded up to 1957; All staff since 1955

Source: Post Office, *Statistics of Sickness Absence, Deaths and Retirements*

process of urbanisation. But once workers are in towns mobility seems to be slower. Immigration was also at a lower level into Britain. Some relief was provided through the rise in the numbers of married women working although that increase mainly provided part-time workers and tended to swell the service industries and public sector and gave rise to the belief that Britain had too large a public sector and too small a manufacturing base.

So the first criticism of Handy's thesis is that the rises in absenteeism and overtime working were not peculiar to mining. They were general and general phenomena require general explanations. There may, of course, have been factors peculiar to mining but Handy's analysis was not conclusive. The rise in absenteeism occurred before the onset of the depression in 1957 and that had to be explained in the context of mining. Handy neglected the influence of the redistribution of the labour force brought about by the decline in the demand for labour. He proposed a 'macro' explanation because he alleged that it was difficult to account for differences in attendance and absenteeism between coalfields and pits. Now a noticeable feature of the sixties was that, though the mining labour force fell, the effect of redundancies was to raise the relative numbers employed in coalfields which had high absence rates, such as South Wales and Yorkshire, and to reduce employment in low absence areas, such as Scotland, Northumberland and Durham.

The lack of correlation between changes in absenteeism and social security benefits and between changes in absenteeism and changes in wages may have been due to the fact that both wages and social security benefits changed together in some periods, leaving absenteeism unchanged. Handy seems to have treated the two influences separately. He also used a simple lag analysis which may not have captured the slow rise in absenteeism which arises as information on changes in benefits is slowly disseminated through the labour market. Nor did his investigation take into account the effect of taxation on the inducement to work as earnings slowly rose and miners lost many social security benefits when they began to pay the standard rate of income tax. This issue became crucial towards the end of the sixties and affected not merely low-paid surfaceworkers but also faceworkers who, owing to the relative decline in miners' wages, were low-paid compared with skilled workers in other industries.

A crucial strand in Handy's analysis was his suggestion that miners might recoup income losses created by absenteeism through overtime working. Armchair reasoning would suggest that in a period when miners were asking for their industry to be protected, they would be in a weak bargaining position. Managers would be more likely to have offered overtime to regular attenders than to persistent offenders and any attempt to combine absenteeism and overtime would have strengthened the Board's resolve to close pits and to weed out persistent absentees during redundancy and redeployment exercises. And these speculations are supported by the facts. A 1965 Coal Board survey revealed a strong negative correlation between absenteeism and overtime working and a further survey in 1973 showed no evidence that overtime working was used to compensate for absenteeism by those with high absence rates. All of which is not to deny that there was a collapse of morale after 1957 but it does cast doubt on the manner in which pessimism revealed itself.

THE STRUCTURE OF ABSENTEEISM

So far we have concentrated upon trends in absenteeism and ignored the fact that the trends are composed of patterns created by daily, weekly and seasonal variations in absenteeism as well as differences in absence rates between coalfields and pits.

The incidence of absenteeism tends to vary between shifts being highest on the day shift and least on the night shift, although there are divergences from this pattern in some coalfields. Authorised absence due to sickness and union or local government meetings tends to be highest on Mondays and Fridays whereas unauthorised absence shows no weekly peaks. However, unauthorised absence does tend to be high before or after annual or statutory holidays. Authorised absence tends to be highest between December and February, then falls to a low level in May and begins to rise again in September. Voluntary and involuntary absences are, of course, linked in the sense that the incidence of voluntary absence tends to be highest for those who have the most involuntary absences. This suggests that some workers are chronically sick and work just sufficient days to qualify for sick pay benefits. Voluntary and involuntary absences are also linked as, for example, when managers attempt to reprimand voluntary absentees who subsequently present medical certificates for future absences and a manager may allow a miner to use up one of his rest days to cover an absence. But, in general, there is a marked difference in the ages of voluntary and involuntary absentees. Voluntary absentees tend to be the younger workers, between the ages of 25 and 35, and voluntary absence then tends to fall with age until the onset of late middle age. In contrast, involuntary absentees tend to be older workers.

Geographically, there are strong differences in absenteeism. The rankings of the coalfields between 1954 and 1966 show a high degree of stability at the extremes. Scotland, Cumberland, Northumberland and Durham were areas of low absenteeism whilst Yorkshire had high absenteeism. Other coalfields, however, showed diverse patterns. Lancashire and South Wales began the period with moderate absenteeism and ended it with high absenteeism. Thus, the notion of absence-proneness resulting from unequal liabilities needs to be qualified. After 1966 analysis is affected by administrative changes which broke up the divisions and replaced them with areas. But allowing for these changes Yorkshire and South Wales are areas of high absence while Scotland, Northumberland and Durham remain areas of low absenteeism. And within Yorkshire it is the Doncaster pits which have the highest absence rates.

Table 5.2 throws some light upon the concept of absence-proneness among the 40 'live pits' of the South Wales coalfield over the period 1969 to 1975. A preliminary analysis confirmed that a simple Poisson distribution did not provide an adequate explanation whereas a modified Poisson did. This implied a rejection of randomness but still left a choice between hetero-

TABLE 5.2 Biennial Rank Correlation Coefficients of Absence in 40 Pits in South Wales, 1965–75

1965/6	0.89
1966/7	0.88
1967/8	0.82
1968/9	0.82
1969/70	0.86
1970/1	0.81
1971/2	0.80
1972/3	0.68
1973/4	0.78

Source: based on raw data supplied by NCB (South Wales Area)

geneity and contagion. The biennial rank correlation coefficients and the Kendall coefficient of concordance do suggest heterogeneity but measures of dispersion also revealed a tendency to widening during the period. Contagion as well as heterogeneity was present.

COMPARISONS WITH OTHER INDUSTRIES

So far we have concentrated upon absenteeism in the coal industry with little reference to absenteeism in other industries. Yet attitudes towards absenteeism in the mining industry could be influenced by comparisons with absence rates in other industries. But it was not until the end of the sixties that information on absence in other industries became available through the *New Earnings Surveys* and *General Household Surveys.* In 1968 the *New Earnings Survey* revealed that 15.1 per cent of male manual workers in all industries were absent for a variety of reasons as compared with 26.6 per cent in mining. The *Survey* also revealed that there were considerable differences in the causes of absenteeism. Few miners lost pay as a result of late arrival or early finishing – 0.6 per cent – while 14.6 per cent of absence in all industries was due to those causes. Presumably the difference reflected the fact that entering or leaving a factory is relatively easy compared with entering or leaving a mine. A miner who missed the time of descent would be classified as absent under another heading. Late arrivals or early finishing was the commonest cause of absence in all industries but in coalmining sickness and voluntary absence were the greatest causes of absence. The *Survey* also revealed a high and significant positive correlation, 0.76, between absence due to sickness and voluntary absence in manufacturing industries which reinforces the hypothesis derived from mining that some workers are chronically sick and put in enough appearances to safeguard their jobs and justify their claims for sick benefits. Finally, the regional distribution of absence indicates that sickness, voluntary absence and late arrival and early finishing tend to be higher in the northern industrial areas, Scotland and Wales.

In addition to information on other UK industries, there is some statistical evidence on miners' absenteeism in the EEC countries for the early seventies. This revealed that miners' holidays in the UK were of about the same duration as in Belgium, Holland and West Germany, but somewhat lower than in France; that unauthorised absence was about the same as in Belgium, but much lower than in France and West Germany; and that authorised absence was higher in France but lower in West Germany, Holland and Belgium. But how much can be gleaned from these statistics is difficult to say. Many of the European countries employ a great deal of foreign labour and much voluntary absence in Britain would probably have been classified as authorised absence on the Continent – a fact which is now being corrected as a result of the revised definitions introduced by the Coal Board in 1973.

THE OPTIMALITY OF ABSENTEEISM

Examination of absenteeism in the coal industry and comparison with other industries forces us to consider whether absence in the coal industry is optimal. To the extent that management anticipates the trend and structure of absenteeism, absenteeism will be optimal given wages and other conditions of employment. Furthermore, the major part of absenteeism does not create large outlays for the Coal Board because it is financed by the state out of taxation. There is an element of cross-subsidisation and the Board's outlays – the difference between expected costs and accounting expenses – arise out of unanticipated absence and involve manpower redeployment and lost output.

Optimality of absenteeism has a bearing on the early retirement programme introduced in 1977. Given that older miners are often involuntarily absent and are often employed on 'button jobs' at haulage junctions or on the surface, then early retirement need not result in a loss of productivity. There would be a reclassification of payments for sickness to payments for pensions by the state. But not all elderly workers fall into the category of semi-workers and early retirement could create shortages of faceworkers and supervisors. Maintenance of output would then depend upon the attractiveness of the coal industry to workers outside the industry. Hence early retirement could be considered as a means of increasing wages and a method of overcoming the limitations of pay norms imposed by incomes policies.

ACCIDENTS

There is a connection between accidents and absenteeism, but the association is not always a strong one. Some absences are not caused by accidents and not all accidents result in absences. Thus, the correlation between accident and absence rates in pits in South Wales over the period 1969–75 was 0.4 and it was 0.6 in the South Nottinghamshire coalfield over the period 1970–75. It is because of the intrusion of other factors that the frequency and severity of accidents merits separate attention.

Figure 5.5 reveals broad trends in three types of mining accident. The numbers of fatal and serious reportable accidents show a continuous decline until 1970 and thereafter tend to be stable. In contrast, the trend for 'over three-day injuries' shows a strong upward movement. These same trends can also be observed in factories; the number of fatal accidents has declined while that of per over three-day injuries has risen. Figure 5.6 shows the trends in the ratios of minor to fatal injuries in mines and factories over a twenty-year period. Both show a strong upward movement; both are strongly correlated.

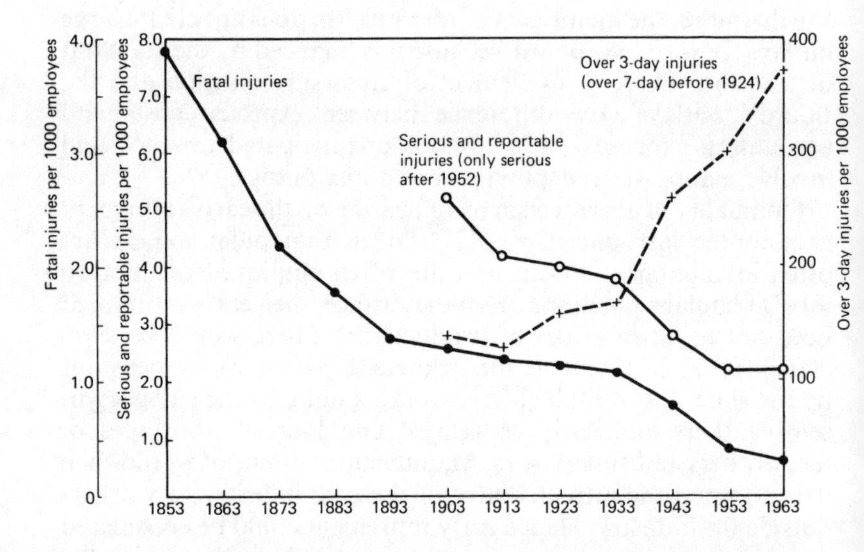

FIGURE 5.5 Decennial injury rates per 1000 employees in British coal mines, 1853–1972

Figures 5.5 and 5.6 suggest some interesting conclusions. First, there appears to be some long-run tendency for the level of injury severity at which people decide to stay away from work to fall. This is a tentative conclusion which may be influenced by better reporting over time. But, although it is tentative, it does seem plausible to assume that there can be a change in attitudes about what types of injury a person should suffer and still continue to work and it is reasonable to think that changing attitudes are related to rising real incomes and the emergence of the welfare state. Secondly, the fact that the trends in mines and factories are similar reinforces the views expressed in the previous section on absenteeism in the sixties. Absence due to minor injuries has been a large component of all absences. Thirdly, the differences in the amounts of minor injuries in mines and factories suggest the importance of particular kinds of accidents in mines, such as those due to loss of balance, falling objects, fires and explosions.

The more radical conclusion, however, is that, given the possibility of a shifting threshold which determines the willingness of a worker to stay away from work, accident statistics may not reveal how effective accident measures are. Only in the case of fatal accidents and serious reportable accidents might any firm conclusions be drawn. Indeed, the rise in absences because of minor injuries – indicating short absences – may be a means of preventing long absences. There may be a trade-off between the frequency of absence and the length of absence. Such a trade-off was detected for 1968 by Harper, Lister and Middleton between the number of accidents and the number of days taken off for each accident in the Coal Board areas.[6] They also found that the declining coalfields tended to have high averages for the number of days lost per over three-day injury and attributed this to low morale being reflected in long absences. This second finding seems to be in conflict with the view that workers who were in the greatest danger of losing their jobs would be the most reluctant to have time off work. However, a complete analysis of absence would include unauthorised as well as authorised absence and a comparison of the two would indicate that voluntary absence was lower in the declining coalfields. Furthermore, the same trade-off can be detected in relatively homogeneous industries, such as the railways and the Post Office. There need not, therefore, be a contradiction between the hypothesis that there is a trade-off

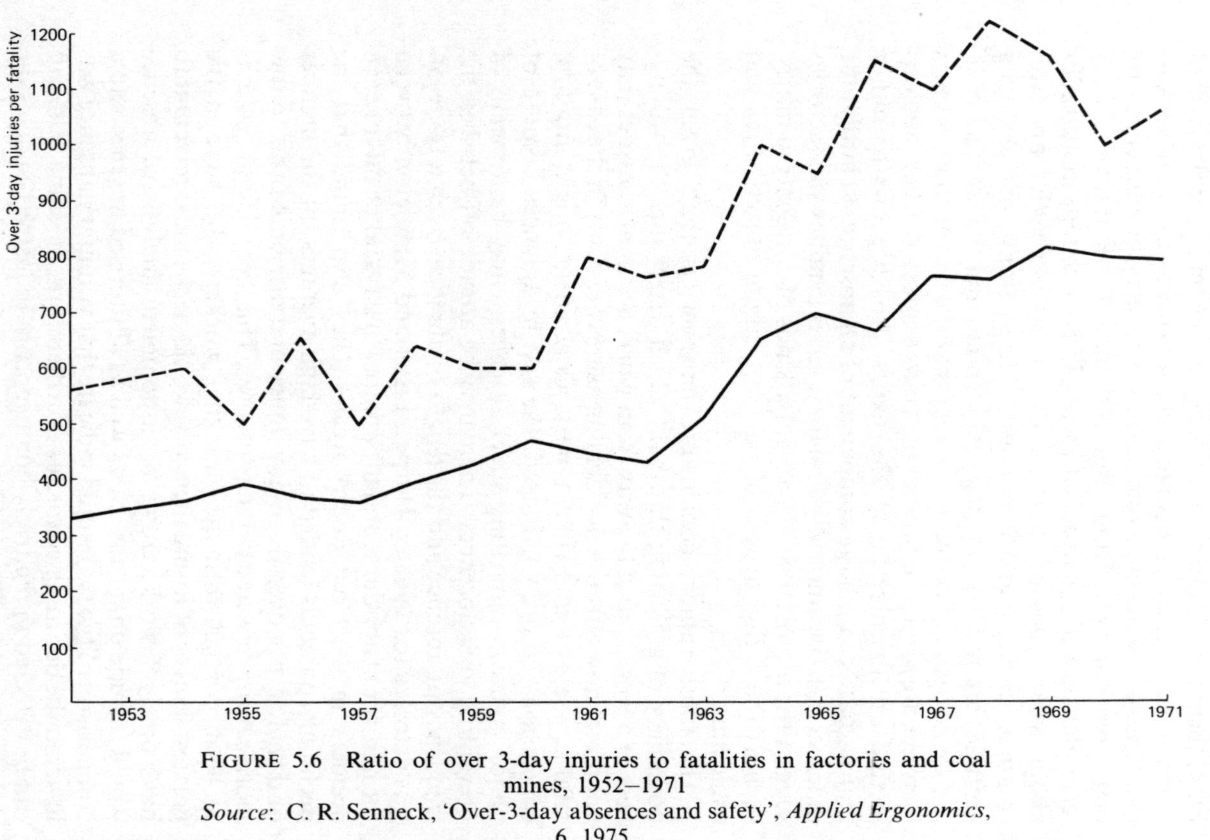

FIGURE 5.6 Ratio of over 3-day injuries to fatalities in factories and coal mines, 1952–1971

Source: C. R. Senneck, 'Over-3-day absences and safety', *Applied Ergonomics*, 6, 1975.

between the frequency and duration of absence which is shifting over time and the evidence of a different trade-off relationship at a point of time between the coalfields. And some areas, such as the Barnsley area and the eastern section of the South Wales coalfield appear to have both a high frequency and a high severity rate of accidents.

ACCIDENT-PRONENESS

The work of Harper, Lister and Middleton provides a useful introduction to the study of accident-proneness. There has, in fact, been considerable variation in the rankings of the coalfields. Thus, South Wales and Kent have the most accidents and Scotland has the least. But the other coalfields display diverse trends. Lancashire shows a rise between 1947 and 1960 whilst accidents declined over the same period in Nottinghamshire. Within coalfields there is some variation in rankings. The Kendall coefficient of concordance for the 40 live pits of South Wales between 1965 and 1975 was 0.69 and it was 0.53 for the South Nottinghamshire coalfield between 1970 and 1975.

THE OPTIMALITY OF ACCIDENTS

The divergence of trends in major and minor accidents poses interesting questions concerning the methods of reducing the frequency and severity of accidents (and we can also add diseases and sickness). Two methods are at present available – a market and a statutory arrangement – and both intertwine prevention and compensation. The market method comprises the ordinary workings of the labour market supplemented by common law action. The labour market relies heavily upon the assumption that most workers shy away from risk and have to be compensated for working in dangerous situations and the payment of high wages raises product price and tends to discourge consumers from purchasing the commodity. To what extent this process is efficient is difficult to judge. Ghosh, Lees and Seal examined the inter-industry relationship between accident rates and weekly earnings for the years 1969 to 1972 and found no significant correlation due to the intrusion of other factors, such as the immobility of labour.[7] In the case of coalmining there have been considerable changes in the level and structure of wages. As a result of the 1966 Power Loading Agreement a uniform wage was introduced which eliminated inter-pit differentials and intra-regional differentials between mining and other industries. The effects of these changes on accident rates are, however, difficult to unravel.

The labour market mechanism is supplemented by common law actions and these have, in recent years, been the subject of considerable criticism and agitation for reform. Briefly, it has been argued that the common law system does not work efficiently because most payments for accidents bear no relationship to possible discounted earnings and family circumstances even when allowance has been made for contributory negligence. Hence, common law does not provide the incentive for employers and workers to be safety-conscious, leaves injured persons heavily dependent upon the state and enables lawyers to pocket the greater part of the insurance premiums as litigation fees. It has, therefore, been suggested that actions at common law should be abolished and that the state system should be amended so as to give higher income payments to the injured. Firms would cease making private insurance payments and instead would make larger contributions to the state scheme. Since injured persons would receive an income maintenance benefit irrespective of the cause of the accident, the task of accident prevention would rest upon an enlarged factory inspectorate plus measures to increase safety consciousness at the workplace; the trade unions would become a factory inspectorate.[8]

The implications of these changes would be very interesting in the case of the coal industry and throw interesting light upon the provisions of the existing system and what Beveridge envisaged in his blueprint for a welfare state. In the original proposals Beveridge suggested uniform benefits but stipulated that each industry's premiums should be based on its accident record. The Miner's Federation objected on the grounds that it would place an intolerable burden on the mining industry and create unemployment.[9] The proposal was withdrawn. Whether a new state scheme would incorporate differential payments is therefore an interesting question. And it points to other anomalies in the welfare state. For example, in 1931 the TUC objected to an unemployment insurance scheme on the grounds that workers could not afford to make contributions to it. In 1942 they accepted a contributory scheme despite their early resistance. One wonders what caused the change of mind and what had happened to Keynesian economics.

STRIKES

At all times and in all countries mining, particularly coalmining, has been characterised by a lot of strikes. Table 5.3 reveals that in the UK coalmining accounted for 56 per cent of all days lost in disputes from 1893 to 1914; 66 per cent between 1919 and 1939 and 13 per cent between 1947 and 1976. And the high degree of militancy is all the more surprising when account is taken of the relatively small percentage of the labour force employed in mining. Thus, in the post-war period coalmining has employed about 2 per cent of the labour force. Similar results can be found for other countries and what international comparisons suggest is that regardless of ownership – public or private – coalmining is an industry which has a lot of strikes; something more fundamental than property rights appears to be involved.

Kerr and Siegel attempted to explain the propensity to strike of

TABLE 5.3 Stoppages of Work due to Industrial Disputes, 1893–1974 (Annual Averages)

	Number of stoppages beginning in year		*Number of workers involved in stoppages beginning in year*		*Total number of days lost in stoppages in progress in year*	
	All industries	*Coal*	*All industries*	*Coal*	*All industries*	*Coal*
1893–1913	653	133	358	186	9,207	5,178
1914–18	814	116	632	254	5,360	1,601
1919–29	691	153	1,076	498	32,412	22,857
1930–8	604	218	323	175	3,152	1,003
1939–45	1,527	740	464	273	1,896	894
1946–57	1,962	1,363	620	229	2,678	582
1958–68	2,370	1,050	1,184	149	3,402	334
1969–74	2,983	198	1,579	164	12,872	3,117

Source: *British Labour Statistics Yearbook* (1974).

workers in different industries by what they called the *isolated mass hypothesis.*[10] According to them, miners, sailors, dockers and loggers – those who have been the most willing to strike – form socially isolated masses. They live apart from other workers in the pit village, on the ship, in dockland or the logging camp. Their grievances are collective rather than individual. Their skills are specific and not easily usable in other industries. Their jobs are dangerous, labour costs form a high percentage of total costs and their industries are extremely sensitive to the trade cycle so that wages undergo violent fluctuations. The isolated mass hypothesis accounts for the visible confrontation of masters and men, the emergence of unions and the tendency of the strike, for this isolated mass, to become a 'kind of colonial revolt against far-removed authority, an outlet for accumulated tensions, and a substitute for occupational and social mobility'.[11] Subsequently, Rimlinger suggested that not all socially isolated masses were militant and cited the Saar miners as an example.[12] But despite the counter-example, the isolated mass hypothesis does contain a grain of truth. The strikes of 1972 and 1974 did appear to be a form of colonial revolt and, despite the massive contraction of the coal industry in the sixties, the destruction of many pit villages and the emergence of commuting, there are many miners who have had no experience of jobs in other industries and who still live a life which separates them from other workers.

MEASURES OF STRIKE ACTIVITY

The significance of strikes can be measured in a variety of ways. First, there is the number of disputes which can be taken as a measure of the frequency of strike action. Secondly, strikes can be measured by the numbers of workers involved. Thirdly, the severity of strikes can be measured by the number of man-days lost or output lost. Each of these statistical measures has its advantages and disadvantages and there are problems in their interpretation. Output lost may be difficult to measure; indeed it is a guess if care is not taken to eliminate the effects of other factors, and is meaningless if the output could not have been sold. Ideally, all methods of measuring strike activity should be used since there is sometimes a tendency for the frequency and severity of strikes to move in opposite directions; the frequency of strike action tends to rise in boom periods while its severity tends to rise in slumps. But often all measurements of strike action are not available and conclusions must be based upon one measurement. However, sufficient inferences can often be drawn from other general background information to draw conclusions about the behaviour of all three indicators. Thus, in the fifties most strikes in the coal industry lasted for less than one day and involved small groups of men so that measures of frequency were often a good proxy for solidarity and severity.

Since nationalisation coalmining strike statistics have been unusually comprehensive. The official strike statistics collected by the Department of Employment are based upon a definition which excludes small strikes; the minimum duration of a strike must be one full day and the minimum size must be ten workers except where the aggregate days lost exceeds 100. In contrast, the Coal Board attempts to record all strikes. If, however, attention is concentrated on the trends in the Department of Employment's data then, as Table 5.2 reveals, strike activity in the coal industry rose to a peak in 1955, then declined until 1968 and then rose to new peaks in 1972 and 1974. This pattern differs markedly from that in other industries where strike activity was rising continuously throughout the fifties and sixties. And the effect of these divergent trends was, as Turner observed, to create an apparent withering away of all strike activity since mining tended to account for about 80 per cent of all strikes.[13]

The Department of Employment did not supply regional data until 1976 but if the Coal Board's statistics are used then it is apparent that Yorkshire loses more coal per man through strikes than any other coalfield, that Scotland and South Wales are the next most militant coalfields while Nottinghamshire, Northumberland and Durham are relatively quiescent. In its evidence to the 1965 Royal Commission on Trade Unions and Employers' Associations, the (then) Ministry of Labour observed that four industries – motor vehicles, shipbuilding, port transport and coalmining – were responsible for 44 per cent of time lost in disputes between 1960 and 1964 and for over half the number of strikes. The Ministry went on to observe that: 'In coalmining Yorkshire has accounted for 46 per cent of all days lost in coalmining during 1960–64, though the proportion of mining employees in that region averaged only 20 per cent over these years'.[14] A subsequent analysis by the Department of Employment revealed that over the years 1966 to 1973 coalmining, shipbuilding, vehicles and port transport still had the most strikes, accounting for 81 per cent of all time lost in disputes, with coalmining accounting for 29 per cent. And Yorkshire was still an important contributor to the coalmining total.[15]

A noticeable feature of Coal Board statistics is that all the coalfields tend to exhibit the same post-war pattern of fluctuations in strike activity – a rise to the mid-fifties, a decline through the sixties and then a rise in the early seventies. This uniformity of behaviour differs from that which obtained under private ownership. The pre-nationalisation distribution of strikes was strongly influenced by the distinction between the inland and the export coalfields. Strike activity in the inland coalfields tended to rise in the booms and fall in the slumps, whereas the relative absence of a cycle of activity in export markets reduced fluctuations in strike activity in the export coalfields. In Northumberland and Durham there was no noticeable trend in strike action whereas South Wales displayed an upward trend. These differences may reflect the fact that comprehensive statistics only became available in the 1890s by which time the North East's main period of militancy was over and past activity provided a frame of reference by which coal-owners and miners judged each other's actions; the relative absence of strikes did not indicate a lack of militancy but the absence of a necessity to strike. In contrast, South Wales's main phase of militancy was about to begin and coincided with the expansion of the coalfield. And, as between the two export coalfields, there were other noticeable differences stemming from institutions, profitability and geology. Northumberland and Durham had few strikes, but when they occurred they were big ones. In South Wales there were big strikes, such as that over abnormal places, but there were also large numbers of small strikes. In both booms and slumps strike activity in South Wales was always high, although it tended to alternate between small strikes and big strikes. These differences in regional patterns owe something to the nature of unionism in the two coalfields. In the North East decision-making was centralised at a relatively early stage and although centralisation was mainly confined to the sliding scale and still left pits free to negotiate basic rates, there was a tendency for the full-time officials to influence pit bargaining. There were also large coal-owners with whom to bargain. In contrast, South Wales's period of militancy began just before the First World War. The difficulties of communication between the valleys meant that Welsh unionism remained on a federal basis for a long time and the relative absence of a few large coal-owners was another factor inhibiting coordination of collective bargaining. Scotland, like Wales, also had problems in organising workers over a large area.

After nationalisation the differences between the patterns of fluctuation in the former export coalfields and the inland coalfields disappeared because the export markets disappeared. Consequently, all the coalfields had to sell in the home market and all were subject to common ownership which, as a result of cross-subsidisation, tended to dampen differences. But since the degree of subsidisation might often be determined by the degree of militancy, reasons for high strike rates in Scotland and South Wales might still be found.

STRIKE-PRONENESS

Strike-proneness is an interesting concept because of its widespread use in public discussion. During the sixties it was alleged that Britain was strike-prone and the Royal Commission on Trade Unions and Employers' Associations was established to unravel the causes of industrial unrest. The 1971 Industrial Relations Act was passed to curb strikes and its subsequent repeal, as a result of vigorous trade union agitation, seemed to confirm that Britain was strike-prone. Some observers, however, disputed this view of Britain as compared with other countries and suggested not merely that such strikes as did exist were concentrated in a few industries, for which blanket legislation was irrelevant, but that the volume of strikes might be Pareto optimal or more amenable to specific policies within industries concerned.[16]

In this section we shall, therefore, concentrate on two aspects of strike-proneness – heterogeneity and contagion – in the Yorkshire and South Wales coalfields, both of which have been responsible for a large part of the industry's strike record. Subsequently we shall look at strike-proneness in other British industries.

We begin with an examination of strike activity in the Yorkshire coalfield over the period 1947 to 1963. The year 1963 was chosen because it marked the changeover for record keeping purposes from the calendar year to the fiscal year (April to March). It is, however, sufficiently close to the introduction of NPLA in 1966 to provide a complete record of strike activity in the period of price lists. During the period the coalfield was divided, for administrative purposes, into 8 areas. The biennial rank correlation coefficients for the areas were high and the Kendall coefficient of concordance for the entire period was 0.80. Areas 2 (Doncaster) and 3 (Rotherham) consistently came top of the list while areas 6 (North Barnsley) and 7 (Wakefield) came at the bottom. This suggests that the South Yorkshire miner is inherently an 'awkward type' and supports the hypothesis of strike-proneness arising from heterogeneity. The pits in the Doncaster Area had certain features in common. They were all developed at about the same period in the inter-war years. They obtained their labour mainly from outside Yorkshire and so were cosmopolitan. They were often under the same private ownership and experienced harsh wage policies, the encouragement of rival unionism by the employers and the quota system in the inter-war years, which restricted profitability and hence wages. And just as the quota system of the thirties had involved cross-subsidisation, so the average-cost pricing policy of the Board in the fifties and sixties involved cross-subsidisation. Finally, they were all big pits and big pits, it was alleged, were more prone to strikes than small pits.

Variance analysis, however, revealed that the differences within the areas were greater than between the areas. There were, of course, periods when intra-area homogeneity was strong, but that suggested that contagion as well as heterogeneity was present. And Table 5.4 suggests that any attempt to link strike-proneness with social isolation (a possible cause of heterogeneity) runs into difficulties. There were some areas where social isolation was low and yet strikes were frequent — although it could be argued that the geographical concentration is not fine enough to capture the high concentrations within the areas.

When the inter-pit variations in strike activity were examined it was found that there were high correlations between the frequency and severity of strikes; pits which had a lot of strikes per 100 faceworkers lost a lot of tonnage per 100 faceworkers. There were high biennial rank correlations although the Kendall coefficient for the whole period fell to 0.47. Furthermore, the degree of dispersion of strike activity varied according to the general trends

TABLE 5.4 Mining Concentration Ratios and Strike Activity, 1949–63

Employment Exchange	*Average Percentage of male labour force in coalmining*	*Average number of strikes per 100 faceworkers*
Askern	71.0	1.8
Barnsley	42.1	1.2
Castleford	61.2	1.1
Chapeltown	23.2	0.7
Dinnington	70.3	0.2
Doncaster	32.4	2.3
Dewsbury	9.6	2.2
Goldthorpe	61.6	2.0
Hemsworth	77.2	1.1
Hoyland	75.6	0.8
Huddersfield	2.0	0.8
Leeds	0.7	0.4
Maltby	69.3	1.4
Mexborough	61.0	2.3
Morley	2.2	0.2
Normanton	73.1	0.7
Pontefract	47.9	1.0
Rotherham	17.9	1.1
Rothwell	28.2	0.5
Royston	74.6	0.6
Sheffield	3.2	0.4
Spcn Valley	3.9	0.1
Wakefield	23.4	0.5
Wombwell	78.6	1.8

Notes: Omitted from the table are:-

1. Thorne Employment Exchange which embraces Hatfield and Thorne, the latter pit being temporarily closed in 1957.
2. Manton, Shireoaks and Steetley pits come under Exchanges in the Midlands Arca of the Ministry of Labour.

Source: B. S. McCormick, 'Strikes in the Yorkshire coalfield, 1947–1963', in D. M. Kelly and D. J. C. Forsythe (eds.), *Studies in the Coal Industry* (Pergamon, London, 1969).

in the coalfield. During the years of high strike activity, 1955–61, dispersion fell and this suggested the presence of inter-pit contagion or a general response to external forces.

The distinction between heterogeneity and contagion is, however, more clearly revealed in Table 5.5 which indicates the pits which appeared in the upper quartile of strike frequencies in at least half of the years 1949–63. In some cases strike activity appears to follow the same path as the coalfield average, although

TABLE 5.5 Strike-prone Pits: Yorkshire Coalfield, 1947–63 (Strike rates as a percentage of the coalfield mean in each year)

	1949	*1950*	*1951*	*1952*	*1953*	*1954*	*1955*	*1956*	*1957*	*1958*	*1959*	*1960*	*1961*	*1962*	*1963*
Area 2 (11 pits)															
A	92	*167*	*155*	*141*	*233*	*343*	*252*	*210*	*195*	*151*	*173*	76	91	63	85
B	*275*	*584*	*590*	*615*	*718*	*506*	*515*	*414*	*477*	*455*	*350*	*239*	*286*	*379*	*255*
C	52	*149*	*206*	*205*	*262*	*264*	*250*	*274*	*216*	*251*	*271*	*153*	*230*	*195*	*206*
D	*156*	0	0	*445*	*176*	*216*	*558*	*628*	*489*	*228*	*354*	*133*	*248*	*182*	*298*
E	*252*	*155*	*216*	*111*	*208*	*164*	*140*	*332*	*272*	*278*	*225*	*196*	*289*	*182*	112
F	62	108	76	*188*	*329*	*451*	*387*	*221*	*245*	*407*	*324*	*313*	*235*	99	*333*
Area 3 (10 pits)															
G	*179*	*519*	*226*	*278*	*165*	*167*	*128*	*155*	*152*	68	78	67	75	*123*	69
H	*400*	*255*	*343*	93	86	82	*154*	*175*	*217*	*330*	*224*	*288*	*173*	*263*	*246*
I	*450*	130	*142*	71	*200*	120	*213*	*255*	*196*	*202*	*163*	*169*	*171*	*151*	*214*
J	*345*	*878*	*825*	*1044*	*153*	*329*	*405*	*293*	*330*	*370*	*406*	*285*	*619*	*351*	*285*
K	*200*	*243*	*224*	*211*	*292*	*349*	57	73	41	*143*	*131*	*210*	*220*	*333*	*324*
Area 4 (12 pits)															
L	*442*	*429*	*227*	*103*	*105*	*289*	81	123	*237*	*348*	*564*	*446*	*216*	73	*157*
Area 5 (10 pits)															
M	*171*	*408*	*422*	*344*	*285*	*249*	*165*	88	*198*	*195*	*302*	114	*255*	*175*	*204*
N	*213*	*246*	*170*	*400*	*153*	*553*	*176*	*462*	*324*	*400*	*357*	*236*	47	70	*148*
Area 6 (17 pits)															
O	119	*47*	31	*139*	24	116	*244*	*323*	*222*	117	*254*	*379*	*219*	254	111
P	*140*	*357*	140	*106*	*169*	*163*	*179*	*163*	79	*167*	*207*	*267*	*149*	52	93
Area 8 (16 pits)															
Q	*237*	*165*	122	*130*	*329*	*544*	283	128	52	*226*	85	110	111	*142*	*296*
R	92	0	0	*143*	*179*	*276*	118	85	*210*	*149*	*137*	*150*	*328*	*509*	*130*

Note: Percentages in italic occur in years in which the pit appeared in upper quartile.
Source: McCormick (1969), cited in note 19.

at a much higher level; for example, pit A. In such instances it is possible to detect the presence of heterogeneity. On the other hand, there are a number of interesting variations. Some pits, such as G and O, are active in the early or late years. Others, such as L, sublimate themselves at the peak of coalfield activity. Only two pits, B and J, have a consistent record of high strike activity and both exhibit two curious features. First, they both reveal a secular downswing in activity from the early fifties. Secondly, they both have a large variable strike component. The conclusions that can be drawn from the study of strike activity in the Yorkshire coalfield between 1949 and 1963, would therefore seem to be as follows. Heterogeneity was present in the sense that there was a preponderance of pits from the Doncaster and Rotherham areas in the upper quartiles of strike activity, but not all pits from those two areas had a lot of strikes. Contagion was also present and, in some instances, gave rise to a large variable component which made it implausible to attach significance to the notion of persistent, immutable strike factors such as the heterogeneity assumption would suggest. Indeed, it would be more plausible to define 'strike-proneness' as meaning simply a tendency for there to be a lot of strikes, rather than to convey the impression of a theory of inter-organisational differences in strike activity.

After 1963 there were some closures of pits and a reduction in the number of areas from 8 to 4. In addition, the introduction of NPLA in 1966 removed wage disputes from the pit level to the national level, although Yorkshire became important in the wage disputes of 1972 and 1974. The new Doncaster and South Yorkshire areas contain pits which have a lot of strikes, and strike-prone pits tend to be those which appeared prominently in the earlier period, such as Bentley, Brodsworth, Markham Main and Cadeby. But there is also a tendency for fluctuations in strike activity to occur.

But rather than continue with a detailed analysis of strike activity in Yorkshire it seems more interesting and useful to consider other coalfields. South Wales has had a long history of industrial militancy. Geologically its seams have been much more difficult to work and have made for much smaller pits than in Yorkshire. The dry nature of the seams gave rise to dust problems and a high incidence of lung diseases. The coalfield experienced a high rate of expansion in the eighties and nineties which brought immigrants from the surrounding regions and gave the coalfield a cosmopolitan nature. The huge influx of labour into the long narrow valleys created social problems of cramped housing and lack of social amenities, such as libraries and recreation grounds. The South Wales coalfield expanded dramatically before the First World War and contracted painfully in the inter-war years. And the process of contraction and migration to the newer industries, to the coastal belt and to England has continued. But although the South Wales coalfield has been declining and unprofitable compared with Yorkshire, it is still a large employer of labour.

Table 5.6 suggests that over the period 1964 to 1975 heterogeneity was present but only to a limited extent in the South Wales coalfield. Year to year correlation coefficients were low and the Kendall coefficient of concordance was 0.32. The measures of dispersion were also wide. The low degree of heterogeneity was also coupled with a low degree of contagion.

TABLE 5.6 Strike-proneness in the 40 'Live Pits' of the South Wales coalfield, 1964–75

1964/5–1965/6	0.23
1965/6–1966/7	0.45
1966/7–1967/8	0.36
1968/9–1969/70	0.53
1969/70–1970/1	0.46
1970/1–1971/2	0.32
1971/2–1972/3	0.11
1972/3–1973/4	0.49
Kendall coefficient of concordance	0.32

INTERRELATIONS OF ABSENTEEISM, ACCIDENTS, STRIKES AND LABOUR TURNOVER

So far we have been seeking to establish the presence of heterogeneity and contagion in absenteeism, accidents, strikes and labour turnover. Before examining the causes of heterogeneity and contagion, particularly in strikes, it may be useful to examine the possible interrelation of the phenomena we have been analysing. In the case of absenteeism and strikes Knowles found a negative correlation in the coal industry during the years 1943 to 1945.[17] Turner and Handy also found a negative correlation in the sixties.[18] On the other hand, McCormick discovered a positive correlation in the Yorkshire coalfield in 1963 and suggested that the relationship might be non-linear and that in periods of acute unrest both high absence and high strike rates might be experienced.[19] Table 5.7 indicates a virtual absence of negative correlations between absenteeism, accidents and strikes in the South Wales coalfield between 1965 and 1974.

TABLE 5.7 Interactions of Strikes, Accidents and Absenteeism in the 40 Live Pits of the South Wales Coalfield, 1965–74

	Strikes/ absenteeism	*Strikes/ accidents*	*Absenteeism/ accidents*
1965/6	0.22	n.a.	n.a.
1966/7	0.35	n.a.	n.a.
1967/8	0.88	0.09	0.54
1968/9	0.15	0.39	0.41
1969/70	0.40	0.37	0.50
1970/1	0.32	0.43	0.54
1971/2	n.a.	n.a.	n.a.
1972/3	0.10	−0.70	0.42
1973/4	0.32	0.48	0.30
1974/5	0.18	0.09	0.31

To the observations on strikes and absenteeism in the coal industry we can add Turner's inability to find any association in the car industry and the evidence of the 1970 *New Earnings Survey* of a positive association, 0.83, between voluntary absence and strikes and 0.76 between involuntary absence and strikes in manufacturing industry.[20]

Table 5.8 throws some light upon the interactions of absenteeism and accidents in the South Nottinghamshire coalfield. No analysis of strikes was undertaken because the Notts coalfield has been traditionally strike-free. During the period of observation the only strikes to occur were those concerned with the national strikes of 1972 and 1974 and those which were associated with a fairly widespread protest in the Notts coalfield against the Third Day Wage Structure which represented the final step in the abolition of the Notts wages differentials over the other coalfields.

Just why the Notts coalfield should have been so strike-free is difficult to determine. The coalfield forms part of the continuous

TABLE 5.8 Interactions of Absence and Accidents in the South Nottinghamshire Coalfield, 1970–75

	Absence/ accident frequency	*Absence/ accident severity*	*Accident frequency/ severity*
1970/1	0.66	0.47	0.88
1971/2	0.52	0.57	0.63
1972/3	0.36	0.35	0.63
1973/4	0.56	0.61	0.66
1974/5	0.56	0.62	0.58

coalfield which runs from Yorkshire into the Midlands. Geologically, there is not much difference between the various sections of the coal belt and given the similarities the question arises; why are there regional variations in militancy? There are undoubted regional differences and the dividing line occurs between Yorkshire and Derbyshire. Yorkshire miners do appear to be more suspicious and awkward than Derbyshire miners, but such an observation merely begs the question; how did the differences arise? South Yorkshire pits tend to be deeper and hotter than those in Nottinghamshire and Yorkshire had a considerable export trade through Immingham before the Second World War which may have accounted for its militant stance compared with South Wales and Northumberland and Durham. Perhaps the greater militancy of the Yorkshire miners has something to do with Yorkshire temperament – as exemplified in such Yorkshire sporting personalities as Freddie Trueman, Geoffrey Boycott and Harvey Smith. Further evidence for such a hypothesis comes from the fact that all industries in South Yorkshire tend to have more strikes than the same industries in other regions.

That a positive association should exist between absenteeism and accidents is perhaps not surprising; many accidents give rise to absences. But the lack of firm conclusions on the interrelations between absenteeism and strikes stems not merely from the existence of different statistical findings but also from the presence of different hypotheses concerning their relationship. Knowles regarded absenteeism and strikes as substitutes. Scott *et al.* considered absenteeism, accidents and strikes as indicators of morale which could be linked to the degree of social organisation of conflict.[21] Thus, absenteeism, accidents and labour turnover could be regarded as measures of unorganised conflict since they tend to be individual actions receiving little or no support from the working group, while strikes were a measure of organised conflict. Furthermore, absenteeism and accidents were indicators of low morale whereas strikes were indicators of high group morale. But the views of Scott *et al.* need to be heavily qualified. They recognised, but did not consider important, the fact that absenteeism may be a group phenomenon. Indeed, it is difficult, in the context of the coal industry, to regard absenteeism as other than a group phenomenon since absence disrupts the work and earnings of other workers. And a great deal of absenteeism may reflect the desire to maximise lifetime earnings and reveals nothing about morale.

Positive correlations of absenteeism and strikes may arise for a variety of reasons. Thus, strikers and absentees may not be the same people. And closely connected with this explanation is a 'Catch-22' phenomenon. Some miners may not go to work because others are on strike or there has been an accident. Retaliation may also occur; because a group of miners was absent on one shift the next shift goes on strike. Retaliatory strikes were common on the old hand-filled system because withdrawals from work disrupted the cycle of operations and forced workers to do alternative jobs. A further reason for the coexistence of high absence and high strike rates may be found in the tendency to substitute authorised absence for unauthorised absence in order to claim income when an anticipated strike occurs. But the main reason for the possible coexistence of high strike rates and high absence rates is simply the failure to realise that not all strikes involve the whole workforce but, typically, concern a small group of men; there has been a tendency to confuse the frequency and severity of absenteeism and strikes.

On the other hand, the substitutability of absenteeism and strikes can be detected in small strikes. Many strikes occur at the beginning of the week and in the spring and for many of these strikes the distinction between working and not working may have been slight. Similarly, strikes on afternoon shifts are much commoner than on other shifts.

Hence at certain times, and sometimes over periods of time, low absence and low strike rates may exist while other occasions may yield high absence and high strike rates. And the application of simple regression techniques may reveal linearities in non-linear systems.

MORALE

In the previous section it was pointed out that Scott *et al.* had used absenteeism, accidents, strikes and labour turnover as indicators of morale. This idea was subsequently adopted by Pencavel who used principal components analysis to examine the movement of morale in the coal industry over the period 1949 to 1963. Morale was considered to be a negative function of absenteeism, etc., and morale was assumed to influence output.[22] The determinants of morale were financial returns, degree of mechanisation, and the average age of miners. Pencavel found that his index of morale explained regional variations and the movement of morale over time. Morale was high in Northumberland and Durham, Scotland and the East Midlands and low in South Wales and Yorkshire. Over time it remained high until 1958 and then declined as the industry contracted. His interpretation of the decline in morale after 1958 is the same as that of Handy which we have suggested attaches too much importance to the rise in absenteeism without observing that there was a national rise in absenteeism in the sixties.

CAUSES OF HETEROGENEITY

SIZE OF PIT

Having sought to define the problems involved in establishing relationships between absenteeism, accidents, strikes and labour turnover we can now pass on to an analysis of the possible causes of heterogeneity or, more simply, why some pits have more strikes than others. In the fifties research workers in the coal industry sought a link between the size of pit and the frequency of absence, accidents and strikes. Revans, for example, found a tendency for the frequency and severity of strikes to rise as the size of the pit rose and also a tendency for non-wage issues to become more important as the size of pit rose.[23] The increase in strike activity he attributed to the problems of communication in large organisations and he also observed that as the supervision ratio increased strike activity tended to decline. Revans's findings referred to the period 1949 to 1954 and with particular force to the

Yorkshire coalfield. A decade later, McCormick found that the interrelations of strikes, size of pit and supervision ratio still persisted in the Yorkshire coalfield.[24] Table 5.9 throws some light upon the influence of pit size (numbers of miners employed) in the South Wales coalfield between 1965 and 1975. Most of the coefficients are not significant and many are negatively correlated although absenteeism is positively correlated with size.

TABLE 5.9 Pit Size, Absenteeism, Accidents and Disputes in the 40 'Live Pits' of the South Wales Coalfield, 1965–75

	Correlation coefficients of pit size on		
	Absenteeism	*Accidents*	*Disputes*
1965/6	0.31	n.a.	–0.21
1966/7	0.32	n.a.	0.13
1967/8	0.26	0.25	0.04
1968/9	0.30	0.20	–0.08
1969/70	0.30	0.30	–0.03
1970/1	0.23	0.11	–0.03
1971/2	0.34	n.a.	n.a.
1972/3	0.40	0.08	0.12
1973/4	0.38	0.13	–0.23
1974/5	0.29	–0.09	0.09

In another context Ingham attempted to provide a theoretical framework which could explain differences in the behaviour of workers in large and small plants.[25] He put forward the hypothesis that large and small units attract and employ workers who have different needs. Large plants cater for workers who want large money incomes whereas small plants exist to provide for those workers who seek to satisfy non-monetary wants. Ingham based his hypothesis upon: (i) an observed correlation between size and absenteeism and (ii) the lack of any relationship between labour turnover and the size of industrial organisations. Ingham was careful to state that he wished to restrict his hypothesis to absenteeism and did not intend it to be extended to strikes and accidents although he does concede that the period of absence following an accident may be influenced by the size of the organisation.

Ingham's hypothesis rests upon the assumption that workers have different wants and that there is relatively costless mobility of labour so that workers can satisfy those wants by moving between employers rather than seeking to satisfy them with their existing employer. In effect, workers with different wants constitute non-competing groups. If, however, workers have the same wants and are immobile then different interpretations of the facts become possible. If workers have the same wants initially then the problem is how do those wants or aspirations become altered in the work situation and workers become content with what they get. Unfortunately, the early studies of behaviour in large and small pits did not record labour turnover. But they did demonstrate that strikes over non-wage issues were relatively more important at large pits and that would seem to indicate that workers in such pits were interested in things other than money and that no sharp differences in wants might exist.

But however interesting are the studies of the fifties, they diminish in importance when placed alongside the changes that have taken place since the mid-sixties. These are;

1. the reduction in pit sizes;
2. the closure of small pits and the disappearance of many closed pit villages;
3. the introduction of power loading which has eliminated the large gangs of fillers previously employed on large wall faces; and
4. the NPLA which substituted time-rates for piece-rates.

The first point is that the size effect is still present although less pronounced than in the early period. The big pits of Yorkshire — Cadeby, Silverwood, Brodsworth, Markham Main and Kellingley — still appear near the top of the league table where they are joined by other big pits, such as Monktonhall in Scotland. In the case of a particular coalfield, South Wales, positive correlations between size and strikes and absenteeism obtain over the period 1965 to 1975 but most of the correlations are not significant. In the two areas where an appreciable range of pit sizes can still be found – Barnsley Area and the Durham coalfield — Ingham's hypothesis was not substantiated; absence was not associated with pit size and turnover rates tended to be higher at the smaller pits in 1975 and 1976. But this is not surprising because Ingham's hypothesis is an equilibrium hypothesis and not one purporting to explain disequilibrium. The effect of the pit closure programme was to destroy the social control that existed over absenteeism, accidents and strikes that existed in the small pits. And although the big pits have tended to become cosmopolitan with inflows of miners from the declining coalfields and commuting from the areas which have declined, the big pits are the pits with a future and they also tend to have better working conditions and a younger workforce.

The distinction between the fifties, sixties and seventies is important. With the transfer of wage negotiations to the national level all pit disputes tend to be organisational disputes and place greater strains upon management. Disputes about working conditions and organisational arrangements are as prevalent as they were under the hand-filled/price lists system despite the belief that the payment of a common wage would eliminate such disputes and increase the mobility of labour.

Differences, therefore, exist between recent and earlier observations. But differences also existed in the earlier periods and were concealed by bias in the observations. The big pits of Nottinghamshire and the West Midlands were always relatively strike-free. And what was most striking about Revans's analysis was its emphasis upon Yorkshire pits and its lack of discussion of the influence of size upon pits in the militant coalfields of Scotland and South Wales and the strike-free Nottinghamshire pits.

STRIKES IN OTHER COAL INDUSTRIES

In the coal industries of other countries there can be observed the same decline in strike activity in the sixties followed by a rise in the late sixties and seventies. This pattern arose through the effects of competition from other fuels so that even if NPLA had not been introduced strike activity would have risen in the UK in the seventies although its severity might have been different. The pattern of strikes – a fall and then a rise – was common to the privately-owned coal industries of America and West Germany and the publicly-owned industries of Britain and France and could be observed in the piece-rate coalfields of Australia, Belgium, France and West Germany as well as the time-rate coalfields of the United Kingdom and the United States.

There were, however, slight differences. In the early post-war years there were large-scale political strikes in France against American (Marshall) Aid. There were strikes against closures in the mid-fifties but it was not until the end of the fifties and the sixties that strike activity assumed importance. In Belgium the main wave of strike activity was against closures in the sixties. The most spectacular strike against closure, however, occurred in Japan where a strike at the Miike Mine in 1960 involved 1200 miners and lasted eleven months. It was a struggle between a prominent Japanese company, one of the Zaibatsu, and a major union in the left-wing section of the Japanese labour movement. During the strike a new union was formed within the company and was supported by the Japanese right-wing labour movement. The strike ended with the defeat of the workers, the virtual disintegration of the Japanese Coal Miners' Union and the demoralisation of the left-wing labour movement.

The most interesting country, however, is America, because of its use of time-rates for wage payments and its earlier encounter with competition from other fuels. In the fifties and sixties every measure of strike activity declined. This was a result of the decline in the demand for coal, the introduction of time-rates and the introduction of long-term wage contracts. In both decades the peak of strike activity occurred in the years when contracts were being renegotiated – a characteristic of other American industries. During the seventies the decline was reversed and there was a tendency for strikes to occur within the period of a contract. The other notable feature of the industry has been the preponderance of strikes over non-wage issues such as working conditions, unionism, job security and safety. Over 90 per cent of all strikes, irrespective of the method of measurement, have been about non-wage issues. Furthermore, most of these strikes were unofficial and involved only local branches. The pattern of disputes reflected the lack of interest by the UMWA under Lewis and Boyle in non-wage issues and their tendency to let wildcat strikes blow themselves out. But the upsurge of interest in safety, the change in union leadership and the rise in the demand for coal may give rise to a change in attitude to unofficial strikes. What is significant, however, has been the high rate of unofficial strikes over non-wage issues coupled with industry-wide bargaining on time-rates which has been in marked contrast to British experience.

Australian strike experience has been rather similar to that of Britain, Western Europe and America. The industry met competition from other fuels partly by contraction and partly by an expansion of exports. But the effects of competition were to cause a fall in strike activity despite the traditional militancy of Australian miners and the continuance of a left-wing, communist-dominated leadership. The pattern of strike activity shows a preponderance of strikes over non-wage issues.

STRIKES IN OTHER INDUSTRIES

So far our analysis has been confined to the coal industry but it can be extended to other industries. There was a decline in strike activity from the mid-fifties until the end of the sixties but if coalmining stoppages are excluded then the trend in all other industries was upward and reached a peak in the period 1970–75. There was a high degree of correlation between frequency and severity in strike activity for the major industrial groups (0.88 for the years 1971–75).[26] In terms of both frequency and severity the most strike-prone industries in the period 1950–75 were docks, motor vehicles, iron and steel and engineering as well coalmining and the inter-industry ranking of strike-prone industries showed a high degree of stability. There are, however, two qualifications. First, there were considerable year-to-year variations in the frequency and severity of strikes in particular industries. Secondly, there was a tendency for the inter-industry dispersion of strike activity to contract in the late sixties and early seventies – this reflected the general decline in real wages due to inflation.

Geographically, there was a tendency for particular regions to be strike-prone but this was not merely a result of particular industries being concentrated in certain regions but was also due to some regional factor. The most strike-prone regions tended to be Merseyside (docks and motor vehicles), Glasgow (shipbuilding and motor vehicles), South Yorkshire (coal, iron and steel and engineering) and South Wales (coal and iron and steel).

The third feature of the strike data available from the Department of Employment is that even within the strike-prone industries most plants seemed to be strike-free.[27] Thus, between 1971 and 1975 only some 2 per cent of all plants were involved in stoppages and even then they were not always the same plants.

From 1945 to 1965 the majority of strikes were over non-wage issues whereas wage disputes tended to predominate from 1965 onwards. The existence of a watershed reflects the fact that in the early period inflation was less severe and wage increases were easy to obtain on the shop floor. Most workers were concerned with fighting managerial prerogatives over such issues as redundancy, transfer and promotion. Over a twenty-year period the frontier of control shifted as workers sought to parallel achievements in industrial democracy comparable to the gains attained in the political sphere. By the middle sixties the problem of managerial prerogatives was reaching a temporary solution. Productivity bargaining was forcing managers to make concessions and legislation was extending conditions of employment security to the unorganised. The second half of the sixties and the early seventies witnessed a switch to wage disputes precipitated by inflation and to disputes over the Industrial Relations Act which represented a general attack on the principle of unionism.

In the light of the evidence from a series of studies of strike activity the Department of Employment *Gazette* concluded:

> Studies of industrial stoppages by industry have often concluded, on the basis of a fairly stable ranking of industries in terms of working days lost from stoppages, that particular historical, technological or organisational factors make certain industries more or less prone to industrial conflict. The current research shows, that, within industries that have higher aggregate levels of stoppage activity, many plants are still free of stoppages. Consequently, while historical, technological or organisational factors general to any one industry may increase the probability of stoppages occurring in that industry, they do not automatically lead to stoppages in all plants.[28]

Three observations can be made on this quotation. First, the conclusion can be regarded as a generalisation of our earlier findings for the coal industry. Secondly, it fails to draw the obvious political conclusion that legislation on industrial relations, such as the ill-fated Industrial Relations Act, is not the most efficient method of tackling industrial unrest. Thirdly, in its emphasis upon contagion rather than heterogeneity the *Gazette* fails to indicate the nature of the factors giving rise to strikes and their interaction with structural features. It is to this later problem that we now turn in a review of the existing literature.

In an analysis of strike frequency in construction, transport, metal goods and coal mining over the period 1950 to 1967,

Pencavel applied the Ashenfelter/Johnson theory of collective bargaining. Essentially, the theory assumes that union leaders will be influenced by political factors, such as the desire of their members to get the same wage increases as other groups of workers, as well as economic factors operating in the factor and product markets. Pecavel found that in all the four industry groups a high rate of strike activity was associated with a high level of demand for labour. Tight labour markets enabled workers to obtain alternative jobs and gave them the opportunity to press their current employers for higher wages. In each industry there was a seasonal pattern of strike activity which was similar to that for all industries and which reached its peak in the first quarter of the year. In coal mining there was a negative time trend but in other industries the trend was towards increasing militancy. Some 94 per cent of strike activity in mining was explained by the level of demand, changes in real wages, incomes policies and the time trend. In construction the national, as well as the industry's, unemployment rate, was significant. In the engineering industry much of the explanation of strike activity came from the time trend and seasonal factors.[29]

Bean and Peel sought to explain differences in the frequency of strikes over wages in engineering, vehicles, shipbuilding and marine engineering and construction. Wage disputes in these industries were responsible for 64 per cent of all wage disputes, excluding those in coalmining, in the period 1962 to 1970. Bean and Peel discovered significant correlations between strike activity and the level of unemployment (negative), productivity (positive) and the expected level of real profits (negative). Anticipated changes of earnings, however, performed badly as compared with anticipated price changes despite Pencavel's belief that wage and price changes would be symmetrical in their effects; a 1 per cent rise in the expected rate of price changes was associated with a 12 per cent increase in the number of strikes and a 1 per cent increase in the rate of earnings relative to overall earnings resulted in a rise in strike activity of 3.5 per cent in the following period.[30]

The final time-series analysis of strike activity to be considered is by Shorey, who examined strikes in the inter-war years (1920–39) and the post-war period (1950–67). In the inter-war years the outcome of the General Strike was found to have a significant effect on strike frequency and unemployment and prices were also important. For the post-war period Shorey used the rate of change of wage differentials, rather than the ratio of levels of inter-industry wages adopted by Bean and Peel. The movement of wage differentials, incomes policies, profits and prices were found to be important determinants of strike activity.[31]

In addition to time-series analyses, there have been cross-section investigations, notably by Shorey. He used data averaged for the years 1963–7 for 33 industry groups. His results revealed that strike activity was related

– negatively to the proportion of women in the labour force
– positively to the percentage of workers paid under payment-by-results schemes
– positively to the rate of productivity increase and the rate of change of capital formation
– positively to differences in the inter-industry wage differential and the rate of change of money wages.[32]

Shorey failed to find any significant relationship between strikes and the demand for labour (as measured by unemployment or vacancies), the degree of concentration of industry or the percentage of the labour force which was skilled. Furthermore, he obtained confusing results with respect to plant size and firm size; an increase in plant size tended to increase strikes but an increase in firm size tended to reduce them. His explanation of his apparently unusual results was that large firms might experience fewer strikes but they would be of greater severity than in large plants.

Shorey's analysis suffered from several defects. He used the 1961 survey of piece-work by the (then) Ministry of Labour and ignored the results of the 1968 *New Earnings Survey* which revealed a large fall in the numbers of workers in manufacturing on piece-work and a rise in piece-workers in non-manufacturing. The *Survey* also revealed that the piece-work bonuses as a percentage of pay had declined. The paradoxical results on plant size were probably due to three factors. First, most large British firms have grown through horizontal merger and may therefore have small plants. Secondly, if large firms are multi-product firms then disputes in one plant may not have wider repercussions. Thirdly, Shorey's measure of firm size double counts those firms which do control plants operating in more than one industry.

Some further light is thrown on the effect of plant size by a series of articles in the Department of Employment *Gazette* covering the years 1971 – 5.[33] The frequency and severity of strike activity tended to rise with plant size for all industries although the severity of strikes was less pronounced in large plants – suggesting that most disputes involve small groups of workers. Furthermore, the simple positive correlation between plant size and strikes did not always obtain when individual industries were considered. The *Gazette* articles did not consider Revan's second hypothesis which suggested that not merely will large plants have more disputes than small plants but that they will tend also to have proportionately more non-wage disputes. However, from the detailed records of the Department it was possible to extract some conclusions about the incidence of non-wage disputes. The data for the years 1966–73 revealed a marked concentration of disputes about supervision and manning and work allocation in a few industries – coalmining, vehicles and docks with other engineering and electricity supply as runners-up. This incidence suggests that size *per se* was not a sufficient explanation on non-wage disputes and is confirmed by a more detailed analysis within industries. An analysis of disputes in the car industry revealed that stoppages rose to a peak in the size group 1000–1999 and thereafter fell. These results differ from those for wage disputes but should occasion no surprise. Large plants are not monolithic in character and non-wage disputes frequently involve only small groups of workers. In the chemical industry there were few wage disputes in the large plants although stoppages over manning and working conditions were common. In contrast, large plants in electrical engineering had more strikes over both wage and non-wage issues than did smaller plants. These results, coupled with those mentioned earlier for coalmining, suggest that it is not size *per se* which accounts for disputes and this leads to the question of why large plants in some industries tend to have more disputes than those in other industries.

The lack of association between strike activity and concentration should occasion no surprise. There is no *a priori* reason why changes in the degree of product market concentration should affect the elasticity of derived demand for labour. In the case of unions, those which had achieved a monopoly position would have located themselves at a point on the factor demand curve where the elasticity of derived demand was unity. Insofar as changes in monopoly do increase the likelihood of strike activity, then it would be as a result of other factors operating. Thus changes in the degree of product market concentration have, in the sixties, been brought about largely by horizontal mergers rather than by internal growth and they have brought together plants with different wages structures and prompted pressures for wage equlisation. Brown and Sissons have drawn attention to the consequences of mergers in the vehicle and newspaper industries.[34]

The final problem for consideration is the influence of trade union organisation upon the level and pattern of strike activity. The crude evidence suggests that strike activity is positively related to the density of trade union membership in different industries but that within manufacturing industry this relationship is reversed. An explanation for these results may lie in the fact that the overall relationship is strongly influenced by heavily unionised, non-manufacturing industries, such as coal-mining, docks and railways. Any result can, of course, be criticised on the grounds that not only is it extremely difficult to measure the degree of trade unionism in each industry but it is also impossible to specify the relationship between union membership and militancy. The Department of Employment assigns the whole of a union's membership to the industry in which it thinks that the majority of members is employed and it fails to allocate the memberships of the general unions to different industries. Attempts to cope with the difficulties of the Department's data have been attempted by Bain and Burkitt but they have not been wholly successful.[35] Thus, Bain has not been able to disentangle the 'metals' engineering' complex which accounts for a substantial part of the labour force and trade unionism and Bukitt's data is no more satisfactory even though its author justifies its usage in the analysis of wage movements on the grounds that it yields results similar to those obtained by other research workers using different methods. The problem of the relationship between union membership and militancy is sharply revealed by the example of the NUM which has never had less than 100 per cent union density in the post-war period but whose militancy has varied considerably over the period. There is also the problem of determining at what level of organisation measurement should be conducted. In 1973 there was a lack of association between the percentage of workers covered by national agreements and strike activity but a positive association between the percentage of workers covered by national and local agreements and strike activity which suggests that it is the interrelations of national agreements and shop floor activity which are crucial for strike activity.

Many of the statistical problems arise from a lack of a satisfactory theory of trade union behaviour: there is too much measurement without theory. Traditional economic theories of union behaviour emphasise the union non-union wage differential and most of the empirical work does not link this crucial differential to the measures of trade union density.

SUMMARY

In this chapter we have examined the problems of absenteeism, accidents, strikes and labour turnover within the coal industry and within other industries. We found that the explanations of absenteeism in the sixties were wrong. We concluded that there were big variations in strike activity by so-called strike-prone pits and we observed that in all industries only a few plants were ever involved in strike activity at any period of time. We also found that economic factors could throw light upon strike activity.

6 The Big Strikes

Big strikes attract public attention, and in this chapter we shall examine those which have occurred since nationalisation. Three of them were specific to Yorkshire and Yorkshire played a major role in the others. For each of the strikes we shall describe the course of events and analyse their causes and effects. And because the strikes of 1969–74 were official and national we shall place them in a wider perspective by examining their implications for economic and social policy.

THE GRIMETHORPE STINT STRIKE, 1947

The Grimethorpe stint strike started on 11 August and finished on 15 September 1947. The strike arose over the application of the Five Day Week Agreement to the Meltonfield Seam at Grimethorpe, a pit in the Barnsley Area. The agreement reduced hours of work by eliminating the Saturday morning shift, but in order to maintain total output it was agreed that there should be a rearrangement of work loads on the five shifts. At most pits it was customary for faceworkers to be allowed out of the pit when they finished their work. There was, however, an attempt to discourage early finishing on the grounds that it encouraged men to neglect safety precautions. By refusing to let men out early it was possible that there could be enough time to make up the lost Saturday shift output.

In the Meltonfield Seam it was proposed to increase the length of the stint by two feet. The 200 faceworkers in the seam refused to accept the increase in the stint and argued that it would mean older workers would have to work harder or be forced to retire from face work. As a result the 2,600 miners at Grimethorpe came out on strike. Ten days elapsed before miners at the neighbouring Ferrymoor Colliery came out in sympathy. But the strike suddenly began to increase in severity on 26 August when the divisional chairman, Major-General Noel Holmes, announced that all strikers would be considered to have terminated their contracts. The strike was therefore turned into a lockout. On 28 August there were 10 pits out on strike and the dispute had spread into the Doncaster and Rotherham Areas, despite pit meetings with the Minister of Fuel and Power, Emanuel Shinwell. At a meeting on 30 August only 43 miners at Grimethorpe voted to return to work out of a total vote of 433 miners – out of a total labour force of 2600!

On 1 September Major-General Holmes promised that there would be no victimisation following a return to work, but there were still 29 pits idle, and the following day the number rose to 46. By 3 September the strike had spread into West Yorkshire, to Dewsbury and Featherstone. On 7 September another vote was taken but only 700 bothered to vote and the verdict was to continue the strike. By 8 September a third of all Yorkshire pits were idle though it was difficult to disentangle the effects of the holidays and absenteeism associated with the Doncaster Race Week. The strike finished with a return to work on the pre-stoppage terms pending the report of a fact-finding committee.

Interest in the Grimethorpe stint strike arises because it was, in many ways, a forerunner of the 1972 and 1974 disputes. At the centre of the dispute was a national agreement whose implementation demanded changes in working conditions. It was a national productivity bargain. But the bargain over hours and effort was not negotiated at the local level by the workers concerned. Instead, the hours were negotiated nationally and then there was an attempt to change effort locally by what, to the workers, seemed to be a unilateral decision. The determination of conditions of work appeared to have been taken away from the face-workers and this was the parallel with the 1966 National Power Loading Agreement. There was a breakdown in communications between national leaders and the rank and file.

The more immediate effect of the strike was that it led to an increase in negotiations at pit level and an exploration of the newly-established conciliation machinery. And as a result the wages of face workers which had been frozen since 1944 started to rise in Yorkshire. And the stint strike had repercussions in other fields. It led to local bargaining on wages and working conditions which was to cause a gap to open between the wages of piece-workers and time-workers, to create problems for the union and the Board and to instigate the search for new wages structures.

THE MARKHAM MAIN DISPUTE, 1955

The Yorkshire coalfield strike of 1955 has to be put in a national context. The boom in economic activity in 1955 and 1956 was the first since the Korean War boom of 1950 and 1951. And it was a rise in economic activity that was accompanied by an increase in strikes and the re-emergence of official strikes. By 1955 unions were becoming aware of the implications of full employment and markets cleared of controls. Through 1954 and the first few months of 1955 the trend of strike activity in Yorkshire rose and sharply accelerated. The basic issue was wages. There had been no major revisions of prices lists in Yorkshire since nationalisation and wage adjustments took the form of *ex gratia* payments called allowances. The increasing importance of allowances reflected two aspects of wage determination in Yorkshire: first, the cost-consciousness of the divisional Board, and secondly, the legalistic outlook of the union which accepted the conciliation machinery, created queues of pits wanting price list revisions and thereby prompted strike action in order to queue-jump. Cost-consciousness followed from coal-pricing policy. The fixing of a coal price below the free market price meant costs had to be kept down. But the excess demand for coal meant there was an increased demand for labour and in Yorkshire there was a tight labour market. The response was sluggish and took the form of increased allowances. The allowances reduced the incentive element in the price lists and most pits became *de facto* day-wage pits. And allowances, being *ex gratia* payments, were resented because they depended upon managerial discretion.

In January, 1955, the turning point came. Barnborough in the Rotherham area struck and eight pits came out in sympathy. Between January and April there were 234 strikes in the coalfield. On 2 May Markham Main fillers came out on strike and received the support of the other pits in the Doncaster area. On 14 May, when there were 33 pits on strike, the area council voted by 93 votes to 14 to recommend a return to work. The next day the strike had spread to all areas. At various times there were 89 pits out of 116 on strike, though there was a tendency, except in the Doncaster area and parts of Rotherham area, for pits to strike, return to work and then come out again. The strike ended on 14 May, when the Doncaster panel recommended a return to work;

the following week was the Whitsuntide bull week when miners boosted output and earnings for their holidays.

We must now examine the part played by the area panels in the 1955 strike. On nationalisation the Yorkshire area of the NUM was a federation of pits, each pit possessing an intense individuality deriving from geology and period of development. Geologically, the Yorkshire coalfield forms part of the eastern limb of the great Pennine anticline. The rocks dip away towards the east. On the west side of the coalfield there runs a strip, about 10 miles wide in the central area, which forms the exposed coalfield and on which the coal measures, though not necessarily the coal seams, form the surface rocks. This exposed area was the first to be exploited and the history of exploration, sinking and getting in Yorkshire is a record of an eastward movement and expansion from the foothills of the Pennines. Around Tankersley, near Barnsley, can be seen the remains of bell pits. And on the slopes to the west of Barnsley can be found villages virtually lying in the pit yard. In a later stage of exploitation, as the frontier moved east, the pit villages were built around the old agricultural villages, which they gradually encroached upon and strangled, though remnants of the old villages can still be discerned. These were the pit villages of the period from 1850 to 1880. Finally, there began, as at Denaby in 1868, the emergence of the model village or company town. The full-scale development of 'the model' was however, a product of the opening up of the concealed coalfield around Doncaster at the turn of the century. A characteristic of the Doncaster area is the 'model village', without long lines of terraced houses, lying at some distance from the existing villages so that the traveller encounters, for example, New Rossington, Edlington and Moorends.

In addition to the varying characteristics of pits and communities as one travels from west to east, there are north to south differences too, though of a more subtle form. The Yorkshire coalfield consists of two coal basins whose divider is Woolley anticline, the axis of which runs from Woolley towards Asken. The northern coal basin, often referred to as West Yorkshire, tends to have thinner seams than South Yorkshire. But even within West Yorkshire there can be found the east-west distinction noted earlier, and West Yorkshire tended to have a greater preponderance of smaller pits often integrated into the textile area of the West Riding. South Yorkshire also contained sharp differences. The Don Faults created a distinct group of pits—Kilnhurst, Denaby and Cadeby—which differed from the pits of the Dearne Valley. And to the south of the Don Faults lay some exceptionally deep pits, such as Dinnington and Thurcroft, and pits such as Shireoaks and Steetley, which in character and temperament were more akin to those of Derbyshire and Nottinghamshire.

The sheer size and complexity of the Yorkshire coalfield had made for a federation of pit villages. But was Yorkshire any different from South Wales or Scotland, both of which appeared to consist of large numbers of pits in diverse localities? The distinction lay in the evolution of unionism. South Wales and Scotland came late to unionism and the intense struggles to achieve recognition brought about a greater degree of discipline and centralisation than in Yorkshire. In Yorkshire union development was steady from the seventies and the steadiness of growth allowed for more local autonomy. At nationalisation the number of area officials was small in relationship to the total membership.

Nationalisation created the need for some change in the county union's organisation because there existed no layer of command equivalent to the Board's areas, of which the Yorkshire division possessed eight. From the point of view of the County officials the introduction of an intermediary between Barnsley and each pit was something to be avoided since it created the possibility of an alternative union leadership. In the nineties pits in the Rotherham Area had formed their own breakaway union and on various occasions since the twenties there had been fears of a breakaway of the Doncaster pits. Nor was the idea of an organisational layer at Area level viewed with equanimity by the pits since it would have implied a loss of autonomy. Consider, for example, the difficulties of imposing an organisational structure in the Rotherham Area (Area 3). Kilnhurst, lying deep in the Don Faults, was an old pit. Sunk in the 1850s it was very much 'a Lancashire pit' with its steep dips and inclines. South of Kilnhurst, across the Don Faults and up 'a mountain', lay the more modern pit of Silverwood. Downstream from Kilnhurst, and near the junction of the Don with the Dearne, lay Manvers, a cosmopolitan pit, possessing no village and drawing its workers from the Mexborough district. But Mexborough was also a railway town. A few miles up the railway track from Manvers lay Wath which was very much an old, solid pit village. North east of Manvers and Wath lay Barnborough. When Barnborough struck it tended to be 'all out', there were few of the small scale 'rag ups' of the other pits. Up the Dearne Valley lay Elsecar and Cortonwood. Elsecar, with its sister pit, New Stubbin, was an Earl Fitzwilliam pit characterised by a higher degree of paternalism. Cortonwood also tended to be quiet. Down the Don from Mexborough lay Denaby. To be sent to Denaby was to be sent to a ghetto. To have been born in Denaby and to work down the pit was to possess a fierce pride born out of the oral tradition of past militancy. A mile away lay Cadeby, Denaby's sister. Cadeby was different from Denaby; natural selection produced a slightly quieter pit.

The lack of cohesiveness of the Rotherham pits contrasted sharply with those north of the Woolley-Askern line. The big pits of the Castleford area achieved unity within their own panel but also dominated the pits to the west – in the North Barnsley area – and in the south – the Wakefield area. These pits tended to vote for the same candidates in Union elections, whereas the vote in South Yorkshire was fragmented. The West Yorkshire pits' control of the full-time posts in the Union also gave them an influence over the pits in the Barnsley area. Many of the pits in the northern area were small, closed-community pits in which mining was combined with smallholdings and miners worked on a 'cut and finish' basis – as soon as the coal was cut and filled they were allowed to go home.

The only area where there was a high degree of militancy and a high degree of social cohesiveness was the Doncaster area. What characterised the pits around Doncaster was the absence of the pit village. There were model housing estates but as pits were built in the age of motor transport there was a tendency to use Doncaster as the social centre, rather than to look inward to the social life of the pit village.

The high intensity of strike activity through 1954 and early 1955 gave rise to the possibility that a coalfield strike would develop and that it might be irrelevant where the leadership came from. It could, for example, have been given by Barnborough in January 1955. And even when Markham came out on strike there was a lag before the Doncaster Panel coalesced to give support. Once the strike started it tended to run away from the leadership.

These points need to be emphasised because there was a tendency to attribute the strike to the presence of communists and other extreme left-wingers. It is true that there was intense activity by the Communist Party in the Doncaster area in the middle fifties and there was an attempt to swing Yorkshire into the left-wing fold with Scotland and South Wales. But left-wingers were often viewed with suspicion especially when, as in the case of Jock Kane of Markham, president of the panel, they had gone over to the Board for a few years as industrial relations officers. There was also a strong Catholic influence in the area. What was important and most striking about the pits in the Doncaster area was how the strike created a magnificent cohesion in their panel and between the pits. The Doncaster miners came out together and went back together. And this solidarity was also to be exhibited in the 1961 strike when they were defeated.

The movement of the strike front, like earthquakes and epidemiological processes, was as much a product of geographical proximity to the Doncaster epicentre and individual pit susceptibility, as of direction by the Doncaster panel. The pits immediately affected were in the Rotherham and Barnsley areas and within those areas it was the pits which had had a record of many disputes in the previous six months. At its height the strike wave lapped around the West Yorkshire pits beyond Barnsley and towards Huddersfield, but did not penetrate very far into the Worksop area. At no time during the strike did the county officials or the Board concede recognition to the strike leaders despite their pleas for a hearing.

After the strike the union responded to organisational deficiencies by introducing area agents. Elections were held for the posts. There was a high turnout in West Yorkshire and a poor response in South Yorkshire where there was suspicion that the agents were the agents of the county officials. The area agents did not supplant the panels which represented a natural response to the existence of a vacuum in much the same manner as district councils had arisen in the National Union of Railwaymen in the inter-war years as a result of railway reorganisation. A more interesting result was the drastic changes in officials in both the union and the NCB at all levels from division and county down to pit and coalface. Another response was for the Board and the union to increase basic tonnage rates by about £2 per week in an attempt to counteract the effect of allowances. Finally, there was an attempt to improve the conciliation machinery. But the strike proved the potency of the strike weapon. Out of 301 price lists,

291 were revised following the strike. And strike activity persisted throughout 1955 and 1956, until the recession in 1957 caused a diminution in militancy.

THE WATER HAIGH/BRODSWORTH DISPUTES, 1961

Although the 1955 coalfield strike had highlighted the problems posed by wages systems in Yorkshire, progress in reforming price lists was slow. In effect, and by virtue of its size, Yorkshire was a microcosm of the industry's wages problems. There were enormous variations within and between pits in the levels of earnings and the composition of earnings. More importantly there were tremendous differences in that elusive phenomenon – effort. In 1961, the Deputy Director of Industrial Relations for the division reported that at some pits men were being paid 55s for 20 tons and at other pits men were being paid 70s for 8 or 9 tons. This report did not go unnoticed. Nor was the 'new' conciliation machinery working. The number of adjourned pit meetings rose from 400 in 1956 to 700 in 1958 and stayed around the 500 mark through 1959 and 1960. The union had failed to solve its organisational defects. The jurisdictions of the area agents did not coincide with those of the area general managers. The union allocated a fifth of its membership to each agent with the result that some agents spanned two Coal Board areas. Moreover, the ballots for agents revealed a lack of interest bordering on contempt. Finally, there was a new element in the situation – the fall in the demand for coal. At the Yorkshire area council meeting on 2 May 1960, there were numerous allegations of cuts in allowances. Subsequently, miners at Upton struck against wage reductions and eight pits came out in sympathy.

In 1966 the union and the Board entered into negotations to revise the wages structure. It was intended to raise wages where they fell below 60s per shift but to defer examination of those earning 65s or more. These proposals were attacked on the grounds that the proposals amounted to a 'wage freeze' at the high-wage pits. The Price List Sub-Committee's report revealed that there were 39 pits with 101 units earning less than 60s and 42 pits with 112 units earning 60s or more and 23 pits with earnings above and below 60s.

In August 1960 the Doncaster panel decided to press for a 65s fall-back rate plus a 10 per cent increase in allowances and that Brodsworth should submit the claim to the Disputes Committee.

Although the strike threat appeared to emanate from the Doncaster area, its first outburst came in February 1961 from Water Haigh in the Castleford area. The strike at Water Haigh took the union and the Board by surprise for it was one of the 39 pits where earnings were below 60s and productivity was high. Indeed, agreement on revisions had virtually been reached. However, Water Haigh intended to steal Doncaster's clothing and got the support of 8 pits in West Yorkshire plus Markham in the South. But there was no strong support. Meanwhile Brodsworth's claim failed and on 27 February the Doncaster panel called their 12 pits out on strike and brought 60 pits in their wake. The strike lasted until 13 March and ended with the defeat of the Doncaster panel.

The 1961 strike was a triumph for collective mediocrity. Bullough, Collingridge, Schofield and Ashman, the county officials, were average men possessed of fragile abilities. They came from the West Yorkshire, mainly from Glass Houghton, but they lacked the qualities of Glass Houghton's greatest collier – Herbert Smith. And they could not match Alwyn Machin, the Thorne collier, who was president of the Yorkshire area in the late fifties. But what they lacked individually they managed to acquire through collective action. Their decision to write a letter to each miner was a stroke of genius. It by-passed the constitutional machinery of the branches and appealed over the heads of the panel's members. The Doncaster policy was a right-wing, aristocratic policy and owed nothing to socialist principles, as was revealed by Bill Kellher, the Brodsworth delegate, during the course of the dispute. 'We have evidence,' he stated, 'that a Trotskyist movement is trying to jump on the bandwaggon and make political gain over this dispute over the price list.[1]

The area officials wrote to each miner and they called meetings with the members of all the panels except Doncaster, which they isolated. And their position was strengthened by the divisional Board, which refused to meet the strikers. At the end of the strike Jock Kane, Chairman of the Doncaster panel, stated that: 'The panel discussed all the issues involved in the strike after talks with officials from Barnsley. There was strong disappointment at what the officials had to offer and there was considerable discussion with the union leaders in which we impressed upon them the seriousness of the issues with which we are confronted.'[2]

In 1961 the higher-wage pits struck and lost. In 1970 and 1972 the high-wage pits of South Yorkshire were to lead national strikes which were to succeed. And from 1972 onwards the high-wage pits of South Yorkshire were to form the forcing house of union policy.

THE DISPUTES OF 1969–1974

The disputes of 1969–74 marked a significant phase in NUM decision-making. They comprised unofficial and official strikes, go-slows and overtime bans, and there was a shift, over time, from unofficial to official action as the leadership was propelled into taking control of a groundswell of militancy which threatened in 1969 and 1972 to engulf it. In 1972 the union called its first official strike since 1926 and it was a stoppage which matched the earlier one in importance. In 1974 the union called a strike which toppled a Conservative government and thereby obtained what seemed to be retribution for the defeat of 1926. The disputes of 1969–74 came at the end of a decade of contraction of the industry in which miners had experienced competition from oil, had to adapt to power loading and other organisational changes, and faced redundancy or transfer to other coalfields. In 1959 when Alfred Robens was made Chairman of the National Coal Board, there were rumours that the industry was to be decentralised and the coalfields were to be forced to compete against each other. Spencerism threatened to emerge and although there were denials the reorganisation of 1966 did seem to suggest a movement towards decentralisation – which the National Power Loading Agreement only partially allayed. There was, above all, a philosophy of *laisser faire* in successive Conservative governments which revealed itself in attempts to make nationalised industries stand on their own feet. It was against such a background that the disputes of 1969–74 made an impact on the thinking of governments and the public. What should be the appropriate policy for nationalised industries? What should be the public's attitude to picketing and secondary boycotts? Should strikers and their families receive social security benefits? Should the problems of low pay be corrected through collective bargaining or through fiscal policy? What criteria should be embodied in an incomes policy? When do industrial strikes become political strikes? What are the relative merits of piece and time-rates? What should be the appropriate organisational structures for the NUM and NCB? These were the questions brought for consideration by the events of 1969–74.

1969

In 1968 and 1969 coal stocks were still high despite a decade of run-down of the industry. Mining wages were low as compared with those in other industries and at the 1968 annual conference Sydney Schofield, the Yorkshire area president, said that low-paid workers were leaving the industry. Lawrence Daly, the Scottish area general secretary, reiterated some of the points made in his pamphlet, *The Miners and the Nation*, and suggested that miners might have to consider go-slows, like the railwaymen and the women workers at Fords, in order to get higher wages. But there were no obvious signs of militancy and Daly's remarks were construed as electoral ammunition in his campaign to succeed Paynter as general secretary. Though the conference proposed wages of £15 a week for surface workers and £16 a week for underground workers, the union accepted the Board's offer of £13 for surface workers and £14 for underground workers in the October. Later in 1968 Daly defeated Gormley for the post of general secretary.

The causes of discontent did, however, emerge in 1969. In Yorkshire there were problems over the payments to market men; that is, workers who did not have regular face jobs but who covered for absentees. In the Doncaster area market men were paid £4.20 a shift whereas at other pits they got £2.60 a shift. In the Doncaster area they were paid as if they were task-workers, but elsewhere they were paid as day-wage men. A request in February 1969 by the Yorkshire area NUM to have a coalfield ballot to strike over the wages of market men was however, deferred by the offer of an interim award pending agreement on the Third Day-Wage Structure which covered task-workers. The other coalfields were relatively quiet in the first half of the year and a ballot to determine whether the South Wales coalfield should strike over the closure of the Avon Colliery was decisively rejected by the rank and file.

What finally brought about the rise in militancy was a demand for a reduction in surfacemen's hours of work. In 1968 the NUM placed a claim for

1. an increase in the surface minimum weekly wage to £15 a week and £16 for underground workers;
2. an increase in the power-loading rate;
3. the introduction of a new wage structure for craftsmen and the reduction in the number of grades to two, skilled and semi-skilled, but allowing for differences in pay according to place of work;
4. a reduction in the hours of work of surfacemen to 40 hours *inclusive of meal times.*

A brief history of surfacemen's hours is set out in Table 6.1. The renewal of interest in hours reflected diverse attitudes and moods. Surfaceworkers' wages were low compared with those in other industries. They were low because the run-down of the industry had pressed particularly heavily on a group of workers, many of whom were disabled and elderly. Mechanisation had also displaced many faceworkers and forced them to take lower-paid surface jobs. Many of them were prepared to work overtime in order to boost their earnings. A reduction in hours could have increased earnings by about 25 per cent and cost the Board about £1m a year. There was also another side to the hours issue. A reduction in hours could be a means of spreading work and a safeguard against further falls in the demand for labour. Policies which have more than one possible effect have the attraction of appealing to a wide audience and the shorter hours campaign was such a policy.

Dissatisfied with delays over market men's wages, miners at Cadeby came out on strike on 16 September. The position of market men was particularly acute at Cadeby because the closure of Denaby in 1968 had resulted in a transfer of miners and swelled the numbers without a face job to 200. The Cadeby dispute was supported by other pits in the Rotherham area and might have spread to the neighbouring Barnsley and Doncaster pits but for the decision of the Doncaster panel to support the claim of the surface-workers and that of the Barnsley panel to support Doncaster. On 10 October the Yorkshire area council passed a

TABLE 6.1 Movement of Hours of Work, 1946–1969

1946	Miners' Charter: 40 hours exclusive of mealtimes. Prevailing hours were 48 exclusive of mealtimes with some local variations.
1947	Claim for $42\frac{1}{2}$ hours exclusive of mealtimes except for those whose hours were less and who should retain their shorter hours.
1953	A claim for mealtimes to be included when calculating hours was rejected.
1955	A claim for the inclusion of mealtimes was withdrawn in favour of amending the 5-day week bonus disqualification clause.
1957	Claim for 40 hours rejected by the National Reference Tribunal.
1959	Claim for 40 hours rejected by the NRT. The NRT reduced by one hour and, subsequently, the NCB reduced them by an extra quarter hour. Surfacemen's hours became $41\frac{1}{4}$ a week, $8\frac{1}{4}$ a shift. Underground hours became $7\frac{1}{4}$ a shift plus one winding time of about half an hour.
1961	Claim for 48 hours for surfacemen and 7-hour shift underground.
1962	Board offered 40 hours exclusive of mealtimes and 7 hours underground if output per manshift reached 34 cwt.
1963	Board offered 7 rest days in lieu of shorter working day. This was agreed and came into effect on 1 May 1964. The rest days were calculated to be equivalent to a 40-hour week and a 7-hour shift underground.
1968	Claim for shorter hours.
1969	NCB offer 40 exclusive of mealtimes.

strike resolution by 85 votes to 3. By 14 October all the Yorkshire pits were stopped and the pressure for strike action spread to other coalfields. In South Wales a resolution for strike action was defeated but it did not stop pits coming out on strike. On 17 October 100 pits were out in Yorkshire, South Wales, Scotland and the Midlands. The Coal Board Chairman, Lord Robens, made a revised wage offer and there were rumours that the Cabinet was considering the stoppage. But the following day the Board announced that they were not prepared to alter their offer of 40 hours exclusive of mealtimes and Lawrence Daly recommended acceptance.

The suggestion that the rank and file accept the Board's offer met with increasing hostility in some coalfields. In Derbyshire the area council passed a vote of no confidence in the leadership of the NUM, in Yorkshire there were demands for Ford and Daly to resign and in South Wales there was an unofficial strike conference. And while some pits, such as Betteshanger, returned to work, there were still 128 pits out on strike on 20 October. But the following day the National Executive recommended acceptance and, though the decision had still to be ratified by a coalfield ballot, there was a drift back. Lancashire area council decided by 28 votes to 2 to accept the Board's offer, and a call by South Wales delegates for a national strike failed to get a hearing. The Yorkshire area council voted by 80 votes to 8 to reject the offer, but a face-saving exercise whereby the TUC General Secretary, Vic Feather, agreed to come to Yorkshire to discuss grievances, enabled a return to work to take place.

The intensity, duration and extensive spread of the strike surprised the leadership and had its origins in many factors. The fundamental point was, however, made by Cliff True, a surface-worker of Fernhill Lodge, in South Wales: 'One over-riding factor in this dispute is the brainwashing of miners to accept pit closures. Morale among miners has reached rock bottom with everyone afraid of militancy in case their pit was closed. Now the men are realising that the pits will be closed whether they strike or not and we might as well get the best out of it while we can.' What was there to lose? Nothing. And much to gain, since wage increases could influence redundancy payments.

The strike revealed many weaknesses in the union's structure. The effect of the Board's reorganisation programme in 1966 had been to strengthen the powers of the area panels in Yorkshire and to weaken those of the county officials because there was no longer a divisional board. The situation was therefore different from 1963 when the divisional board stiffened the county officials in the unofficial strike. But elsewhere the organisation managed to retain some control. In most coalfields the relationship between NCB areas and county unions remained unchanged. The Nottinghamshire coalfield became divided into South and North Notts. areas but that did not have much effect on a traditionally peaceful coalfield. South Wales was split into two areas and the stoppages were confined to a few valleys in East Wales and never penetrated West Wales. In Scotland there was only a limited reponse. And South Wales and Scotland throw some light on the strength of tradition and the role of the Communist Party. The struggle to establish unionism in both coalfields resulted in strong resistance to unofficial strikes. But the fact that neither strongly supported the hours movement suggests that the communist leaderships were 'caught out' by the speed of events. The final comment must be reserved for the new General Secretary, Lawrence Daly. During the strike he was criticised for his lack of militancy and his reluctance to meet the unofficial strikers. In reply, Daly stated that the Yorkshire area did not request official strike action but indicated that unofficial action would continue until the Board conceded the full claim on hours. A request for official action would have meant a delay while a coalfield ballot was held. Furthermore, he argued that he was not a prisoner of the NEC, but he was bound by the union's rules and it was not customary for the general secretary to visit coalfields when there were unofficial disputes.

The fundamental question remains unanswered: why did the strike fail? There were many reasons why it might have succeeded. The real wages of miners had deteriorated, there were defects in the organisational structures of both the Board and the union. To answer the question, therefore, it is necessary to go back to the union's original claim. It consisted of two parts; a claim for an increase in wages and a claim for a reduction in the hours of surfaceworkers. Both claims had constitutional support, but the claim for shorter hours was also supported by unofficial strikes. What the Board did was to concede the wage increase in full but only offered to cut hours by 15 minutes. This offer split the union. There was nothing in the hours claim for the faceworkers, who dominate the union. In effect, the Board threw its weight behind the union leadership in much the same way as the Yorkshire divisional board had thrown its weight behind the county officials in 1961. The effect was to contain and roll up the strike front. But the policy had its dangers. To grant a wage increase in full was unprecedented. It suggested that there was more money available than the miners had anticipated. Next time the demand would be for more and even the moderates would be asking for more. The Board was to lose the war; it had mauled but not destroyed the Doncaster panel and in Yorkshire there had been an unprecedented official vote for strike action.

1970

1970 opened with proposals to introduce a Third Day Wage

Structure despite protests from Nottinghamshire and some concern at a possible connection between stagnant productivity and the Power Loading Agreement. In April a conference decision proposed a new claim of 38¾ hours, including meal breaks, for surfaceworkers, which the Board rejected. But the most important indication of a change in mood occurred at the annual conference in July when delegates defied the Executive and supported a South Wales resolution that there should be a national strike if the Board rejected the union's wage claim. The conference also passed a resolution that there should be a £5 increase in the minimum wages and the NPLA rate should be £30 a week. The claim, if conceded, would increase wages by about 30 per cent. On 16 September the Board made an offer which would have raised wages by 6 per cent for faceworkers and 17 per cent for surfaceworkers – an average increase of about 10 per cent, which compared favourably with the 7 per cent recently obtained by dockers. The meeting between the Executive and the Board was subjected to intense lobbying by miners from various coalfields. On 17 September the NEC rejected the offer and recommended strike action to members. On 26 September the Prime Minister, Edward Heath, was interviewed on Thames TV and indicated that the Government was prepared to face a general strike in order to reform industrial relations. A subsequent proposal for a two-year wage agreement was rejected as a gimmick.

The result of the coalfield ballot was announced on 24 October. It revealed a majority of 55.5 per cent in favour of strike action but the necessary two-thirds was not achieved. A breakdown of the voting figures revealed problems, tensions and conflicts within the NUM. On the one hand, the vote of the manual members was in favour of strike action by more than the necessary two-thirds and it was the white-collar vote of COSA members which swayed the total vote against strike action. Hence, there were comments that the union was dominated by petticoat government. On the other hand, within the manual vote the Midlands coalfields of Nottinghamshire, Leicestershire and South Derbyshire voted against a strike and Derbyshire only agreed by the narrow margin of 66 votes. On 28 October the Executive voted by 13 to 11 to accept the Board's offer.

The response to the ballot result and the Executive decision was a spate of strikes. There was a call for strike action in South Wales and the Scottish Area rejected the Executive decision. Pits in the Doncaster area came out on strike on 30 October despite an area council vote against strike action. By 3 November the unofficial strike had spread to South Wales (23 pits), Scotland (21 pits) and Yorkshire (25 pits). In Yorkshire the Doncaster panel held meetings with the other panels and on 5 November the Barnsley panel voted to join the strike. The following day there was a Scottish vote to join the strike and in Lancashire there was a proposal to hold an overtime ban. The peak of strike activity occurred around 10 November when 116 pits were out on strike – 42 out of 72 pits in Yorkshire, 21 out of 32 in Scotland, all 50 pits in South Wales, Pleasley in Derbyshire, Wolstanton in Staffordshire, 4 pits in Durham and all 3 pits in Kent. Thereafter, the strike front receded, with Daly pleading for a return to work and Robens denouncing the strike leaders as communists. The strike front collapsed between 14 and 19 November and the Doncaster panel recommended a return to work on 21 November. Subsequently, there was a pithead ballot on a revised offer of about 12 per cent, which was accepted by a 2 to 1 majority though there were majority votes against in Scotland, South Wales and Kent.

The second phase of strike activity revealed several differences from 1969. There was a shift towards militancy in the NUM leadership. The Executive recommended to the rank and file a vote for strike action and Daly emphasised the necessity of a two-thirds majority. But once the result of the ballot was revealed, there was an attempt to support the constitutional position. And this attempt to maintain the constitutional position was to have a decisive influence on Daly's thinking and attitudes. In 1969 he declared it was not customary for the general secretary to meet areas where there were unofficial strikes. In 1970 he visited Doncaster and was howled down when he attempted to address the strikers. This treatment shook him and forced him into increasing militancy in 1971 and 1972. The other important feature of 1970 was that South Wales and Scotland voted to strike and joined the unofficial strike action. The two most disciplined coalfields had now swung behind Doncaster. The third feature was the extent of militancy as revealed in the ballot figures and in the fact that pits in Durham and the Midlands joined the strike.

1971–2

1971 began with the retirement of Lord Robens as the Chairman of the National Coal Board and his replacement by Derek Ezra. The change meant that the leaderships of both the NCB and the NUM were comparatively new and inexperienced since Lawrence Daly had only been appointed General Secretary of the NUM in 1968 and Joe Gormley became President of the union in 1971. Thus there was the likelihood that the NUM would be testing Ezra's capabilities and there was also the possibility of mistakes because Gormley had fought Daly for the secretaryship in 1968. On the one hand, there was the new chairman of the Coal Board, who had been recruited from within the industry, a man who did not obviously possess the political skills of Robens but who did seem to fit more easily into the Conservative government's view that the nationalised industries should be run on commercial lines and should not be dependent on government subsidies. On the other hand, there was the political commitment to nationalisation of the new NUM leadership which, although differing in its interpretations of that commitment, did not readily accept commercialism which would jeopardise wages.

The second major event of 1971 was the Conservative government's Coal Industry Act. The previous Labour government had drafted a bill for the industry in the session 1969–70 but it fell when the Conservatives were elected in 1970. The Conservatives' Act differed from the Labour proposals in several important respects. First, it required the Coal Board to separate the accounts of its subsidiaries from those of colliery undertakings and allowed the minister to discontinue or restrict any non-commercial activities. Secondly, the minister could allow the Board's accumulated deficit to rise to £75 or £100 m. Thirdly, the Labour government's proposals to reimburse the NCB for any losses resulting from delaying colliery closures and to reimburse the electricity industry for burning excess coal were omitted. The purpose of the Act seemed clear although its detailed provisions might appear ambiguous. The Board was to become a commercial organisation. Unfortunately, the restrictions placed upon the Board's activities – the use of its computer facilities for hotel bookings, for example – meant that profits had to be made from coal production only. There was to be no hint of cross-subsidisation. The actual effects of the Act, however, were muted by the failure to implement the hiving-off proposals, and coal shortages reduced the pressure on the electricity industry to burn excess coal. There were also the later effects of the rise in oil prices. But even if the purpose of the Act was not translated into action, its symbolism served as a threat to the NUM.

The next major events occurred at the NUM annual conference. The problems created by the 1970 ballot led to resolutions to change the two-thirds rule. One resolution proposed that a simple majority rule be introduced. It failed to obtain the necessary two-thirds majority and conference passed a rule that a 55 per cent majority would be required in future ballots. Conference also passed a wages resolution which demanded:

1. a substantial increase in wages for all members and minima of £26, £28 and £35 a week for surface, underground and NPLA workers respectively;
2. renegotiation of all differentials and realistic measures of all job values;
3. in the event of an unsatisfactory response the NEC should consult the members with regard to various forms of industrial action.

On 20 July 1971 Lawrence Daly wrote to G. C. Shephard, the Board's member responsible for industrial relations, and outlined the union's wage claim:

1. a minimum wage of £26 for surface workers, £28 for underground workers and £35 for workers covered by the NPLA;
2. wider wage differentials because it was considered that they were now too narrow given the behaviour of prices;
3. the claim to be operative from 20 July 1971;
4. a more detailed claim would be submitted at the next joint national negotiating committee meeting.

On 22 July J. C. G. Milligan replied to Daly on behalf of Shephard and rejected the idea that the operative date could be decided in advance of a settlement. On 7 September Daly wrote to Shephard indicating the union's views on differentials. The union wanted the differential between craftsmen at the face and elsewhere underground reduced to 50p a shift and differentials in the Third Day-wage Structure reduced. The NUM also wanted a working party to be set up to review the industry's wages structures and job gradings.

The NUM's case for wage increases was presented at the JNNC meeting on 14 September. It was based upon changes in the cost of living which were not fully reflected in the official index. And the union also claimed an increase based upon prospective rises in prices as a result of entry into the Common Market and forthcoming rises in rail and bus fares. The claim for reduction in craftmen's differentials was due to pressure from the craftsmen, while the review of wages structures was deemed desirable because mechanisation and changes in methods of work had drastically altered job descriptions beyond the definitions laid down in the 1955 Day-wage Agreement. The case for the adult wage being granted at 18 years had been part of union policy for a long time and would help recruitment. The NUM also argued that the industry was in a sound economic position, productivity was rising and the union had cooperated with the Board in introducing changes. The Union pointed out that the existence of day-wage structures meant minimum rates now became maximum rates with no opportunities for raising wages locally and, often, few opportunities for overtime working. The union referred to wage increases in other industries and concluded by saying that the claim was on behalf of workers in the coalmining and coking industries.

On 12th October the Board replied to the NUM's claim:

1. The cost of narrowing differentials was estimated to be £14 million for craftsmen and £1 million for the Third Day Wage Structure. But the Board felt that since both wages structures had only been recently introduced it was too early to make changes.
2. There were no recruitment problems and therefore the payment of the adult wage was not a priority.
3. The NUM's full claim was estimated to cost about £20 million and could not be contemplated. The Board had only just broken even in the previous financial year.
4. The Board could probably find £25 million which might be used to give surface workers 9 per cent and underground workers 8 per cent but with 5 per cent to Kent and

Nottinghamshire and 6 per cent to Scotland and South Wales.

5. The Board welcomed the proposal to set up a working party on the wages structures and job gradings.

On the same day as the Board's reply, the *Daily Telegraph* reported Mr John Davies, the Minister for Trade and Industry, as saying that, although the Government had not interfered in the negotiations it had expressed its views on the claim. The NUM Executive rejected the Board's offer on the grounds that it was both 'shabby and insulting'. It took the view that if high wages meant higher prices then prices should be raised and the Board should ask the Government to improve the offer. The Executive proposed an overtime ban to commence on 1st November and a pit-head ballot on strike action.

Following the decision to call an overtime ban the NUM Executive laid down six guiding principles:

1. liaison committees were to be established to supervise the ban and to communicate with other unions:
2. no cover was to be provided for absentees except with the approval of the committees:
3. there was to be no production, transporting, bunkering or preparation of coal in overtime or mealtimes;
4. no overtime work was to be carried out unless it was for the safety of men or the preservation of the mine;
5. clerical workers were to work overtime only when it was to provide assistance to other members;
6. no weekly paid industrial staff were expected to work overtime.

NACODS were invited to attend liason committees but declined, stating that:

1. NACODS could not in any circumstances sit on any liaison committee even in an advisory capacity but would carry out the duties laid down by legislation;
2. NACODS would not do NUM work unless the safety of the mine was imparied;
3. NACODS would make every effort to carry out safety inspections.

An overtime ban was intended to start on 1 November, but as this was a Monday there was some confusion. At many pits the ban took effect on the Sunday evening. And in Nottinghamshire an overtime ban had operated at some pits since 2 August as a protest against the Third Day Wage Structure and the replacement of district autonomy by central control. The liaison committees were a new feature and there were difficulties in reconciling their decisions with those of management and branches. Restrictive practices crept in and in the Barnsley area winding-men were told their cars would be damaged and they would be attacked if they worked overtime to maintain safety regulations. In some areas, such as South Durham and Rotherham, there was a complete ban on overtime. At the Manvers coal preparation plant at Mexborough, near Rotherham, a complete ban on overtime caused considerable disruptions not merely at the plant, but also at the four pits which supplied it with coal. At some pits men refused to move machines to places of safety if it meant that coal had to be cut and there were refusals to repair belts in overtime. The significance of overtime working lay in the fact that, although work was no longer a cyclical process, jobs were still interdependent and because most shifts were production shifts there was a need for weekend work in order to carry out maintenance.

The effects of the overtime ban are a matter of debate and confusion. The elimination of overtime cut total hours by 3 per cent. The Board's deputy chairman, Sheppard, claimed that:

1. NCB stocks increased;
2. stocks held by coal users increased;
3. pits have been saved heavy stocking costs;
4. costs have been cut by the elimination of overtime.

on the other hand, Gormley stated: 'I am more than satisfied with the tremendous response to our appeal for an overtime ban. I realise that there have been one or two local difficulties, but in general the ban has been operated successfully. And it is, in my opinion, having a greater effect than the Board estimated or are willing to disclose'.

Nevertheless, 'the local difficulties' caused Daly to issue a circular on 10th November reminding members that: 'the objective is to curtail *production* outside the normal five shifts while preserving the future of the mine or plant, and the right of members to work a basic five day week.' On the same day there was no overtime worked at 20 of the 72 Yorkshire pits.

The drastic effects of the overtime ban caused the Board, in some areas, to send men home because there was no work for them. In North Derbyshire the loss of wages caused resentment and there were claims for the payment of the guaranteed wage. During the subsequent strike the NUM North Derbyshire Area stated that unless its members got their guaranteed pay they would continue the overtime ban after the strike ended.

The ballot on strike action was announced on 2 December and gave a 58.8 per cent majority to the NEC call for strike action if the situation warranted it. At the end of November coal stocks stood at 34 m tons: 11 m were at pit-head end, 23 m were in the hands of customers, of which power stations held 17.6 m tons – equivalent to about 10 weeks supply. The NEC recommended a strike to take place on 9 January 1972. The threat of strike action brought an improved offer from the Board. The Board also asked that the proposal be put to a pit-head ballot. Both the offer and proposal were rejected.

The decision to strike meant that instructions had to be sent to branches on strike behaviour and assurances had to be sought from other unions that picket lines would not be crossed. On 28 and 30 December Daly wrote to Area secretaries outlining the strike procedures:

1. pickets were to guard against infiltration by non-Union members;
2. only NUM strike literature was to be handed out;
3. all offers of help had to be carefully scrutinised; (the National Union of Seamen, National Union of Railwaymen, the Amalgamated Society of Locomotive Enginemen and Firemen, the Transport and General Workers Union and the Amalgamated Union of Engineers and Foundry Workers had offered assistance);
4. all picketing was to be peaceful;
5. the only men allowed to work were pumpsmen, winding men, fan attendants and telephone operators, though in emergency others would be allowed to work;
6. essential supplies were to be maintained to, for example, hospitals;

7. cokemen were to work to the minimum.

The reasons for the elaborate instructions lay in the criticisms of the behaviour of pickets in the strikes of 1969 and 1970 and the uncertainties arising from changes in the law. There were many adverse comments on the presence of non-union members in the picket lines and it was alleged that it was the undisciplined behaviour of students and members of extreme left-wing organisations that had led to many acts of hooliganism and violence. Furthermore, the new Industrial Relations Act was due to come into force on 31 January and there was uncertainty as to how the courts would interpret the sections on peaceful picketing.

On 5 January the Board made a final attempt to avert a strike and offered:

1. an increase of £2 per week for all adult day-wage men under the 1955 Day Wage Structure and £1.90 for all other adult workers with comparable increases for juveniles. All increases were to back-dated to 1 November.
2. Five extra individual holidays were to be introduced from 1 May.
3. There were proposals for productivity bonuses with (a) an interim scheme back-dated to 1 January 1972, if productivity between January and October 1972 was 3 cwt more than the same period in the previous year, and (b) discussions of long-term productivity schemes.

The offer was coupled with letters from Ezra and Sheppard to Gormley and Daly suggesting that if informal talks did not lead to satisfactory conclusions the Board would be willing to submit the dispute to the National Reference Tribunal on the grounds that the NRT had resolved differences in the past and that if there was a strike then the solution would be some form of arbitration. On the following day Daly replied: 'In line with many other Trade Unions in this country, the NUM no longer has any confidence that reference to an Arbitration Tribunal would secure an unbiased hearing. The Government's directions have undermined the whole principle of free negotiation.' Throughout the negotiations the Board had, of course, been constrained by the government's pay limit of 8 per cent although the cost of living had increased by 10 per cent over the year. Subsequently, the

Executive rejected the offer because the five extra holidays only gave miners parity with workers in other industries, whilst the wage offer was not appreciably different from that which the membership had already rejected.

The strike began on 9 January with the NUM leadership uncertain as to its outcome. Coal stocks stood at a record level of 17 m tons as a result of precautions taken by the government and consumers. The distribution of stocks was as shown in Table 6.2.

TABLE 6.2 Distribution of Stocks

	Million tons	*Weeks' supply*
NCB-held	6.63	–
Power stations	12.84	7.2
Gas works	0.05	2.3
Coke ovens	1.38	3.0
Industry	1.30	4.8
Domestic		
House coal	0.72	2.7
Anthracite	0.37	5.5
Other	0.27	–
Total distributed	16.94	

During the first week only 46 out of the 289 pits were following the instructions concerning pumpsmen, winding-men and other workers. A request to the TUC for a 'round table discussion' of support for the NUM by other unions met with a lukewarm response although the TUC did state that other unions had agreed that their members would not cross the picket lines. Commenting on the TUC decision Gormley said: 'I am extremely disappointed to know that they did not consider this serious enough to get together to form some concerted ideas. I would have thought that this was one time when the TUC could have shown itself to be united. I would not say we are on our own yet. I know some of the individual unions will react favourably, but it would have been better if action had been centralised'. The TUC's recommendation did, however, allow the NUM to disperse its pickets throughout the country to all major power stations, ports, coal depots and steelworks. But the government stood aloof and the impression was that the miners' strike would collapse in similar fashion to that of the postal workers in the previous year.

Everywhere there was a feeling that the miners would lose, go back to work for a slight increase in pay and then there would be more pit closures.

Throughout most of January the strike had little effect and it became apparent in the second week that power stations were conserving coal and burning extra oil; it was therefore decided to instruct pickets to disrupt the flow of oil. It was also in the second week that picketing started to produce violence. At Cadeby, in Yorkshire, officials were turned away on 17 January. On 16 January Ezra made a plea for an independent enquiry. There was a joint meeting with Vic Feather, General Secretary of the TUC, on 18 January and the following day the Minister of Labour, Robert Carr, considered intervening but then decided that the two sides were 'too far apart'. The popular press was, however, tending to side with the miners. On 14 January the *Daily Express* headline shouted: 'Give 'em the money Ezra' and the *Mirror* on 17 January demanded: 'End the bitter silence!'. At the end of the second week only 36 out of the 289 pits had safety cover.

In the third week the intensity of the violence on the picket lines increased. At Coal House, Doncaster area HQ, clerical workers were jostled, thumped and spat on by an estimated 700 pickets and similar incidents took place at area HQs in South Wales and Scotland. In the Rotherham area no officials were allowed into the pits. The third week witnessed clashes at pits in Yorkshire, Derbyshire and Nottinghamshire. At some of the pits the liaison committees lost control of the rank and file and at the end of the third week the Doncaster panel was attempting to give re-assurances that there would be no further violence. But in relation to the number of picket lines in operation the amount of violence was slight.

In the fourth week, which spanned the end of January and the beginning of February, the strike began to have some effect. The winter had been exceptionally mild but a sudden cold spell caused major power reductions and the closure of some firms. Both inside and outside the coalfields pickets were effectively blockading power stations and preventing not merely the entry of coal but also other essential supplies, such as oil and liquid hydrogen. By the fourth week industry was relying wholly on stocks held by users since the beginning of the strike. By 5 February the *Guardian* was urging that the miners be treated as a special case and the Coal Board Chairman Ezra announced on television: 'I think some third party will have to intervene. We would very much like an arbitration arrangement.'

On 8 and 9 February there took place the picketing and closure of the Saltley coal dump in the Midlands. 'Saltley' acquired significance because of the coverage by the press and television of scenes of mass picketing by miners and local factory workers. The Chief Constable of Birmingham closed the coal depot for reasons of safety. At the same time the Coal Board made a further desperate offer of £2.50 for surfaceworkers, to be raised to £3.00 in six months, and comparable increases for other grades. The NUM Executive rejected the offer and demanded a minimum wage increase of £6. The NUM reply shattered the Coal Board and left the government's incomes policy in shreds. The *Daily Telegraph* of 8 February summed up the government's dilemma: 'If the government takes emergency powers, troops and military vehicles could be used to get supplies to the power stations and to make sure that pickets keep their activities within the law. Action along these lines would enable the government to at least keep the situation under control, though it would not, of course, solve the problem'. On 8 February the government did declare a state of emergency and a three-day week was imposed on 11 February. During the following week 1.6 m workers were laid off work.

The position at the end of the first week of February was:

Miners on continuous picket duty	about 11,000 per day
Number of pickets arrested	48
Cost of strike to the NCB	£13m per week
Number of pickets injured	9 plus 1 killed
Stocks at power stations	3 weeks' supply without stock movements

It was against such a background that the Wilberforce Inquiry carried out its hearings.[3] The Court received evidence from inside and outside the industry. The Board drew attention to its commercial position and market prospects. During the sixties the industry had managed to achieve some stability largely by holding prices fairly constant. Productivity had risen by about 6 per cent per annum between 1961 and 1968, but since then the rate of productivity increase had started to flag. The recent upsurge of inflation threatened to destroy the Board's financial position. It was worried about being able to maintain its share of the markets in iron and steel and electricity. The Board did, however, believe that if its costs were kept within bounds then it could continue to make a substantial contribution to reducing the dependence upon imported oil.

TABLE 6.3 Possible Pattern of Fuel Supplies to Reduce Dependence on Imported Oil
(m tons coal equivalent)

	1971	*1980*
Total energy requirements	330	430
Nuclear/Hydro	12	40
North Sea gas	24	70
North Sea oil	–	80
Coal	140	140
Imported oil	154	100
Import dependence	47%	23%

The union pointed out that it had cooperated with the Board in introducing mechanisation and carrying out redundancies and yet miners' wages had still fallen below those in other industries. Although it had accepted time rates, the basic rates had not risen sufficiently to maintain earnings at a level comparable with what could be obtained elsewhere. And in the case of surfaceworkers there had been a dramatic fall in real incomes because inflation had carried their nominal incomes into the standard tax rate bracket while means-tested benefits had been withdrawn. Miners, the union argued, were no longer prepared to accept low wages in order to keep the industry viable. Furthermore, the industry should not be expected to finance interest payments on plant and equipment which had been abandoned. Such payments should be financed out of the proceeds of general taxation.

The Court recognised that there were two distinct elements in the miners' claim: one based upon the cost of living and which might, because of inflation, be fairly continuous and one based upon a once-and-for-all fundamental adjustment of miners' wages relative to those of other workers. The Court recommended that:

1. surfaceworkers' wages should be increased by £5 a week;[4]

2. elsewhere underground-workers should receive an additional £6 a week;
3. faceworkers should get an increase of £4.50 a week;
4. all increases to be backdated to 1 November 1971.

The Court did not make any recommendation on the payment of the adult wage at 18, but did suggest that the Board and the union should devise a productivity scheme. Its recommendations left many issues unresolved, such as:

1. the length of time over which miners should be allowed to pay rent arrears;
2. how holiday pay should be calculated as a result of the strike;
3. whether miners were entitled to guaranteed wages during the overtime ban;
4. what should be done about insurance contributions not paid during the strike.

The result was that the union did not accept the Wilberforce recommendations as final and, following further talks at Downing Street, obtained additional concessions:

1. men on personal rates to get the full wage increases;
2. corresponding increases to be granted to cokemen, weekly paid workers and canteen workers;
3. adult wage to be paid at 18 years of age from 1 November 1971;
4. five extra individual holidays;
5. a transport subsidy scheme;
6. consolidation of bonuses into shift payments;
7. rent arrears to be spread over a period.

A ballot on the complete proposals was carried out on 23 February and yielded a majority of over 96 per cent in favour of acceptance. Work was resumed on 28 February. The dispute had been the longest in the coal industry since 1926 and the first official dispute under nationalisation. The NUM attributed its success to:

1. the determination of its members, which had been fostered

by a decade of deterioration in their standard of living;
2. the support of other unions;
3. the picketing of the power stations.

1972–3

The question following the settlement of 1972 was why, in the next wage round, the NUM did not strike and force a further massive wage increase. The Annual Conference in July 1972 proposed a wage increase of 30 per cent leading to minimum wages of £30 a week for surfaceworkers, £32 for workers elsewhere underground and £40 for NPLA operators. And the Conference also insisted that if the Board failed to concede the claim then there should be a pit ballot to determine whether strike action should be taken to force the wage claim.

The Conference decisions placed the leadership in a difficult position because the union and the NCB were still discussing with the government the financial reconstruction of the industry. Financial reconstruction implied a government subsidy, and the amount of the subsidy might be influenced by the union wage. There were also discussions proceeding between the TUC, the CBI and the government on how to tackle inflation. Finally, the union's wages committee had not had time to assess the effects of the 1972 settlement on the rank and file. In the light of these unresolved problems the leadership decided in October to delay wage negotiations even though this was opposed by the left within the Executive. The decision, however, received support from a report of the wages committee in November which suggested the union should move away from the annual confrontation and towards a system of joint decision-making which would give local union officials some part in the determination of policies. The report envisaged a three-phase policy which saw the union and the Board involved in planning, investment, production and even the distribution of coal. Such a joint venture, the report argued, was the only way to increase real wages and would lead to the attainment of a four-day week but with four shifts in each day.

Towards the end of November informal talks began on the claim for increased wages, shorter hours, indexation for changes in the cost of living and alterations in craftmen's differentials. The case for a wage increase was argued on the fact that real wages had deteriorated since the Wilberforce settlement. In January the Board made an offer of £1 plus 4 per cent which was in line with Phase 2 of the government's incomes policy. The NUM negotiating committee unanimously agreed to reject the offer and South Wales demanded a national conference to back the claim. Subsequent discussions between Maurice Macmillan, Minister of Employment, and Derek Ezra brought the possibilities of some concessions on holidays. But these hopes were soon dispelled by the government's insistence on adherence to Phase 2 and the threat contained in the Counter-Inflation Act which outlawed strikes that broke the wage ceiling of £1 plus 4 per cent. The Minister for Industry, Tom Boardman, blocked any possibility of the third week's holiday which the union claimed. Gormley commented: 'We asked the minister to allow us to solve the dilemma in some way. The minister replied that he realised the difficulties but that any promise of a third week's holiday would be able to be valued in cash, and therefore would be outside the scope of Phase 2 and so could not be allowed.' A proposal by Derek Ezra that the Board and the union should agree in principle to a third week's holiday and then consider ways and means of achieving it was also rejected by the Minister who warned the Board against entering into long-range commitments.

The results of the pit-head ballot were announced on 3 April and revealed a 3 to 2 majority against strike action. It was a verdict which surprised the leadership and the militant wing of the union. The union then resumed negotiations on the basis of the Phase 2 offer which gave minimum rates of £25.29 to surfaceworkers, £27.29 to workers elsewhere underground and £36.29 to NPLA operators. The Scottish area, however, announced that it was going to put forward a resolution to the 1973 Conference claiming minimum rates of £30, £35 and £45 respectively.

The 1972–3 negotiations contained some unusual features. First, there was the long delay in taking up negotiations, for which we have found some explanations. Secondly, there was the apparent willingness of the Board to agree with the union's demands. Although the Board began by trying to maintain the phase 2 policy it quickly moved to a position of being willing to concede the third week's holiday despite it giving rise to benefits in excess of the government norm. It seemed as if the traumatic effects of the 1972 strike had pushed the Board into a placatory mood which left the onus of enforcing government policy upon the government. And the government was much more openly and obviously involved in the decision not to concede the third week's holiday. The Board had virtually surrendered to the government the right to negotiate. The third feature of the negotiations was the determination of the rank and file not to strike. In Yorkshire the militant vote dropped to 53.1 per cent as against 75 per cent in 1971. Gormley's explanation of the vote was that: 'Our members are aware of the political situation and the ballot vote has told us not to be involved in industrial action. Perhaps they thought we might be on our own fighting the government's policy . That's what democracy is all about.' And to the political sophistication of the rank and file could be added their instinctive industrial awareness of the costs of strike action. The strike would have had to take place in the summer months when the demand for coal was falling off and stocks were rising. It would have implied the loss of holidays with pay and absenteeism with pay. And while it was difficult to get the troops out two years running it was perhaps inconceivable that those who had been on strike in three consecutive years would relish a fourth encounter so quickly.

1973–4

The wage settlement of April 1973 was quickly followed by the July annual Conference and a decision to press for minimum wages of £35 for surfaceworkers, £40 for underground workers and £45 for coalface workers; that is increases ranging from £8 to £13 a week. The decision to press for an increase so quickly after the last settlement was influenced by the feeling that the Wilberforce settlement had resulted in the union's wages strategies being disturbed. In the negotiations of 1971–2 the union had been able to exploit the demand problems created by the winter months but in the negotiations of 1972–3 the rank and file found themselves having to consider the possibility of a spring or summer strike. Hence there was a feeling that if there had to be another 'Saltley' then it would be better to have it in the winter.

The wage claim, along with demands for shift allowances, holiday pay improvements, sick pay etc., was lodged on 12 September and was based on the deterioration in wages since Wilberforce and the severe voluntary wastage of manpower, particularly in Yorkshire and Nottinghamshire. The Board promised to reply around 10 October when it was thought that Phase 3 of the government's counter-inflation policy would be known. When Phase 3 was published it laid down the following guidelines for wage increases:

1. 7 per cent of average pay bill per head of group for preceding 12 months or £2.25 with a maximum of £350;
2. unsocial hours between 8.00 p.m. and 6.00 a.m. could be paid at a higher hourly rate;
3. 1 per cent could be devoted to holidays and sick pay schemes;
4. weekly hours could not be reduced to 40;
5. improvements in holidays would not count if they gave the equivalent of a third week;
6. efficiency schemes could be introduced and any resulting wage increases would be exempt from the structures of the first guideline;
7. threshold payments to cover changes in the cost of living were to lie outside the structures of the first guideline;
8. settlements were not to be made within a period less than twelve months after the previous settlement.

When the Board replied on 10 October it was obvious that the government's Phase 3 policy had been designed to give the miners a generous wage increase while containing the demands of other unions. The Board offered increases of £2.25 for surfaceworkers and £2.30 for underground workers. In addition, there was an offer to raise the hourly payment for unsocial hours from 2½p to 17p and to raise holiday pay although not to the NPLA rate. The Board's offer averaged about 13 per cent. The Executive rejected the offer and asked for a meeting with the Prime Minister, Edward Heath. Support for the rejection came from the normally moderate Nottinghamshire Area on 18 October. But the NUM president, Gormley, warned his members that a strike could help the Prime Minister in a general election—a warning that earned him a rebuke from the Scottish area.

On the 23 October the NUM negotiators met the Prime Minister but he indicated that the government was not prepared to regard the miners as a special case lying outside Phase 3. Heath's reply summed up the weaknesses of his strategy for dealing with the miners. Conscious that they were capable of wrecking any incomes policy, Heath realised that the miners would have would have to be treated as a special case and in July he had allowed secret negotiations to take place between Sir William Armstrong, then head of the Civil Service, and Joe Gormley, president of the NUM. Heath and Armstrong seem to have got from Gormley an assurance that if the Phase 3 limits included an allowance for unsocial hours which enabled the miners to get a bigger increase than anybody else then the miners would settle within the limits. The plan failed because the government and the Coal Board put their final offer into the initial offer. They failed to realise that in bargaining it is expected that there will be an improved offer at a later stage and that the final offer should have come in dramatic fashion when the NUM negotiators met the Prime Minister at Downing Street. To the NUM the offer appeared so good as to suggest that the Board could give more, and more had to be given because food prices had risen sharply by October.

A special delegate conference was held on 25 October and an overtime ban was proposed. Discussions were also held with NACODS and BACM about safety. Unofficial overtime bans were staged at some pits in Yorkshire, Warwickshire and Staffordshire on 6 November and these seemed to have stimulated a revised offer of £2.30 for surfaceworkers and £2.57 for underground workers. The Board conceded the case for a national productivity scheme instead of a pit productivity scheme. But the offer was rejected and the NUM's determination to get more received a boost from the Arab oil embargo. Despite a plea by Tom Boardman, the industry minister, for the NUM to ballot its members on the revised offer, the overtime ban began on 12 November. A further revised offer was made on 15 November which offered the adult wage at 18 years and £5.70 per day for the 19 holidays other than the two weeks normal holidays. In addition, the Board indicated that it was prepared to consider a sick pay scheme once Phase 3 was over. The offer was rejected by the Executive which objected to a redistribution of the total wage bill in an attempt to 'pack out the day wage'. The government, however, appeared to be opposed to further concessions and on 22 November the Prime Minister appealed to the miners 'not to oppose the will of the people'. This theme was subsequently taken up by other ministers, notably Robert Carr, who said there would be no surrender.

So far the Opposition had confined its opinions to behind-the-scenes discussions and general statements of support for the miners. On 27 November Harold Wilson made an attempt at constructive intervention by suggesting that the time taken for clocking-in and clocking-out should be paid for. (Later, the Coal Board was to argue that the time involved would only yield about 25 minutes of overtime pay.) The intervention did have the effect of prompting an offer of further negotiations provided other unions did not jump on the bandwaggon.

At the turn of the year it was still not clear what would be the outcome of the dispute. The overtime ban had been in operation and from the beginning of December there had been a tightening-up in its severity as miners in some coalfields operated a go-slow in normal hours. But despite the fall in output the economy seemed to be surviving as a result of the restrictions on the use of fuels which had been put into operation since the beginning of the overtime ban and the introduction of short-time working after Christmas.

On 9 January, 1974, the union's negotiators met the Secretary of State for Employment, William Whitelaw. He admitted that there had been mistakes in running down the industry and placing too much reliance on oil and he accepted the view that an election would not solve any problems. But he felt that Phase 3 was sufficiently flexible to accommodate the claims of the miners and in the best interests of the country. If Phase 3 was broken by the miners then it would be broken by all the unions. He believed that there should be discussions of the industry's future and that pneumoconiosis claims and other pensions issues might be considered to be outside the orbit of Phase 3. The union's negotiators, however, insisted that Phase 3 must be broken.

The turning point in the dispute came around 16 January with statements by government ministers and the chairman of the Central Electricity Generating Board that stocks of coal were sufficient to see the economy through to the summer. On 17 January, Lord Carrington, the Energy Minister, announced that discussions would take place to move to a four-day week. It is not clear why these announcements were made. The government may have been hoping to convince the NUM that resistance to the Phase 3 policy was futile. And it could have been putting the ball firmly into the NUM's court by indicating that any strike action would be as a result of the union's intransigence and would allow the government to take sterner measures. Yet, by stating that stocks were ample, the government laid itself open to the charge that the emergency measures had been panic measures. And, in the upshot, the effect of the government's statements was to push the NUM negotiators into recommending a strike. As Gormley put it, 'the overtime ban is not having the effect we thought it would have in the early stages. This can be supported by the coal stock figures quoted by Lord Carrington last week. I feel that we have to be more positive if we are to succeed.' The ballot for strike action took place on 31 January and 1 February and yielded an 81 per cent majority in favour of strike action.

On 5 February the union gave notice of a strike: 'That unless a satisfactory offer was received all members of the NUM who were subject to NUM agreement, with the exception of rescue brigademen, would be on official strike as from 9 February 1974.' The NEC also outlined its policy for the direction of the strike:

1. routine safety work would not be undertaken but BACM members should be permitted to carry out inspections and take remedial action;
2. the present emergency committee would be disbanded and authority for conducting the strike was to be vested in the Finance and General Purposes Committee;
3. liaison committee would not be established at pit level but there would be Area Liaison Committees;
4. in the event of emergencies the Area Liaison Committees were to take action after consultation with the National Committee;
5. priorities for coal distribution were to be established;
6. a National Strike Fund was to be set up.

Following the declaration of strike action NACODS indicated that their members would present themselves for work in order to carry out inspections.

There was a last-minute attempt to avert a strike by referring the dispute to the Pay Board. The Pay Board, a successor to the National Board for Prices and Incomes and the Office of Manpower Economics, published a report on wage relativities on 24 January. At first the government demurred from referring the dispute but at the end of January finally consented to a submission. But the miners still refused to call off the strike. And when, on 7 February, the government announced that a general election would be held on 28 February the NUM still decided to go ahead with the strike on the grounds that it was not politically motivated and a return to work might weaken any chances of getting an advantageous settlement. But the NEC did agree to give evidence.

The Coal Board, in its evidence, supported the views expressed by the NUM and concluded: 'it is clear that the relative importance of coal-mining to the United Kingdom economy has increased and that it will continue to hold new importance in the future . . . Because of this it is the Board's view that corresponding improvements in the wages and conditions of service of the work-force are vital so that the challenge of this new role can be met successfully'. And in support of this view the Board argued that recognition should be given to the physical and psychological aspects of mining; the special skills of mining and the need to improve wages. The Board also pleaded for the restoration of the National Reference Tribunal and the introduction of local productivity schemes.

In its report the Pay Board followed the lines of the evidence it had received.[5] Coalmining was a special case, wages should be increased to improve the manpower situation and those who worked underground should be adequately compensated. The Pay Board suggested that in addition to the Coal Board's original offer there should be a special allowance of £1.20 a shift to underground workers and that there should be a re-adjustment of internal relativities.

But the Pay Board's report did not prove to play such an important part in the final settlement. The general election brought a Labour government to power and the new Secretary of Employment allowed the NCB and the NUM to renegotiate freely without reference to the Pay Board's report. The final settlement resulted in new minimum rates of £31 a week for surfaceworkers, £36 a week for underground workers and £45 a week for faceworkers. In addition, there was to be a 19p an hour premium for unsocial hours, increased holiday pay, increased lump payments to those who voluntarily retired from the industry, and improved death benefits.

The 1974 confrontation ended a period of bitter dispute. In 1975 and 1976 the NUM complied with the Labour government's incomes policies. In 1975 it accepted the £6 limit even though this implied a reduction in real wages and a deterioration in the miners' relative wage. In 1976 the union accepted the Chancellor's proposals for linking wage increases to tax changes. But the acceptance of the 1976 proposals was only carried by virtue of the white-collar vote within the union; the manual vote was strongly against acceptance of an incomes policy and even within the quiet areas, such as Nottinghamshire, there was a noticeable hardening of attitudes. Nottinghamshire has, in fact, become more militant. From 1955 onwards it acquiesced in the erosion of its advantages over other coalfields but the strikes of 1972 and 1974 seem to have caused an awakening to the effect of the losses. In 1976 it led the campaign for early retirement, and in 1977 it led the campaign for large wage increases and, with Yorkshire and Derbyshire, opposed the proposals for a national concessionary coal scheme which would have meant a redistribution to other coalfields.

LESSONS AND PROBLEMS OF THE BIG STRIKES

The big strikes raise many issues, both academic and practical, which are of general interest.

UNION BALLOTS

An assumption of much middle-class thinking in the post-war period has been that unions are undemocratic. Goldstein's study of voting behaviour in one branch of the Transport and General Workers' Union had revealed a few left-wing zealots sitting around a table, armed with many coloured pencils, marking the voting slips of absent brothers.[6] This view was not disturbed by Allen's assertions that unions must be democratic because they are voluntary societies, since that thesis ignored the importance of the closed shop.[7] The ETU trial seemed to confirm the belief that unions were undemocratic and both the Conservative and Labour government's industrial relations legislative measures were based on a belief that unions had to be made more democratic.[8]

In the light of the background beliefs it is not surprising that attempts should have been made to suggest that decision-making within the NUM was undemocratic. In his autobiography, *Ten*

Year Stint, Lord Robens applied the popular view of unionism to the 1970 strike ballot.[9] According to Lord Robens, about 83 per cent of the membership voted despite the fact that 21 per cent of the membership were absent from work. In Scotland, he alleged, there was an excess vote of 14 per cent, in Wales an excess of 13 per cent and for the country as a whole an excess of 8 per cent. Union ballots are not, of course, conducted according to the principles laid down for political elections, but in the NUM the voter usually has sufficient privacy to register his vote. During the 1970 ballot there were no obvious signs of malpractice in South Wales. At Garw and Coegnant the ballots were held at the baths and were secret. The view that only those who are at work should be allowed to vote would be a principle which would be restrictive, if not undemocratic.

The 1970 ballot is also interesting because the detailed branch votes published in *The Miner* (November 1970) throw some light upon the question; if everyone turns up to vote will the ballot result be non-militant? The correlation coefficient for all branches between the size of the militant vote and the total vote cast was positive, 0.360. The white-collar vote of COSA members was, however, negative, −0.220, so perhaps the middle-class view of trade unionists applies only to middle-class trade unionists.

LIFE ON STRIKE

Despite the welfare state and the provision of financial assistance to the families of miners, most strikers experienced considerable hardship. Some, of course, had wives working, but even they got into difficulties if they had mortgage commitments. For many it was an encounter with the hardships experienced by their parents in 1926. Savings were run down and debts were run up, old recipes were revived. Picking coal on spoil heaps became a flourishing industry in some coalfields and many sought odd jobs – although these activities were constrained by the need to man picket-lines. For many it was an exhilarating experience which united families and taught the new post-war generations of miners what it meant to be a miner. In the light of the ways in which most miners and their families managed to sustain themselves the various proposals to refuse social security benefits to miners' families seem irrelevant. In all probability such a step would have intensified the struggle and made a settlement difficult. It would have merely transferred the problems of poverty and vagrancy to the local authorities which were often controlled by the miners. And, as the Conservative government discovered during the disputes, social security benefits to strikers in other countries, particularly in the EEC, were more generous than in Britain – a discovery which the Cabinet hurriedly suppressed.

BARGAINING AND STRIKE THEORY

The strikes of 1972 and 1974 seem at first sight to destroy the economic theory of bargaining and strikes as presented by, for example, Hicks and Ashenfelter and Johnson.[10] According to the theory the union's wage claim should fall the longer the strike proceeds; in both the big strikes the reverse happened: the NUM's demands rose. Has the theory, therefore, been refuted? Must we accept Shackle's criticism of Hicks's theory?[11] The simple answer is no. But acceptance of the theory and the events of the strikes does emphasise the limitations of the theory.

The essential features of the Hicks/Ashenfelter–Johnson theory of strikes can be appreciated from an understanding of Figure 6.1. It is assumed that a firm is attempting to maximise the present value of its future earnings stream and that there is a trade-off between wages and strikes such that a long strike can be avoided by paying a high wage and a low wage can only be paid after a severe strike. Hence there will be a set of indifference curves between wages and strikes, each curve of which will denote a different net present value (Figure 6.1a). Ashenfelter and Johnson assume that in the case of the union a strike is a means of reconciling rank-and-file aspirations with what the employer is prepared to pay; that is, they assume that the union is similar to that portrayed by Ross rather than the simple wage-maximising model of Dunlop. Hicks did not enquire deeply into the behaviour of the union. In Hicks's analysis the strike arises because of irrational behaviour and in Ashenfelter and Johnson's theory the irrational behaviour stems from the clash between the leadership, who know what the employer might pay and the rank and file, who assert what the employer should pay. Both groups of theorists assume that the union makes an initial claim and that its demand falls as the length of the strike proceeds; there is a

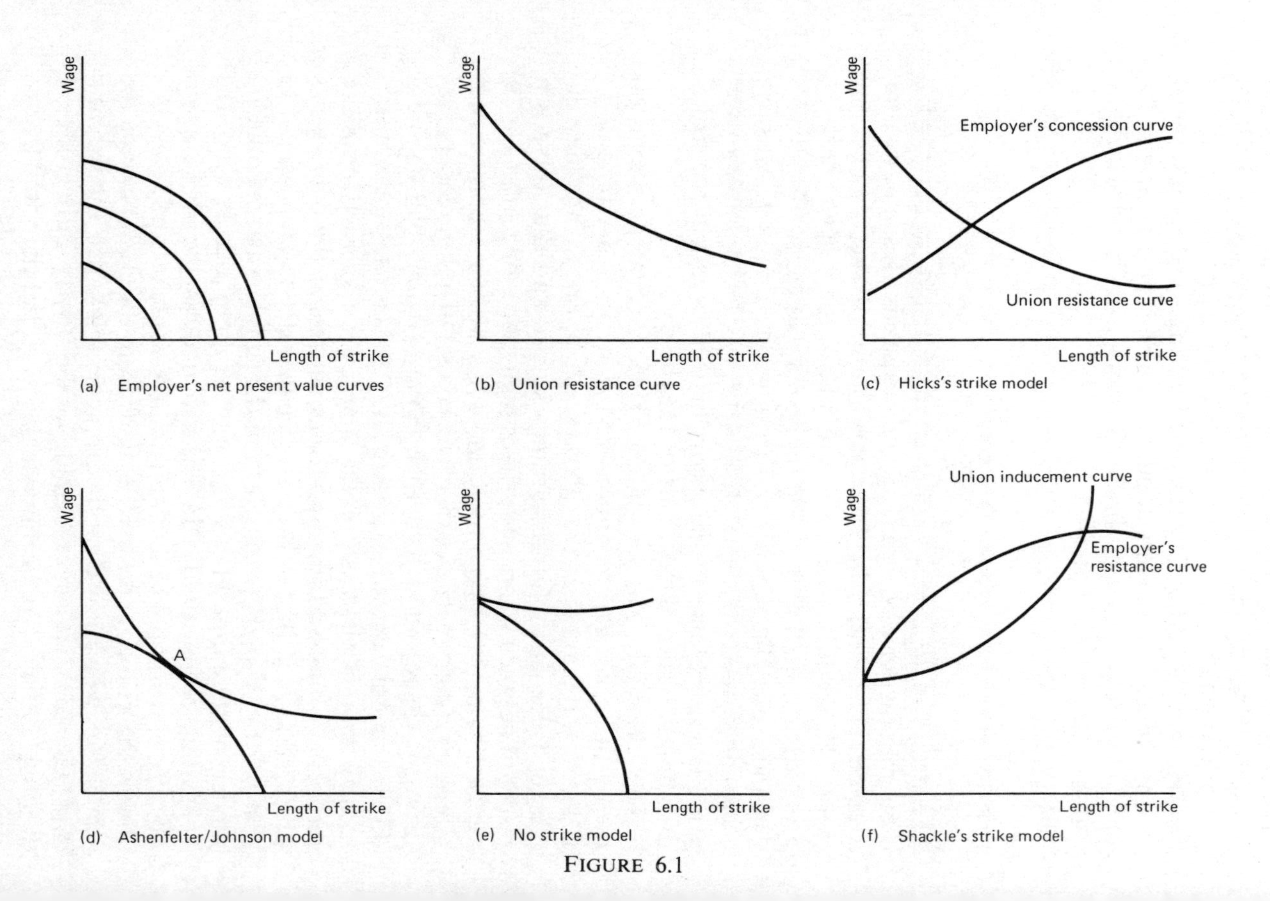
Wage
Length of strike
(a) Employer's net present value curves
Wage
Length of strike
(b) Union resistance curve
Wage
Employer's concession curve
Union resistance curve
Length of strike
(c) Hicks's strike model
Wage
A
Length of strike
(d) Ashenfelter/Johnson model
Wage
Length of strike
(e) No strike model
Wage
Union inducement curve
Employer's
resistance curve
Length of strike
(f) Shackle's strike model

FIGURE 6.1

negatively sloped *union resistance curve* which, if there is no conflict between the leadership and the rank and file as in Dunlop's union monopoly model, may be regarded as the locus of a set of a union net present value curves. And in similar fashion it is possible to trace out an *employer's concession curve* which would cut through the firm's net present value curves. In Hicks's analysis the Pareto optimal solution to the simultaneous determination of the wage and length of strike is given by the intersection of the resistance and concession curves as in Figure 6.1(c). In Ashenfelter and Johnson's analysis the solution is given by the tangency of the present value curve and the resistance curve as in 6.1(d) if there is a strike and as in 6.1(e) if there is no strike.

Now the objection to this theory – and it was first voiced by Shackle – is that it assumes too readily that the union's resistance curve has a negative slope. But during the strikes of 1972 and 1974 the resistance curve appeared to slope upwards or jump to the right. Shackle argued that if union members are asked to contemplate a big strike then they would hope to get a large wage increase. Hence, the union's resistance curve would slope upwards, as in 6.1(f), and cut the employer's concession curve from below; the slope of the curve would increase from left to right because the marginal disutility of the strike would be increasing and the marginal utility of the wage would be decreasing. Hicks accepted Shackle's criticism, but took the view that his model assumed that union negotiators had some idea of what the employer's concession curve looked like. He assumed that a period of bargaining had elapsed and that the capital market had provided information on the employer's concession curve. Hence, the strike was irrational.

The theory, therefore, provides limited assistance in understanding the miners' strikes. There was no capital market to provide information about the financial position of the Coal Board; the limit to wage increases seemed to be the taxable capacity of the community and that was not crystallised until the strike was under way. Furthermore, the concession curve did not stay constant. In 1972 it shifted as a result of the rise in oil prices. In 1974 it shifted because the Board's initial offer, which was intended to be its final offer, was construed by Gormley as an opening gambit which suggested the possibility of an even bigger final offer. Similarly, the analysis provides only limited assistance in understanding the behaviour of firms in the private sector, such as sales maximisers and Galbraith's giant corporations. Indeed, it is curious that Ashenfelter and Johnson do not extend to the firm the idea of a clash between managers and shareholders which would parallel the clash between union leaders and their rank-and-file members. Nor do the models accurately capture those situations of stagflation – where wage and price changes lag behind changes in output and employment – so that strikes coincide with falling employment, as in the period 1969 to 1975.

PICKETING

The strikes of 1969 to 1974 gave rise to problems of picketing. They arose in three geographical contexts and involved issues of inter-union cooperation and conflict. The first group took place at pit level and concerned the rights of access to mines of some members of the NUM, such as winding-men and pumpsmen, and members of NACODS and BACM. The second group comprised clashes with members of APEX and took place usually at area level. The third group involved members of unions, such as the T & G, and non-union lorry drivers attempting to gain access to coke depots, power stations and docks with coal, oil and liquid hydrogen.

Although the examples in Table 6.4 are from newspaper reports and may contain bias through lack of reporting, there is a distinct impression of an absence of picketing problems in some coal-fields. Scotland and South Wales (except at area level), Lancashire and Staffordshire seem to be relatively quiet. In contrast there is a great deal of turbulence at pit level in Yorkshire, Derbyshire and Nottinghamshire.

Peaceful picketing was legalised by the Trades Disputes Act, 1906. Section 2 of that Act specified that picketing was lawful: 'merely for the purpose of peacefully obtaining or communicating information or of peacefully persuading any person to work or to abstain from working'. But the Act did not legalise trespass, nuisance, obstruction or other offences which are virtually inseparable from effective picketing. It was these activities which were the subject of much discussion during the disputes. In some instances pickets were fined and in one case a picket was killed by a lorry which refused to stop. There were also situations, such as at Saltley, where the sheer numbers of pickets could have been

TABLE 6.4 Examples of Violence in Picketing, 1972

Pit level (clashes with officials and police)		
17 Jan	Cadeby	(Yorkshire)
19 "	Calverton	(Nottinghamshire)
20 "	Gedling	(Notts)
21 "	Gedling	(Notts)
25 "	Lynemouth	(Durham)
26 "	Ellington	(Durham)
	Donisthorpe	(Leicester)
31 "	Clipstone	(Notts)
1 Feb	Rockingham	(Yorks)
	Renishaw	(Derbyshire)
	Ireland	(Derbyshire)
	Penrikyber	(South Wales)
	Bevercotes	(Notts)
3 "	Kilnhurst	
	Cadeby	(Yorks)
8 "	Cortonwood	(Yorks)
9 "	Brookhouse	(Yorks)
10 "	Manton	(Yorks)
11 "	Manvers	(Yorks)
Area level (clashes with members of APEX and police)		
20 Jan	Doncaster	
21 "	Doncaster	
	Tondu (E. Wales)	
25 "	North Durham	
Coke depots and power stations (clashes with lorry drivers and police)		
4 Feb	Longannett	(Scotland)
9 "	Saltley	(Birmingham)

construed as intimidation and obstruction but it is doubtful whether the police could have arrested all those who took part or that the government would have called out the militia to shoot over the heads of the pickets. The problems were aggravated by the existence of secondary boycotts of oil and liquid hydrogen. It would have been possible for the CEGB to have sued for inducement breach of contract, but such an action might have aggravated the strikes. Moreover, by one of those ironies of decision-making the NUM could have legalised its picketing by registering under the 1971 Industrial Relations Act; in order to maintain the Post Office's monopoly of carrying mail the Act allowed unions to picket other agencies which carried goods during disputes.

The law was not extensively used during the miners' disputes, not because it was not available but because the injured parties chose not to use it. It was, of course, possible that changes in the law to allow pickets to stop vehicles in order to make the drivers aware of the issues involved in the miners' disputes might have reduced some of the conflict but it is doubtful whether it would have persuaded the miners that they should not prevent the movement of coal. The law could have been used only if public opinion was prepared to support its use and in the miners' disputes there was no evidence that the government enjoyed widespread support in its policy.

WHY THE GOVERNMENT LOST

At first sight it is not obvious why the government lost in 1972 and 1974. Allusions to a miners' revenge for the defeat in 1926 might satisfy left-wing historiography but there were no portents for such a view in 1971. Coal was no longer the important source of energy that it was in 1926 and oil and gas were still making inroads into coal's markets, even into the sheltered market of electricity.

There were, however, significant features of the seventies which favoured the miners. Although coal was no longer so important, its uses were concentrated in vulnerable situations. In 1926 coal stocks were widely dispersed; every household had a cellar full of coal. In 1972 stocks of coal were concentrated at fewer points – coke depots and power stations and at pit heads. This reduction in the number of points which had to be controlled becomes important when the shift in strike strategy is noted. In 1926 the miners stayed in the coalfields whereas in 1972 and 1974 they came out of the pit villages and picketed ports, power stations, coke depots and urban manufacturing areas. In doing so the miners effectively controlled supplies and communicated the nature of their grievances to other workers.

In the seventies the miners were supported by public opinion. Memories of 1926 seemed to awaken feelings of guilt. In 1972, 57 per cent of a Gallup Opinion Poll expressed sympathy with the miners while 45 per cent said their opinion of the Prime Minister had gone down as a result of his manner of handling the dispute. And even in 1973 and 1974 the percentage of miners' sympathisers remained high; in December 1973 it was 41 per cent and in February 1974 it was 52 per cent. This volume of approval remained high despite strong disapproval of the miners' picketing tactics.

Public opinion reflected the failure of the government to pursue a coherent case. Within the government the hawks favoured standing up to the miners in order to defend incomes policies. Yet it was not clear throughout 1969 and 1970 that the miners' claims constituted aggression as much as embittered defence. And a more sensible policy might have been to allow miners' wages to rise to a level which would have restored parity with other industries and to have also allowed the price of coal to rise.

The weaknesses of the government's position stemmed from a lack of clear policies about incomes, the mobility of labour and the control of inflation. Throughout the sixties the policy had been one of attempting to have an orderly run-down of the mining industry by letting the labour force fall gradually and at the same time keeping the costs of employment low by holding down wages. Unfortunately, wage restraint did not force workers out of the industry at a fast rate but, instead, it impoverished workers. Furthermore, there was no active manpower policy which would have attracted workers into other industries. This lack of a policy about the allocation of labour led to a long drawn-out contraction of the industry which created bitterness. When the government failed to control the rate of inflation the situation was exacerbated.

The government had also no clear understanding of the effects of the reorganisation of the industry in 1966. The abolition of the divisions removed concentrations of power in the hands of a few divisional chairmen and permitted the Board to confront numerous area managers. But, at the same time, it reduced the effectiveness of the NUM's area officials because they could not rely upon support from a coordinated NCB at coalfield level. The wages reorganisation also reduced the importance of local management and could be considered to have been in the NUM's interests because it suggested that wages were not to be used as a means of ensuring competitive efficiency between the coalfields. But, although Spencerism appeared to have been banished, the reorganisation of wages increased the potential power of the National Executive, and by the process of redistributing income from the high-wage to the low-wage coalfields meant that discontent would be channelled into a national confrontation rather than a few local disputes.

SUMMARY

The major strikes in the coal industry have stemmed, in the main, from failures in communication and in the institutions through which communications were conveyed. This point of view finds support in 1947 and 1969 when the effects of national decisions upon local custom and practice were not anticipated. However, in 1955, 1961 and 1972–4 it is possible to take an alternative view that strikes were to be expected given management's decisions about wage policy. The strikes of 1972 and 1974, however, seem to be most ably summarised by Edmund Burke's observations on the American colonial revolt of 1776.

> 'Through a wise and salutary neglect, a generous nature has been suffered to make her own way to perfection'.
>
> (*On Conciliation with America*)

7 A Postscript and Some Conclusions

In November 1977 the miners rejected a proposal for a productivity bonus scheme by 55.75 per cent to 44.25 per cent. The scheme would have led to the establishment of norms by method study for coalfaces and the incentive bonus would have been based on individual faces or the average for all faces in a pit. Haulage and surfaceworkers would have received their bonuses on the basis of productivity in their pits and workers at workshops, area and national levels would have obtained a bonus based upon the appropriate geographical unit. Following the ballot Joe Gormley, the NUM president, announced that he would never again attempt to introduce a national productivity bonus scheme. In December, however, the NEC voted to allow Areas to introduce schemes. The NEC decision caused considerable furore and controversy because it seemed to flaunt the verdict of the pit-head ballot. The militant coalfields of Kent, South Wales, Scotland and Yorkshire attempted to obtain an injunction restraining the NEC but it failed. Through December 1977 and January 1978 the various coalfields voted to accept productivity schemes. Despite their massive votes against bonuses Yorkshire, Scotland and South Wales succumbed to internal pressures from workers at highly productive pits and to the pressure of comparisons with the benefits being received by miners in neighbouring coalfields. The *volte face* of December 1977 represented a triumph for the right wing and created considerably disunity within the NUM.

The events which led up to the decision to introduce piece-work were as follows. The Wilberforce Court of Inquiry recommended that the NCB and the NUM consider methods for increasing productivity. Following the 1974 dispute and in the light of the rise in oil prices, the reports of the Coal Industry Examination Committee suggested that an incentive scheme be introduced. The Board and the NUM introduced a scheme based upon the total output for the whole industry but it proved a failure because the bonus was seldom achieved. When the Early Retirement Agreement was introduced in 1977 and NUM agreed to do all it could to minimise the effects of any fall in manpower. Finally, the Government's White Paper, *The Attack on Inflation after 31st July 1977* permitted self-financing productivity schemes to be introduced at any date after 31 July 1977.

From the point of view of the Board the industry had been on a productivity plateau for several years. Despite increased mechanisation there was a very slow rate of increase of productivity on haulage systems and this acted as a brake upon the effect which improvements in face productivity could achieve. British pits tended to be small and had antiquated underground layouts as compared with their German and Polish counterparts. Indeed productivity showed a tendency to increase when pits were closed which suggested that it was the poor haulage and surface installations of the smaller and older pits which held back productivity advance. Some improvement might be expected to come from a switch to retreat mining and through an increase in the number of drift mines but these were the only immediate and foreseeable technical changes. The main increase in productivity had to come through the more efficient use of manpower.

The National Power Loading Agreement was supposed to permit greater mobility of labour but a striking feature of the years after 1966 was the increase in the number of stoppages over methods of working. Some increase in strikes might be attributed to the euphoria following the victories of 1972 and 1974 but the upsurge may have reflected a return to the patterns of the fifties and an unwillingness of miners to give up custom and practice. It might have been possible to increase productivity by giving work groups greater autonomy but absenteeism meant that managers were continually involved in redeploying men and disrupting the autonomy of groups. A switch to incentives might reduce absenteeism, give work groups more autonomy and increase productivity.

The Labour Government had an interest in persuading the miners to accept a productivity scheme. Attempts to control inflation were continually threatened by the possibilities of a coal strike. The acceptance of incomes policies over the period 1975 to 1977 had led to a fall in real wages and restlessness in some coalfields. The problem was therefore how to give the miners more money without creating pressures for comparable wage increases by other unions. In 1977 the attempt to give miners more was to take the form of a generous incentive scheme. The problem was: would the miners accept it?

From the point of view of the NUM the Power Loading Agreement and the victories of 1972 and 1974 had posed a variety of problems which led to some members, particularly within the NEC, being persuaded to accept the idea of an incentive scheme. There was the problem of what the Union should do next for its members. It attempted to introduce a national concessionary coal scheme but this ran into difficulties comparable with those which followed NPLA. Yorkshire, North Derbyshire and Nottighamshire threatened to strike if they were required to redistribute some of their concessionary coal to miners in other areas. For the time being the issue of concessionary coal has been shelved although the growing importance of miners' 'free coal' as a percentage of total output means that it cannot be left undiscussed for long. As a result of closures output has fallen whilst the numbers of claimants (pensioners and widows) has risen – particularly in such areas as South Wales. The NUM also considered the possibility of securing for its members a greater say in the running of the industry but a proposal in 1975 that miners should be allowed to select their managers was quickly dropped. Ostensibly it was voted by BACM but even within the NUM the idea never got strong support. To the left wing it was impossible to have workers' control in a capitalist society: to the right wing collective bargaining was a sufficient condition for industrial democracy.

The NUM was therefore left with the traditional policy of raising wages. But raising wages at national level seemed inevitably to lead to confrontations. Whilst the public was sympathetic in 1972 and 1974 there could be no guarantee that such support would be extended into the future. North Sea oil threatened to make inroads into the market for coal. There was also a considerable lobby in favour of a nuclear energy programme and this group pointed to the fact that West Germany, France and Belgium were allowing their coal industries to wither away. Despite the fact that Britain rested on a bed of coal there was no obvious reason why it should be mined.

A proposal to adopt an incentive scheme was rejected by a pithead ballot in 1974 and by the annual conference in 1977. At the

1977 Conference a Yorkshire resolution that the Union should seek to obtain a wage of £110 for faceworkers, if necessary by strike action, was defeated and replaced by a Nottinghamshire resolution that the Union should seek to obtain a wage of £135. Despite the fact that Nottinghamshire proposed a higher wage the resolution did allow the NEC to obtain that increase through an incentive scheme. Later in 1977 the NEC returned with a proposal to ballot the membership on a productivity scheme. Kent sought an injunction which failed because the conference decision had not been based upon a specific proposal and because there was a strong case for a ballot to be taken, given the lack of representativeness of the NEC.

The pit-head ballot of December 1977 revealed a majority against incentives. The campaigning which led up to the ballot, however, revealed weaknesses in both the left and right wings of the NUM. Although a semblance of unity had been created after 1966 power still lay in the coalfields. Gormley and Daly campaigned on behalf of the scheme but they did not go into the coalfields. The members of the NEC who were opposed to incentives mounted a very strong campaign not merely in their own coalfields but also in the traditional right-wing areas. There was nothing in the scheme for the unprofitable coalfields of South Wales and Scotland. Yorkshire voted against the scheme because of a realisation that the Power Loading Agreement had created unity within Yorkshire and also solidarity with miners in other coalfields. Even with the profitable areas the majority in favour of incentives was not always substantial.

The voting reflected national, regional, local and occupational issues. The scheme was vague and left many problems unresolved. If face productivity increased could the extra coal be raised to the surface? If the coal could not be raised was the scheme simply a means of closing pits and coalfaces? Could the increased coal be sold? Would the scheme mean a surrender of custom and practice? There was also a belief that an increase in the basic rate would lead to an increase in productivity comparable with those achieved after 1972 and 1974.

But the left had its problems. There was a reluctance to strike and there was loyalty to the Labour Government. It was these difficulties which permitted the NEC to propose that the areas should be allowed to introduce incentive schemes. The success of the NEC however raises the question: can there be another step?

In 1947 the NUM obtained security of collective bargaining rights and in 1966 it obtained the right to treat the total wage bill as a pool which could be shared equally amongst all miners irrespective of their working conditions. Yet miners still suffered from instability of incomes. In the sixties there was a fall in wages, there was a rise in the seventies and there could be a further fall in the eighties. The achievement of a trade union state has not been accompanied by stability of incomes. In the sixties the Board and the NUM attempted to cope with the problem through increased stocks and closures but wages still fell. What should be the policy for the eighties? One possibility would be to subsidise miners' wages on the grounds that it is essential to ensure a supply of miners at the turn of the century. But such a subsidy could only be applied to the English coalfields: it could not apply to Scotland and South Wales. Another possibility would be to work out the trend of coal prices and then introduce a sliding scale of prices for coal. When prices fell below the trend the State would compensate the Coal Board who could then decide whether to maintain capacity or use the subsidy to pay redundant miners. When prices rose above the standard the Board would compensate the State. Such a scheme could cope with the problems of efficiency as well as equity. But to forecast the trend of prices over a twenty-year period seems to be something that the State is not prepared to undertake.

What the adoption of incentive schemes has done is to allow for an equalisation of wage costs through effort. It has allowed the unprofitable coalfields to survive for a while through increased labour productivity whereas the Power Loading Agreement would have accelerated their demise. The Scheme has also given the Board the possibility of holding labour costs down until the next wave of mechanisation occurs.

Industrial relations in the coal industry are a microcosm of industrial relations in all industries. The problems of ownership, methods of wage payment, wages differentials, strikes and accidents are common features. And they all indicate that industrial relations cannot be divorced from the principles governing social relations. The miners attempted to create a social dividend in one industry but ran into difficulties. Mining, as a microcosm, indicates that problems of particular groups need to be set in the context of national minimum standards of social well-being. Mining also indicates the tremendous inertia that pervades industrial relations. Despite nationalisation, mechanisation and other sweeping changes the NUM is, like its predecessor the MFGB, concerned with the preservation of the individuality of the pit villages.

Appendix: The Theory of Trade Union Growth, Structure and Policy

THEORETICAL PREOCCUPATIONS

Before 1899, when Ashton of Lancashire and Pickard of Yorkshire founded the Miners' Federation of Great Britain and Ireland, trade unionism among miners seemed to expand in the booms and contract or disintegrate in the slumps. Thus, Hepburn's union collapsed in the 1830s, the Miners' Association of Great Britain and Ireland disappeared about 1846, MacDonald's Miners' National Association was founded in 1863 and contracted severely in 1874 whilst its rival, Halliday's Amalgamated Association of Miners, had an even shorter life from 1868 to 1873. After 1889 unionism presumably became more permanent, as Robertson observed, because it took longer to sink pits.[1] All of which suggests a prosperity theory of trade unionism – a thesis endorsed by Griffin for the coal industry.[2] And on a wider canvas the prosperity thesis has been advanced as a general explanation of trade union development. Thus, in the period up to 1850 it is commonly suggested that workers joined unions in the booms and political movements in the slumps – a pendulum theory which derives compelling attention from the sharp contrast between Owen's Grand National and Chartism. In America, Commons put forward the prosperity thesis although he did concede that rising prices might be a more potent cause of trade unionism and subsequently Davis emphasised rising prices.[3] More recently, Ashenfelter and Pencavel have suggested that the growth of American trade unionism between 1900 and 1960 can be explained in terms of change in the demand for labour, changes in prices, the prevailing level of union organisation and the percentage of Democrats in the House of Representatives (a proxy for political support), and Bain and Farouk Elsheik have used a similar explanation for the development of British trade unionism.[4] We appear, therefore, to have a theory which is applicable to all industries as well as mining. Hence we should observe little variation in the patterns of trade union development.

The trouble with the prosperity argument is that it lacks conviction. Why do workers join unions in boom periods when casual observation suggests that they are more in need of unions in slumps? Indeed, Perlman argued that workers join unions because they are conscious of the scarcity of jobs – a theory which presupposes a genetic difference between cartellistically-minded businessmen and trade-union-minded workers and ignores the possibility that scarcity of jobs might be a consequence rather than a cause of trade unions.[5] Yet the only period in which unions appear to have expanded and flourished in a slump was in America in the thirties – and that outburst required massive political support; in the previous decade – the golden twenties – there was a failure of American unionism to expand in the new mass-production industries. So the thesis appears to fail in both boom and slump. And even if the prosperity thesis is qualified by rising prices, the question has to be asked: do trade unions cause rising prices by pushing up wages? There is also the point that the observed difference between unions in boom and slump may not merely be a question of numbers but also of form and direction. The prosperity theory ignores the distinction between formal and informal organisations, between manual and white-collar unions, assumes that a union which has obtained a closed shop monopoly position will readily take in new members when the demand for its members' services increases, and neglects the decisive influence which some unions may exert on the development of unions for other groups of workers. Unionism may survive through slumps at workplace level in a loose but effective fashion, and then suddenly appear to emerge in booms. Thus the Brotherly Union Society was formed in Pemberton, Lancashire in 1794; its rules were apparently amended in 1804 and again in 1830.[6] Even in the twenties and thirties when formal unionism appeared to have collapsed there still existed 'restrictive practices'. Early unionism was often different in its methods from later unionism. Early unionism seems to have been directed against merchants and shopkeepers, rather than employers. Only at a later stage did workers demand compensation from their employers for rising food prices. As to the distinction between manual and white-collar unions, the prosperity thesis suggests that we should expect to find white-collar unions in the last half of the eighteenth century and the first half of the nineteenth century. Finally, the lack of evidence of an association between Chartism and miners, and positive distaste in some areas, suggests that mining unionism may not have collapsed in the 1840s or that miners, at least, did not necessarily turn to political movements.[7]

We need a theory of the demand for trade unionism as opposed to a theory of wanting unions or a number-crunching exercise which finds a statistically significant association between prosperity and unionism but which begs the question of causation. Most of the interview evidence as to why workers join unions supports the idea that they do so in order to obtain protection but that may simply reflect the fact that most of the evidence was culled in the wake of the slump of the thirties. In contrast to statisticians and sociologists, economists would seek to establish that the demand for trade services was related to the price of trade union services, the prices of complementary and substitute goods, income and tastes. Of these factors only tastes may be non-measurable, although it may be possible to find proxies for tastes in education, sex and age, all of which are measurable. Thus, men tend to earn more than women, older workers tend to earn more than younger workers and educated workers tend to earn more than uneducated workers. Hence we might explain differences in the incidence of unionism between men and women as being due to differences in the ability to purchase unionism, although that explanation would not seem to explain the low density of unionism among professional workers. Other factors must intrude.

There are, therefore, two probable reasons why trade unionism expands in booms. During a boom incomes rise and workers can buy more of all goods including unionism. We should, therefore, expect to find an increase in unionism even if the price of unionism remains constant. But there are also reasons for expecting the price of trade unionism to fall. The main cost of joining a union is the possible loss of a job through victimisation and not the trade union subscription. During a boom, when labour becomes scarce, the fear of victimisation will tend to fall. Hence we should expect workers to buy more unionism in a boom because their incomes have risen and the price of unionism has fallen. As for the problems of rising prices, may we not invoke the Keynesian thesis that workers can determine their money wages but not their real wages and feel obliged to press for money wage increases in order not to be left behind?

But although workers' incomes rise and the price of unionism falls we have still to consider the possibility that the prices of substitutes for unionism might also fall. Thus, paternalism or antagonism could fall in price because employers could pass on the costs of wage increases and welfare services in price increases. The price of paternalism may fall but it may not fall sufficiently and it may be an inferior, even a Giffen, good. Workers' attitudes to employers' behaviour may be influenced by that behaviour in slumps and no amount of paternalism in a boom may compensate for its disappearance in a slump.

So far we have analysed a worker's demand for unionism but we need also to consider a union's demand for members. A trade union is a club which seeks to obtain and maximise benefits for its members. Many of the benefits, for example wage increases, are such that it may be difficult for an employer to discriminate between union and non-union employees. Making sure that individuals are treated differently incurs administrative and clerical costs and an employer may not wish to discriminate in order to discredit a union. Union benefits may, therefore, generate an externality or spillover which could undermine the union, and it would be necessary for it to internalise that benefit. A union's demand for members is another way of recognising that there are interdependences in the utility functions of union members which are commonly called solidarity.

Now the trade union's demand for members also depends upon relative costs and benefits and the costs of unionism can be influenced by the geographical spread of potential members. Thus the density of union membership tends to be higher in large plants than in small plants. A union may also prefer to leave some groups of workers unorganised, provided that their wages are determined by minimum wage legislation. And the willingness to organise may be influenced by the existence of rival unions which may compete so intensively as to outweigh the gains from organising and leave workers reluctant to join unions because of the absence of benefits. When benefits are maximised a union will cease to recruit – a point ignored by some writers who, confusing a closed shop agreement with monopoly powers, assume that a monopolist will expand supply when demand increases. Such an assumption overlooks the point that an employer may grant a closed shop agreement to reduce administrative costs of negotiating with numerous workers but he may still expect that he will be able to hire more workers if he needs them; the existence of monopoly power may turn upon whether the union possesses a pre- or post-entry closed shop agreement.

The optimum size of a union is governed, therefore, by the benefits and costs of unionism. In Figure A.1 we measure the total benefit and total cost per person of joining a union along the vertical axis and the number of persons in the union along the horizontal axis. The benefit curve may be thought of as a total net product curve or total net revenue product curve; that is, net of the employer's benefits. As more members are allowed to share in the benefits of unionism the value that an individual places on unionism will decrease. On the cost side, the addition of extra members will reduce the cost per member and the cost curve is shown declining. Where the slopes (derivatives of the total benefit and cost curves are equal) then an optimum size of union will occur. If the number of members is greater than the optimum then some members will voluntarily leave the union or be ejected and will move to other groups – which may be other unions, unemployment, self-employment or non-unionism.[8]

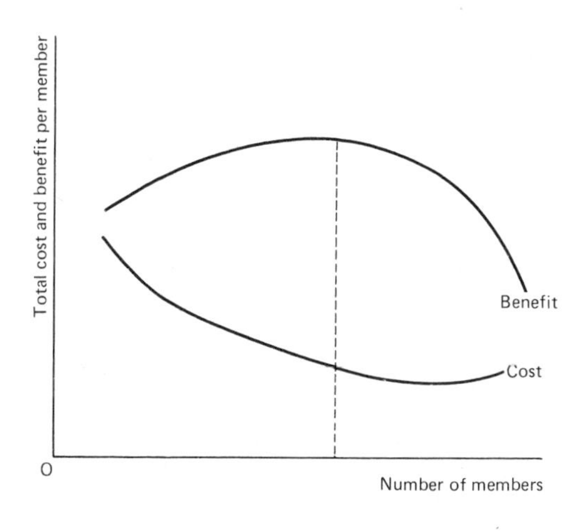

FIGURE A.1

Figure A.1 was drawn up on the assumption that a given wage bill was to be shared equally among a number of trade unionists, the number of which was to be determined. If the wage bill was increased then the benefit and cost curves could be shifted and a new trade union size would be determined. By similar reasoning it is possible to determine the optimum wage benefit per member. Thus, in Figure A.2 the total costs and benefits confronting a member arc measured along the vertical axis and on the horizontal axis is measured the size of wage. We can then trace out the total benefit and cost functions. As more members join, the benefits will rise and then fall, at some point reaching a maximum. Costs will tend to rise with numbers of members joining the union. Hence, we can obtain an optimal wage for each size of union; Q_K is one such wage for a union of size $N = K$.

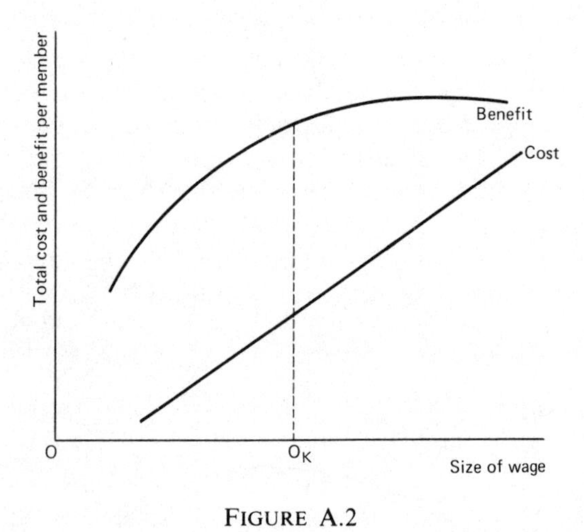

FIGURE A.2

The results derived from Figures A.1 and A.2 are combined in Figure A.3. On the vertical axis is measured the wage and on the horizontal axis is measured the size of the union. The values for the optimal union size for each wage obtained in Figure A.1 allow us to plot the curve TT_1 in Figure A.3. And the values for the optimal wage for each union size allow us to plot the curve QQ_1. The intersection of the two curves, TT_1 and QQ_1 determines the full equilibrium of the union at G. At G the individual member is in equilibrium both with respect to the amount of the wage and

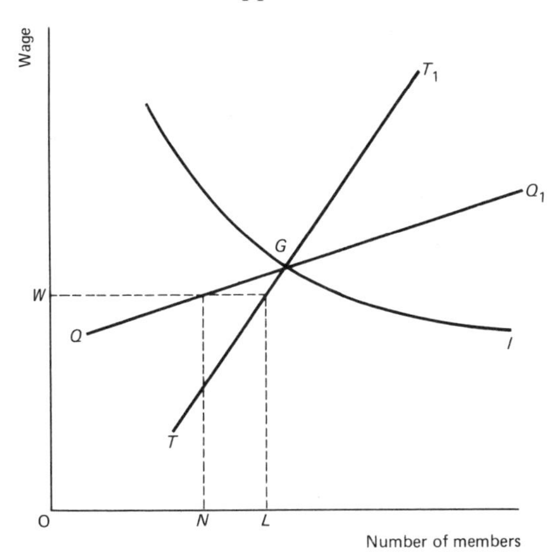

FIGURE A.3

the group size for that wage. If the group size was limited to N then the attainment of equilibrium would leave the individual member wishing to membership to L; he may feel that the presence of non-union members constitutes a threat to the wage. Figure A.3 can also be construed as a standard preference map showing the individual's tastes for size of wage and size of union, and the point where the two curves, TT_1 and QQ_1, intersect at G gives rise to the highest indifference curve attainable. (This underlying construction will form the basis for the indifference curves in Figure A.4 below.) It would also be possible to allow for individuals sharing on an equal basis.[9]

The optimum size of a trade union, and even its existence, is strongly influenced by employers' attitudes because the production function is a joint one. Just as it may be difficult to obtain benefits without forming a union and it may be difficult to avoid non-unionists benefiting from wage increases obtained by a union, so it may also be difficult to disentangle the benefits that an employer derives from the use of his productive serives. It may be difficult to disentangle the contribution of the worker from the contribution of the spade. There is, therefore, a further sharing problem to consider because the employers' attitude to unionism may also influence the location and elasticity of the benefit and cost

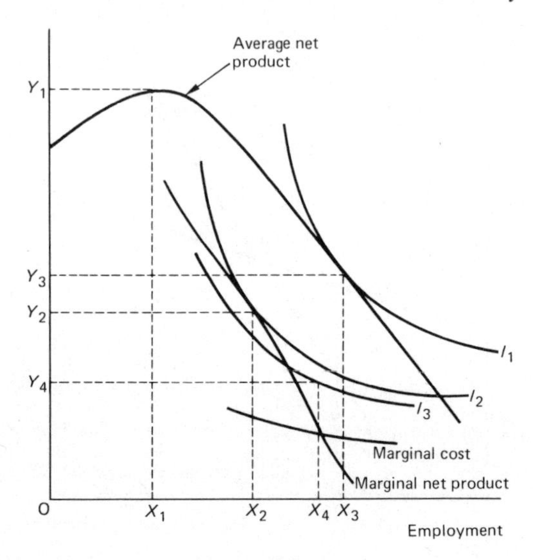

FIGURE A.4

curves drawn in Figure A.1. Formally the employers' attitude is summarised in the Marshallian conditions governing the elasticity of derived demand.

(a) the degree of price elasticity of demand for the commodity produced by union labour;
(b) the degree to which non-union labour or other factors may be substituted for union labour;
(c) the elasticity of supply of other factors of production;
(d) the percentage of total costs constituted by union labour.[10]

These factors, however, should be subsumed in a more general expression governing an employer's 'tastes' for union labour because an employer may dislike union labour even if it adds nothing to his production costs.

Employers' attitudes enable us to distinguish four sharing situations:

1. an open shop in which there is no employer discrimination against unionism;
2. a closed shop in which only union members are employed;
3. employer opposition or discrimination against unionism;

4. bilateral monopoly in which a single union confronts a single employer or employer's association.[11]

1. If, in the case of an open shop, a union seeks to obtain that wage which will maximise the income of its members (that is, it sets the wage at the point on the demand curve where the elasticity of demand is unity) and the demand for union labour is a fixed fraction of the total demand for labour then the union's policy will maximise the income of *all* labour employed. If the wage is set above the level that would prevail in its absence then unemployment will be shared equally by union and non-union workers. In this case union action benefits non-union members who are fortunate enough to be employed.

2. If the union imposes a closed shop then the incidence of unemployment will fall upon non-union members. Furthermore, the existence of a closed shop may enable a union to change its policy from one of maximising the income of labour to one of maximising income per member.

3. If an employer prefers to employ non-union labour at any given wage then the optimum policy for a union would be to maximise the total income of union labour which would equal the demand curve for all labour at each wage rate minus the supply of non-union labour at each wage. How much union labour would be employed would then depend upon the supply of non-union labour relative to the total demand for labour.

If an employer prefers to pay a higher wage to non-union labour than to union members then the resulting wage-employment situation will also depend upon the availability of non-union labour.

4. If bilateral monopoly exists then several possible results may obtain:

(a) If the employer is sufficiently strong he will set a wage equal to the lowest wage acceptable to union members. This wage will measure the usefulness of the union and the wage in non-union employment.

(b) If the union is sufficiently strong and it prepared to ignore the employment consequences of its wages policy then it will set the wage equal to the maximum average net revenue product of labour (OY_1 in Figure A.4). This sub-case corresponds to the worker cooperative of Ward and the trade union state of Meade.[12]

(c) If the union has regard to the unemployment effects of its wages policy then it will opt for a lower wage. A union may have a set of indifference curves relating employment to wage, and, as in Figure A.4, may opt for wage OY_2 and employment OX_2.

(d) A union may be sufficiently strong to ask for an all-or-none contract which fixes both the wage and numbers to be employed. For example, it might ask for wage OY_3 and employment OX_3. If the employer were stronger he might drive the contract down to wage OY_4 and employment OX_3 at which point the marginal net revenue product of labour is equal to the marginal cost of labour, *MC*.

We have produced a theory of the demand for trade unionism which might, in principle, be tested. The benefits from being a member of a trade union can be summarised in the union/non-union differential and the purchase of this benefit is governed by price and income. But this benefit must not be considered over a short period of time, but over a longer period such as the trade cycle. It is true that union membership tends to rise in booms but the evidence on the union wage differential in the upswing is conflicting. Thus, it has been suggested that in upswings the differential contracts and that it expands in slumps, and this is due to the inability of cartels, such as trade unions, to respond quickly to changing circumstances. But if a union recruit is envisaged as investing in a wage and job then he may well be seeking an all-or-nothing contract which gives him a reduced amplitude of fluctuation of earnings and job security. Taking a long-term view of the benefit can also explain the apparent stagnation of unionism in boom periods and when prices are rising, such as in Britain in the sixties. If, as Malcolm Fisher has argued, unionisation creates a once-for-all effect, which may be distributed over time, for existing members, then there may be no gains for outsiders who enter the occupation; the costs of entry may exceed the gains. An expansion of unionism could then only occur as a result of some unanticipated change in benefits or costs such as legislation on industrial relations.[13]

THE WEBBS AND TRADE UNION HISTORY

We have produced an explanation of the demand for trade unions which has some semblance of credibility when applied to the development of mining trade unions. The question arises whether it can be extended to all trade unions or whether the pattern of development of mining unionism differs from that of other unions. This brings us to the Webbs and their critics. G. D. H. Cole seems to have been the first writer to have questioned the Webbs' account of the development of trade unionism when he pointed to the existence of unions of unskilled and semi-skilled workers in mining and textiles alongside the New Model Unions in the third quarter of the nineteenth century. The main body of criticism is to be found in a symposium entitled 'The Webbs and their work' in the Bulletin for the Society of Labour History.[14]

In his critique Allen made the following points:

1. The Webbs neglected ephemeral action and the eighteenth century in which trade unionism was quite extensive.
2. They neglected important causative considerations in the environments of unions such as economic, social and political factors.
3. They exaggerated the importance of the Combination Acts.
4. They attributed the defeat of the Grand National to internal defects instead of the determination of the employers to stamp out unionism.
5. There was nothing new about the ASE, and new Model Unionism was a piece of historical fiction.
6. They exaggerated the importance of the Junta and indulged in the cult of personality, for example, Francis Place.

A. A. Musson's critique incorporated the following points:

1. The Webbs highlighted developments which demonstrated the evolution of socialism and dealt inadequately with the purely trade union aspects which were the most essential, solid and continuous aspects.
2. The influences of Owenite ideology and classical economics were exaggerated.
3. The upsurge of 1833–4 must be attributed to trade recovery. There was no catastrophic collapse after 1834. The trade cycle had more influence on trade union development than ideological fluctuations.

4. There was nothing new about the New Model.

H. A. Clegg made the following observations:

1. The turning point was 1890 and not 1892.
2. In the period 1874–88 trade unions were in retreat yet the Webbs chose to emphasise politics.
3. The craft unions practice mutual insurance rather than collective bargaining.

Now many of the criticisms of the Webbs are misplaced if the two books, *Industrial Democracy* and *The History of Trade Unionism* are read in conjunction for *Industrial Democracy* provides the analytical core to the *History.*[15] In *Industrial Democracy* is contained the distinction between closed and open which Turner was able to use so effectively in his analysis of contemporary trade unionism.[16] The closed unions satisfied the Marshallian conditions with their controls over entry to trades. But the Webbs also emphasised the open unions which were not open in the sense that an employer could exercise favouritism, but were open in the sense that there were no obvious barriers to entry; and once inside a firm there was a definite job hierarchy up which a worker progressed. The Webbs also observed that some of the most successful unions, such as those of miners and cotton weavers, were open unions and that open unions were the most characteristic form of unionism. The Webbs attributed their success to the large area over which an employer might have to substitute non-union labour. This inability of an employer to change his factors of production even when labour was a large proportion of total costs of production was an important qualification of the Marshallian conditions which Robertson later rediscovered.[17]

The differences between the closed and open unions on the control of labour supply were used by the Webbs to explain differences in their methods of negotiating improvements for their numbers and also their attitudes towards specific aspects of the employment contract. Thus the closed unions tended to favour the method of mutual insurance for getting improvements whereas the open unions tended to favour collective bargaining and legislation. The open unions sought to control the length of the working day by legislation whereas the closed unions preferred the methods of autonomous regulation and mutual insurance. The closed unions tended to favour time rates whereas the open union chose piece rates.

The existence of two types of union form raises the question of their relative importance. The Webbs argued that sometimes there is a movement from one form to the other as unions coalesce or fragment. But, by and large, they noted a tendency for some groups of workers to prefer one form to the other. Thus, the printers always preferred the closed form whereas the miners always favoured the open form. And they suggested that the apparent historical alternation between closed and open unions is due to the 'accidental prominence' of certain types of union in particular periods. It is this assumption of accidential prominence which explains the structure of the *History* and which does much to counter the critics. We can now therefore examine the *History*.

In the opening chapter the Webbs pointed out that unionism antedated the factory system and was to be found in the crafts, such as tailoring, woollen manufacturers and cutlery. Secondly, they noted the influence of the technology and the work situation upon unionism:

> Where work is carried on, not by individual craftsmen but by associated groups of highly skilled wage earners, it is practically within the power of these groups, if supported by the public opinion of their community, to exclude any newcomer from admission. The 'group system' goes far, we think, to account for the exceptional effectiveness of Trade Union regulations on apprenticeship among Boilermakers, Flint Glass Makers, Glass Bottlemakers and Stuff Pressers.[18]

Such groups could be formed out of the network of relationships created by the production processes and need not give rise to formally recognisable trade unions. But these latent relationships could suddenly surface and provide the basis for action.

> The historic strikes of the London building trades and the Newcastle engineers in 1871 were both conducted by committees elected at mass meetings of the trades, among whom the trade unionists formed an insignificant minority. In the history of the building and engineering trades there are numerous

> instances of agreements being concluded on behalf of a whole district, by temporary committees of non-unionists . . .[19]

The third point the Webbs made is that there is a connection between the guilds and the trade unions but it is no more than can be observed in many other organisations. What was a rather subtle remark came to be translated by subsequent writers into a bold denial of the connection between the guilds and the unions.

This brings us to the phasing of trade union development. Contrary to the critics, the Webbs are quite explicit that the Combination Acts were not applied to all combinations and that for some groups they were a dead letter, either because the law was inefficiently operated or because the employers were content to negotiate with the unions. But they did make three points which have been overlooked by subsequent writers. First, though the Acts were not always applied, the common law of conspiracy was often applied. Secondly, it was the uncertainty of enforcement that constituted a real threat to some groups. Thirdly, they observed that the Acts were applied to the newer trades such as textiles. There was class distinction:

> The failure of the Combination Laws to suppress the somewhat dictatorial Trade Unionism of the skilled handicraftsmen and their efficacy in preventing the growth of permanent unions among other sections of the workers is explained by class distinctions, now passed away are greatly modified, which prevailed at the beginning of the century.[20]

The same balanced treatment can also be detected in the second phase from 1818 to 1840. Thus, notwithstanding Allen's assertion that the Webbs ignored employers' attacks on the Grand National we read that:

'The great association of half a million members had been completely routed by the employers' vigorous presentation of the "document".'[21]

And despite Musson's complaint of a lack of balance, the Webbs did account for the activities of the builders and did not omit to mention that the printers and engineers stayed aloof from the general movement.

In the third phase of New Model Unionism the Webbs do indicate the antecedents of the unions and why they appeared relatively quiescent in the thirties and forties. They also made it abundantly clear in *Industrial Democracy* that no unions ever accepted the doctrines of political economy. The New Model Unions of engineers and building workers were sectional unions, but, unlike the unions of miners and cotton weavers, they were closed unions which used the methods of autonomous regulation and mutual insurance to alter wages. And it was these methods which were coming under attack during the period because the employers, through the use of lock-outs and legislation, were attempting to destroy the unions and keep them out of their factories. And to defend themselves the unions were forced into wider arrangements. It was because of the changing nature of wage negotiation that the Junta became important. There was no essential difference between the Junta and George Potter except tactics, and all the evidence – that of the Webbs, Coltham and Clements – points to Potter's lack of fitness for conducting the struggles of the period.

The Webbs have also been accused, notably by Flanders, of ignoring the role of employers in the development of industrial relations and so it comes as a surprise to read their comment on the 1892 engineering lock-out: 'It is significant that even in so complete a victory the employers found themselves driven to a system of Collective Bargaining even more systematic and national than before prevailed'.[22]

CONCLUSIONS

What can we conclude from our discussion of the Webbs and the theory of trade unionism? First, trade unions based on different principles can co-exist side by side. Robertson's explanation of Hick's qualification of the Marshallian conditions governing the elasticity of derived demand constitutes a sufficient basis for open unionism. Secondly, open unionism is highly likely to be associated with political activity; the demand for the services of an open union and the state are likely to be complementary rather than competitive. This is a point which tends to be overlooked by some economists, such as Friedman and Fisher, who argue that only craft unions may exert any significant influence on wages.[23]

But by political action, which may be relatively inexpensive for an open union, barriers to entry to a trade may be erected. Indeed, open unionism may be a comparatively inexpensive method of mobilising votes. And looking at the history of mining unionism we are forced to recognise the complementary pursuits of industrial and political objectives. Unlike the craft unions miners had no guild system of controls over labour and hours of work. Indeed, like textiles, mining seems to have inherited the domestic system's lack of controls. Hence the influx of female and child labour and the apparent expansion of hours – both of which had to be curbed by legislation. It is commonly believed that the expansion of hours was due to the employers' desires to use their machines intensively. This is not a complete explanation, because employers could have run their machines continuously by employing workers on shifts. It was also relatively costly to attract, select and retain. Hence, the bond system and also the tendency to lengthen the hours of individual workers. It was only when restrictions on the hours of women and children were curtailed that employers resorted to shift systems and even then there was an attempt to retain long shifts for men; the common response of employers in the big pits of the North-East and in the textile factories was the relay system. It would be interesting to have a complete analysis of hours of work systems. There is, for example, evidence that slaves tended to work shorter hours than free men. Did miners on the bond system work shorter hours than those employed after its abolition? Legal controls on truck had also to be introduced. MacDonald's union appeared to be more successful than Halliday's because it chose to use political methods and through the introduction of checkweighmen created the basis of pit level unionism. Even the MFGB could use political as well as industrial action. In 1893 it conducted a highly successful strike against the coal owners but in 1908 it sought and obtained a statutory limitation on hours of work and in 1912 it obtained a legal minimum wage. Industrial action was, in fact, only likely to be successful on a sectional basis and not on a national scale for the miners. Thus, in the second half of the nineteenth century the miners of Northumberland and Durham were able, for a period to maintain a position superior to that of miners elsewhere because of higher productivity, differences in working arrangements and the acceptance of sliding scales. Halliday's union obtained some success in the inland coalfields but when its methods were applied in the export coalfield of South Wales the union disintegrated. Similarly, in the interwar years, Spencerism was able to emerge in the Nottinghamshire coalfield because of the greater productivity of that coalfield but even there it did not always produce satisfactory results and elsewhere it struck few roots and left the MFGB's policy of pursuing a national minimum wage intact. Nationalism required political support.

The third point is that the law is often only a symbol which is used at the periphery of industrial relations. Thus, the Taff Vale decision was out of line with trends in the organised trades and the subsequent Denaby Main case of 1905 represented the actions of an awkward employer – although had the employer won then, the miners of the Don Valley might well have left the Yorkshire miners and formed their own union. Similarly in the inter-war years the 1927 Trade Union Act was a piece of political symbolism which was not used by most employers. Nor was the 1971 Industrial Relations Act used by the majority of employers and its passing was not mourned. A further point is that in the debate between 'accidental prominence' and 'continuity' what is involved is judgement. Of course, there was continuity – the Webbs do not deny it – but the continuity school produces a plain unvarnished tale which fails to take account of the interactions of unions, employers, governments and the law. Indeed, the politics almost disappears from the story. Yet it is difficult to deny the importance of the vote both for industrial and political development. Once the rural areas got the vote the miners began to support a working-men's party – something that the Liberal revival in Lancashire could not prevent. But one does not have to be a socialist to believe that the printers were relatively unimportant whereas Robert Owen, the Chartists, New Model Unionism, the Junta and New Unionism were.

The final point concerns the relevance of the 'accidental prominence' of either closed or open unions to contemporary society. The present distribution of unionism shows a marked concentration of members into a few unions which have grown as a result of mergers and internal growth. Furthermore, these unions are still expanding and, in a sense, all unions are open unions. The 'accidental prominence' is of open unions but within those unions, as Turner observed, there are significant closed sections, which may exert an interesting influence on the pattern of industrial relations.

Notes

CHAPTER 1

1. J. E. Nef, *The Rise of British Coal Industry* (Routledge, London, 1932), vol. 1.
2. cf. D. Knoop and G. P. Jones, *The Medieval Mason* (Manchester University Press, Manchester, 1933).
3. Op. cit., p. 147. A. Radford, *Labour Migration in England 1800–1850* 2nd edn, (Manchester University Press, Manchester, 1964), Ch. IV.
4. Adam Smith, *Lectures on Justice* (Cannan edition, Oxford, 1896), p. 101.
5. Serfdom and long hirings constitute a qualification to those theories of economic development which postulate unlimited supplies of labour.
6. R. Challinor, *The Miners of Lancashire and Cheshire* (Frank Graham, Newcastle, 1969). Anderson has, however, turned up examples of miners' bonds in the Orrell Coalfield which was to the west of Wigan. See D. Anderson, *The Orrell Coalfield 1740–1850* (Moorland Publishing Company, 1975), pp. 128–9.
7. A. J. Taylor, 'The sub-contract system in the British coal industry', in L. S. Pressnell (ed.), *Studies in the Industrial Revolution* (Athlone Press, London, 1960). For a discussion of later developments see Robert E. Goffee, 'The butty system and the Kent coalfield', *Bulletin* of the Society for the study of Labour History (1977), pp. 41–56.
8. cf. E. Rogers, 'The history of trade unionism in the coal-mining industry of North Wales to 1914', *Transactions of the Denbighshire Historical Society*, (1964).
9. Challinor op. cit.
10. Rogers op. cit.
11. cf. E. J. Hobsbawm, *Labouring men* (Weidenfeld and Nicholson, London, 1964).
12. cf. E. W. Evans, *The South Wales Miners* (Welsh University Press, Cardiff, 1961).
13. For evidence of an association between Chartism and the miners see R. Challinor and B. Ripley, *The Miners' Association: A Trade Union in the Age of the Chartists* (Lawrence and Wishart, London, 1968). For the contrary evidence see E. Rogers op. cit.; J. E. Williams, *The Derbyshire Miners* (Allen and Unwin, London, 1962); C. P. Griffin, *The Economic and Social Development of the Leicestershire and South Derbyshire Coalfield*, (unpublished PhD, Nottingham, 1969). See also the interchange between Challinor, Griffin, and G. Barnsby in the *Bulletin* for the Society of Labour History (1971–3).
14. The 1842 Mines Act prohibited the employment of women underground

and restricted the hours for boys, but its effects are uncertain. Women were certainly excluded from underground working but it was difficult to check upon the ages of boys.

15. cf. P. M. Sweezy, *Monopoly and Competition in the British Coal Trade* (Harvard University Press, 1938). Sweezy develops his analysis using the kinked demand curve which he pioneered. Other writers have come to doubt its applicability to collusive oligopoly. Cf. G. J. Stigler, 'The kinky oligopoly demand curve', *Journal of Political Economy*, LV (1947), 432–49.
16. cf. J. R. T. Hughes, *Economic Fluctuations in Trade, Industry and Finance, 1850–60*,
17. T. Ashton, *Three Big Strikes* (MFGB, 1925), p. 291.
18. J. W. F. Rowe, *Wages in the Coal Industry* (King, London, 1922).
19. R. G. Neville and J. Benson, 'Labour in the coalfields (2)', *Bulletin* for the Society of Labour History (1975); J. H. Porter, 'Wage bargaining under conciliation, 1860–1914', *Economic History Review*, XXIII (1970).
20. Op. cit.
21. A. R. Griffin, *Mining in the East Midlands, 1550–1947* (Cass, London, 1971), pp. 156–7.
22. For the history of Denaby Main see J. E. MacFarlane, 'Unionism versus free labour: the strike at Denaby Main in 1869', (forthcoming); ' "One association – the Yorkshire Miners' Association": the Denaby Main lock-out of 1855', in S. Pollard and C. Holmes (eds.), *Essays in the Economic and Social History of South Yorkshire* (South Yorkshire County Council, Barnsley, 1976); see also the papers by R. G. Neville, 'In the wake of Taff Vale: the Denaby and Cadeby miners' strike and conspiracy case, 1902–06' and J. E. Macfarlane, 'Denaby Main: a South Yorkshire mining village', in J. Benson and R. G. Neville, (eds.), *'Studies in the Yorkshire Coal Industry* (Manchester University Press, Manchester, 1976).
23. 'Symbolism' refers to the use of the law to control collective bargaining. It does not refer to the law on individual contracts.
24. S. and B. Webb, *The History of Trade Unionism* (Longmans, London, 1911).
25. S. and B. Webb, *Industrial Democracy* (Longmans, London, 1902).
26. A. Marshall, *Economics of Industry* (Macmillan, London, 1892), p. 368.
27. The vote was 445,601 for and 115,921 against. The two-thirds majority rule arose because it was the rule which applied in Durham and given the quasi-autonomy of the districts it would have been difficult to have persuaded Durham to come out if a lower majority had been recorded.
28. For Askwith's account see G. R. Askwith, *Industrial Disputes and Problems* (Murray, London, 1920).
29. J. Skinner, *Fair Wages and Public Sector Contracts* (Fabian Research Series, 310, London, 1973).
30. As proposed by Keynes in the twenties.
31. The Triple Industrial Alliance, formed in 1914, was composed of the unions of miners and transport workers and arose out of an awareness that a strike of one group could have serious repercussions on the others. Thus in the 1912 coal strike many railwaymen were sent home because of lack of work. The Alliance did not operate in the war because of an industrial truce and collapsed afterwards because no agreement could be reached on how autonomous each of the sections could be in negotiations.

32. Baldwin's views are discussed in K. Middlemass and J. Barnes, *Baldwin* (London, 1969).
33. The proposals were, in fact, drawn up by Sir Herbert Samuel.
34. There are three good accounts of Spencerism in Nottinghamshire by the Griffins. See A. R. Griffin, *Mining in the East Midlands, 1550–1947* (Cass, London, 1971); *The Miners of Nottinghamshire*, 1914–1944 (Allen and Unwin, London, 1962): A. R. and C. P. Griffin, 'Non-political unionism' in A. Briggs and J. Saville (eds.), *Essays in Labour History 1918–1939* (Croom Helm, London, 1977). Bernard Taylor, *Uphill all the Way* (Sidgwick and Jackson, London, 1962), emphasises the failure of Spencerism to get a foothold in the pits around Edwinstowe. J. E. Williams, op. cit. deals with activities in Derbyshire. W. R. Garside, *The Durham Miners 1919–60*, (Allen and Unwin, London, 1962), has a good account of the spread of Spencerism into Durham. Company unionism in South Wales is treated by D. Smith, 'The struggle against company unionism in the South Wales coalfield, 1926–39', *Welsh Historical Review*, VI, 1973. Scotland is treated in A. Moffat, *My Life with the Miners* (Lawrence and Wishart, London, 1971).
35. J. H. Jones, *The Coal Mining Industry* (Pitman, London, 1939): A. F. Lucas, *Industrial Reconstruction and Control of Competition* (Longmans, London, 1937); M. W. Kirby, 'The control of competition in the British coal-mining industry in the thirties', *Economic History Review*, 2nd. ser. 26 (1973), 273–84; N. K. Buxton, 'Entrepreneurial efficiency in the British coal industry between the wars', idem, 25 (1972), 476–97; M. W. Kirby, 'A comment', idem, 25 (1972), 655–64; N. K. Buxton, 'Entrepreneurial efficiency in the British coal industry between the wars: Reconfirmed', idem, 25 (1972), 658–664.
36. A. Anderson, 'The political symbolism of the labour laws' and 'The labour laws and the Cabinet Legislative Committee of 1926–27', *Bulletin* of the Society for the Study of Labour History (Autumn 1971).
37. Written Evidence of Sir Harold Emmerson, *Report* of the Royal Commission on Trade Unions and Employers' Associations, Appendix 6 (H.M.S.O., 1961).

CHAPTER 2

1. L. Johansen, 'Labour theory of value and marginal utilities', *Economics of Planning*, 3 (1963), 89–103; N. Georgescu Roegen, *The Entropy Law and the Economic Process* (Harvard University Press, 1971).
2. There is a useful collection of articles on participation theory in the inter-war years in K. Coates, *Democracy in the Mines* (Spokesman Books, Nottingham, 1974).
3. J. E. Williams, op. cit.
4. *The Miners' Next Step* (Robert Davies and Co., Tonypandy, 1912) reprinted K. Coates, op. cit.
5. J. E. Meade, *'The theory of labour-managed firms and profit sharing'*, *Economic Journal*, special issue in honour of E. A. G. Robinson (1972), 402–28.
6. The literature of the inter-war years is surveyed in A. Bergson, 'Socialist

economics', in H. Ellis (ed.), *Survey of Contemporary Economics*, vol. 1 (Irwin, New York, 1948).
7. O. Lange, 'The economics of socialism', in B. E. Lippincott (ed.), *The Economics of Socialism* (University of Minnesota Press, 1938), pp. 57–90.
8. A. P. Lerner, *The Economics of Control* (Macmillan, New York, 1944).
9. J. Dupuit, 'On the measurement of the utility of public works', in *International Economic Papers*, 2 (1952), 83–110.
10. W. J. Corlett and D. C. Hague, 'Complementarity and the excess burden of taxation', *Review of Economic Studies*, 21 (1953–4), 21–30.
11. *Report of the Advisory Committee on Organization* (National Coal Board, 1955).

CHAPTER 3

1. *Report of a Committee of Investigation into a dispute between the Yorkshire winding-enginemen and the National Union of Mineworkers*, Cmnd. 3865 (HMSO, London, 1964).
2. S. M. Lipset, M. A. Trow and J. S. Coleman, *Union Democracy* (Free Press, Glencoe, 1956).
3. Bernard Karsh and Jack London, 'The locus of union control', *Quarterly Journal of Economics*, 68 (1954), 415–36.
4. Peter Friedlander, *The Emergence of a UAW Local 1936*–1939: A Study in Class and Conflict (University of Pittsburgh Press, Pittsburgh, 1975).
5. G. S. Bain, *The Growth of White Collar Unionism* (Oxford University Press, 1970).
6. Milton Friedman, *From Galbraith to Economic Freedom* (Institute of Economic Affairs, London, 1977).

CHAPTER 4

1. The Five-Day Week Bonus was introduced as an incentive to good attendance in 1947. The bonus was paid on the basis of five days worked and not on a daily basis. As such it meant that a man who missed one attendance was encouraged to have more days off because he had already lost his bonus.
2. *Memorandum of Agreements*, Part VI, pp. 29–30.
3. I. M. D. Little, *The Price of Fuel* (Oxford University Press, Oxford, 1954).
4. *Report of the Committee on National Policy for the Use of Fuel and Power Resources*, Cmnd. 8647 (HMSO, London, 1952).
5. K. J. W. Alexander, 'Wages in the coal mining industry since nationalisation', *Oxford Economic Papers*, 8 (1956), 164–180.
6. J. Hughes, 'The rise of the militants', *Trade Union Affairs* (Winter, 1960–1).
7. H. A. Turner, 'Trade unions, differentials and levelling of wages', *Manchester School*, 20 (1952), 227–82; Alexander op. cit.; R. G. Searle-Barnes, *Pay and Productivity Bargaining* (Manchester University Press, 1969).
8. E. H. Sealey, 'A statistical analysis of productivity movements in British coalmining', *Transactions of the Manchester Geological and Mining Society* (1962).

9. J. W. House and E. M. Knight, *Pit Closure and Community* (Newcastle University, 1967).
10. *Ryehope: A pit closes* (Department of Employment and Productivity, HMSO, London, 1970).
11. Lord Robens, *Ten Year Stint* (Cassell, London, 1972), pp. 105–6.
12. Because the last Dutch mine closed in 1975 there will be no discussion of Dutch experience.
13. In all the coal-producing countries of Europe there existed a mineworkers' pension fund whose origins went back to before the Second World War. The objective of the pensions was not merely to provide for old age and sickness but also to provide a financial inducement for the recruitment of labour. The funds were financed out of coal receipts but with the fall in the demand for coal the funds were in danger of becoming insolvent. In Belgium the scheme was merged with the national pension scheme. In West Germany it was subsidised. In France it was partly merged and partly subsidised. Similar problems affected the UK and USA. See *The Effects of the Reduction of Manpower in the Mining Industry on Mining Social Security Systems and Pension Systems in Particular* (Commission of the European Communities Social Policy Series, 23, Brussels, 1973).
14. For a discussion of the early crisis see 'Modernisation des mines, conversion des mineurs', *Revue Francaise du Travail*, XVI (1962) 1–201.
15. In 1949 Frenchmen comprised 73 per cent of the labour force, 80 per cent in 1958 and 84 per cent in 1974. The biggest declines in foreign labour were experienced by Germans (6,497), Italians (3,387) and Poles (20,538). Exiled Poles, Czechs and Yugoslavs entered the pits at the end of the war. The numbers of North Africans have remained constant at about 6,000 although Moroccans have tended to become more important than Algerians.

    In the UK there were two attempts to introduce foreign workers. In the late forties there was an attempt to recruit Italians and in 1956 there was an attempt to recruit Hungarians. An unpublished survey by J. Kenyon, a North Gawber, Yorkshire miner, showed that in 1956 resistance to foreigners was based upon lack of consultation and the existence of rising unemployment.
16. cf. M. Barratt Brown, 'Determinants of the structure and level of wages in the coal-mining industry since 1956', *Bulletin of the Oxford Institute of Statistics*, 29 (1967), 139–70.
17. For a discussion of trends in the importance of time-rates and piece-rates in British industries see B. J. McCormick, 'Methods of wage payment, wages structures and the influence of factor and product markets', *British Journal of Industrial Relations*, XV (1977), 246–265. For an American contribution see John H. Pencavel, 'Work effort, on-the-job-screening and alternative methods of remuneration', *Research in Labour Economics*, I (1977).

CHAPTER 5

1. cf. J. M. Buchanan and Wm. Craig Stubblebine, 'Externality', *Economica* 29 (1962), 371–84, reprinted in American Economic Association, *Readings in Welfare Economics* (eds. K. J. Arrow and T. Scitovsky), (London, 1969), pp.

199–212. Although our discussion implies that only one tax/subsidy need be imposed to achieve optimality it is highly likely that more than one measure may be necessary to cover the repercussions of a single measure. Furthermore, the measure imposed need not be a price measure; it could be a standard or prohibition on some activity. Thus in the case of safety measures it may be more efficient to lay down standards for dust, or fencing of machinery.

2. Quoted in *Colliery Guardian*, 21 Jan 1966, p. 73.
3. L. J. Handy, 'Absenteeism and attendance in the British coal mining industry: an examination of post-war trends', *British Journal of Industrial Relations*, VI (1968), 27–50.
4. Office of Health Economics, *Off Sick* (London, 1971); Society of Occupational Medicine, *Proceedings of the Symposium on Absence from Work attributed to Sickness* (ed. A. Ward Gardner), (London, 1968).
5. P. J. Taylor, 'Some international trends in sickness absence, 1950–68', *British Medical Journal* (1969), 705–7.
6. D. G. Harper, E. G. Lister and M. Middleton, 'A study of regional variation in workdays lost through accidents', *Accident Analysis and Prevention*, 3 (1971), 229–36.
7. Debaprya Ghosh, Dennis Lees and William Seal, *The Economics of Personal Injury* (Saxon House/Lexington books, London, 1976), pp. 61–3.
8. cf. *Safety and Health at Work* (HMSO, London, 1972).
9. *Report on Social Insurance and Allied Services*, 2 vols., Cmd. 6404 and 6405 (HMSO, London, 1942).
10. C. Kerr and A. Siegel, 'The inter-industry propensity to strike: an international comparison', in A. Kornhauser, R. Dubin and A. Ross, *Industrial Conflict* (McGraw-Hill, New York, 1954), pp. 189–204.
11. Op. cit., p. 190.
12. G. Rimlinger, 'International differences in the strike propensity of coal miners: experience in four countries', *Industrial and Labour Relations Review*, 12 (1959), 389–405.
13. H. A. Turner, *The Trend of Strikes* (Leeds University Press, 1963).
14. R. C. on Trade Unions and Employers' Associations, *Written Evidence of the Ministry of Labour* (HMSO, London, 1965), p. 39.
15. 'Concentration of industrial stoppages in manufacturing industries', Department of Employment *Gazette*, Feb 1977, p. 115.
16. H. A. Turner, *Is Britain Strike Prone*? (Cambridge University Press, 1969); W. E. J. McCarthy, 'The nature of Britain's strike problem', *British Journal of Industrial Relations*, VIII (1970), 224–236.
17. K. C. J. C. Knowles, *Strikes* (Oxford, 1954).
18. Op. cit.
19. B. J. McCormick, 'Strikes in the Yorkshire coal industry', in M. Kelly and D. J. Forsyth, *Studies in the Coal Industry* (Pergamon, London, 1969), pp. 171–98.
20. H. A. Turner, G. Clack and G. Roberts, *Labour Relations in the Motor Industry* (Allen and Unwin, London, 1967).
21. W. H. Scott *et al.*, *Coal and Conflict* (Liverpool University Press, 1963).
22. J. Pencavel, 'Analysis of an index of industrial morale', *British Journal of Industrial Relations*, XII (1974), 48–55.

23. R. Revans, 'Human relations, management and size', in E. M. Hugh Jones, *Human Relations and Modern Management* (North Holland, Amsterdam, 1958), pp. 177–220.
24. McCormick op. cit.
25. G. K. Ingham, *Size of Industrial Organization and Worker Behaviour* (Cambridge University Press, Cambridge, 1970).
26. Based on material in the Department of Employment *Gazette*, Feb and Nov 1976, Feb 1977 and Jan 1978.
27. Op. cit.
28. Op. cit., Feb 1977.
29. J. Pencavel, 'An investigation into industrial strike activity in Britain', *Economica*, NS 37 (1970), 229–50. The Ashenfelter/Johnson is found in O. Ashenfelter and G. E. Johnson, 'Bargaining theory, trade unions and industrial strike activity', *American Economic Review*, 59 (1969), 35–49.
30. R. Bean and D. A. Peel, 'A quantitative analysis of wage strikes in four UK industries, 1962–70', *Journal of Economic Studies*, 13 (1974), 88–97.
31. J. Shorey, 'Time series analysis of strike frequency', *British Journal of Industrial Relations* , 15 (1977), 63–75.
32. J. Shorey, 'An inter-industry analysis of strike frequency', *Economica*, 43 (1976), 349–63; 'The size of the work unit and strike incidence', *Journal of Industrial Economics*, 23 (1975), 175–88.
33. Op. cit.
34. W. Brown and K. Sissons, 'The use of comparisons in workplace wage determination', *British Journal of Industrial Relations*, 13 (1976), 23–51.
35. R. Price and G. S. Bain, 'Union growth revisited: 1948–74 in perspective', *British Journal of Industrial Relations*, 14 (1976), 339–55; B. Burkitt and D. Bowers, 'The degree of unionization: 1948–68', *Bulletin of Economic Research*, 26 (1974), 79–100; K. Mayhew, 'The degree of unionization: A Comment', *Bulletin of Economic Research*, 29 (1977), 51–3: B. Burkitt and D. Bowers, 'A Reply', ibid, 54–6.

CHAPTER 6

1. *The Star*, Sheffield, 23 Feb 1961.
2. *The Star*, 13 Mar 1961.
3. *Report of a Court of Inquiry into a Dispute between the National Coal Board and the National Union of Mineworkers*, Chairman Lord Wilberforce, Cmnd. 4903 (HMSO, London, 1972).
4. In making its recommendations for surface workers the Court referred to the fact that many of them were disabled and immobile. This was but one instance where a general problem was presented as a special case The correct solution would have been achieved through a negative income tax. The usual state of affairs is that industries are expected to take a quota of disabled workers and their wages are fixed by collective bargaining – a practice which comes close to being an all-or-nothing affair.
5. Pay Board, Special Report, *Relative Pay of Mineworkers*, Cmnd. 5567 (HMSO, London, 1974).

6. J. Goldstein, *The Government of Trade Unions*, (Allen and Unwin, London, 1952).
7. V. L. Allen, *Power in Trade Unions* (Allen and Unwin, London, 1954).
8. C. H. Rolph, *All Those in Favour* (Andre Deutsch, London, 1962).
9. Lord Robens, *Ten Year Stint* (Cassell, London, 1972).
10. J. R. Hicks, *The Theory of Wages*, 2nd edn. (Macmillan, London, 1963); O. Ashenfelter and G. E. Johnson, 'Bargaining theory, trade unions and industrial activity', *American Economic Review*, 59 (1969), 35–49.
11. G. L. S. Shackle, 'The nature of the bargaining process' in J. T. Dunlop (ed.), *The Theory of Wage Determination* (Macmillan, London, 1957), pp. 292–316.

APPENDIX

1. D. H. Robertson, *A Study of Industrial Fluctuations* (King, London, 1913).
2. A. R. Griffin, *Mining in the East Midlands* (Cass, London, 1964).
3. J. R. Common and Associates, *History of Labour in the United States* (Macmillan, London, 1936); H. B. Davies, 'The Theory of trade union growth', *Quarterly Journal of Economics*, 55 (1941), 611–13.
4. O. Ashenfelter and J. Pencavel, 'American trade union growth: 1900–1960', *Quarterly Journal of Economics*, 83 (1969), 434–48; G. S. Bain and Farouk Elsheik, *Union Growth and the Business Cycle* (Blackwell, Oxford, 1976).
5. Selig Perlman, *A Theory of the Labour Movement* (Kelly, New York, 1949); see also C. A. Gulick and M. K. Bers, 'Insight and illusion in Perlman's theory of the labour movement' *Industrial and Labour Relations Review*, 6 (1953), 511–31.
6. R. Challinor, *The Miners of Lancashire and Cheshire* (Frank Graham, Newcastle, 1969). See also E. Rogers 'The history of trade unionism in the coal-mining industry of North Wales', *Transactions of the Denbighshire Historical Society* (1964).
7. For evidence of an association between Chartism and the miners see R. Challinor and B. Ripley, *The Miners' Association: A Trade Union in the Age of the Chartists* (Lawrence and Wishart, London, 1968). For the contrary evidence see J. E. Williams, *The Derbyshire Miners* (Allen and Unwin, London, 1962); C. P. Griffin, *The Economic and Social Development of the Leicestershire and South Derbyshire Coalfield*, (unpublished Ph.D. thesis, University of Nottingham). See also the interchange between Challinor, Griffin and G. Barnsby in the *Bulletin for the Society of Labour History* (1971–3).
8. cf. J. M. Buchanan, 'An economic theory of clubs', *Economica*, 32 (1965), 1–14.
9. cf. R. D. Tollison, 'Consumption sharing and non-exclusion rules', *Economica*, 40 (1972), 276–91.
10. A. Marshall, *Principles of Economics*, 8th ed (Macmillan, London, 1920).
11. cf. Bronfenbrenner, 'Economics of collective bargaining', *Quarterly Journal of Economics*, 53 (1939), 535–61; W. Fellner, *Competition Among the Few* (Knopf, New York, 1949).
12. B. Ward, 'The firm in Illyria: market syndicalism', *American Economic*

Review, 48 (1958), 566–89; J. E. Meade, *Efficiency, Equality and the Ownership of Property* (Allen and Unwin, London 1964).
13. M. R. Fisher, *The Economic Analysis of Labour* (Weidenfeld and Nicholson, London, 1971) ch. 5.
14. V. L. Allen, 'A Methodological criticism of the Webbs as trade union historians'; A. E. Musson, 'The Webbs and the phasing of trade union development between the 1830s and the 1860s', H. A. Clegg, 'The Webbs as historians of trade unionism 1874–1894', *Bulletin* for the Society for the Study of Labour History, no. 4 (spring, 1962); V. L. Allen *The Sociology of Industrial Relations* (Longmans, London, 1970); H. A. Clegg, A. Fox and A. F. Thompson, *A History of British Trade Unions since 1889*, Vol. 1, *1889–1910*, (Oxford, 1964); A. E. Musson, *British Trade Unions, 1800–1975*, (Macmillan, London, 1972); *Trade Union and Social History* (Cass, London, 1974). The earlier piece by G. D. H. Cole was 'Some notes on British trade unions in the third quarter of the nineteenth century', *International Review for Social History*, II (1937) reprinted in E. M. Carus Wilson (ed.), *Essays in Economic History* vol. III (Longmans, London, 1962). See also R. V. Clements, 'British trade unions and popular political economy, *Economic History Review*, 2nd ser., XIV (1961); A. Flanders, *Management and Unions* (Faber, London, 1970).
15. S. and B. Webb, *The History of Trade Unionism* (Longmans, London, 1894) and *Industrial Democracy*, 2nd edn. (Longmans, London, 1911).
16. H. A. Turner, *Trade Union Growth, Structure and Policy* (Allen and Unwin, London, 1962).
17. D. H. Robertson, *Lectures on Economic Principles* (Fontana, London, 1963), pp. 192–3. For an earlier discussion see J. R. Hicks, *The Theory of Wages*, 2nd edn. (Macmillan, London, 1963).
18. *Industrial Democracy*, p. 478.
19. *History*, pp. 300–1.
20. *History*, p. 74.
21. *History*, p. 137.
22. *History*, p. XIX-X.
23. M. Friedman, 'The Significance of labour unions in economic policy' in D. McCord Wright (ed.), *The Impact of the Union* (Harcourt Brace, New York, 1951), pp. 207–15; M. Fisher, *The Economic Analysis of Labour* (Weidenfeld and Nicholson, London), pp. 132–165.

Index